An Italian Home
Settling by Lake Como

Paul Wright

Paul Wright is an award-winning English artist who specialises in large scale murals, Trompe l'Oeil painted furniture, contemporary oil paintings and watercolour landscapes.

In 1982, following a period spent designing theatre sets around the UK, Paul started his own art studio in Surrey, where he specialised in hand painted interiors for private homes and commercial premises.

In 1991 he moved to northern Italy with his partner, Nicola, where he continues to work from his studio and art gallery base in the beautiful medieval village of Argegno on the shores of Lake Como, and from where he travels to other European countries and to the USA.

Paul's work has been featured in many art exhibitions in the UK and on two programmes for Italian television, plus dozens of periodicals and newspapers worldwide, notably *The Sunday Times*, *Architectural Digest*, *The Wall Street Journal* and *The Arts Review*.

An Italian Home is Paul's first book

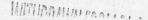

An Italian Home
Settling by Lake Como

Paul Wright

Earslwood Press

This edition published in 2011 by Earslwood Press,
10 Chaldon Close, Redhill, Surrey, RH1 6SX United Kingdom
www.earslwoodpress.co.uk

Set in 11 on 14pt Sabon MT
Typeset by Earslwood Press, 10 Chaldon Close, Redhill, Surrey, RH1 6SX United Kingdom
Cover design by Earslwood Press

This edition printed and bound in England by
CPI Cox & Wyman
uk.cpibooks.com

This story is based on true-life events, although many of the characters' names have been
changed

ISBN 978-0-9562308-1-2

iv

To my daughter, Sammie

I would like to thank Bill Munro of Earlswood Press for his encouragement and tireless work over many weeks, pulling this book into shape

Paul Wright, Argegno, Italy 2011

Contents

Chapter 1

Greener Grass

Back in 1990, I was living in a sixteenth century cottage in Godalming, a small town in Surrey's stockbroker belt, with Nicola, my partner of six years. I was, and still am, a self-employed artist, and our cottage doubled as my studio. I had spent my early career as a stage designer and scenic artist working mainly in London theatres, so living somewhere with a good train service to Waterloo main line station was essential, but for me, work in the UK had been getting irregular. At the onset of the decade, with severe economic recession and interest rates at record levels, it had all but dried up. People were only spending their money on the necessities required to keep body and soul together and art and live theatre weren't, for most people, a necessity.

Nicola was working as a legal secretary for a company of solicitors in Godalming and had done so for five years. Before that, her first job after leaving Godalming College was for an estate agent as a surveyor's assistant. She found working for the solicitors more enjoyable, but was often overworked, under pressure and, as summertime approached, she was in need of her annual break. We were pretty sure we would return to Spain, where we'd had superb holidays for the previous two years, but the time before that, our first experience of anything Spanish, in a timeshare apartment in Puerto de Alcudia in Majorca, had nearly put us off the country for good. The apartment belonged to one of the partners of Nicola's firm, and he had offered us a fortnight there for free by way of a 'thank you' bonus for a pile of extra work she had done on a particularly difficult case.

After two days there, we were wondering what kind of favour this legal partner thought he was doing us, as we were sure we could not stand another twelve days and nights in what we considered to be a truly godforsaken place. All we saw was kilometre upon kilometre of concrete high-rise hotels, shoved up to satisfy the demands of the tens of thousands of tourists who paraded along the seafront in various stages of undress and sobriety and we detested every bit of it. But we were there for a fortnight and as our accommodation was free, we decided to make the best of it and hire a car to explore the rest of the island. What we found was stunningly beautiful; inland, there were mountains covered in pine trees and around the coast were pretty inlets where a cobalt blue Mediterranean Sea lapped against the rocks. Consequently, we spent the rest of our holiday driving away from the coastal resorts to inland villages where the native Majorcans lived, well away from the hordes of sun-worshippers. Here we found peace and sanity, plus some interesting bars where we could hang out until the late evening, when we could return to the relative peace and quiet of our apartment after many of the holidaymakers in the resort had turned in for the night.

The following year we decided to try Girona, in Catalonia on the Spanish mainland. From there, we visited Barcelona, where we admired the astonishing architecture of Antoni Gaudi. We also went to the nearby town of Figueras, where we were fascinated by the museum dedicated to the surrealist painter Salvador Dali. At last we had found what we had been looking for in a holiday; a vibrant atmosphere, interesting cultural sights and, as a bonus, a profusion of tapas bars. We'd been warned that bag snatchers were about, but that did not deter us. We took the risk, had no trouble and enjoyed a truly stimulating holiday. We wanted more like them.

For our third visit, we wanted to visit the countryside of mainland Spain, especially the rural parts the tourist rarely sees, so we chose Andalucia, the home of flamenco, sherry bodegas and dancing horses. We stayed in Arcos de la Frontera, a picturesque village south of Seville, overlooking vast sunflower fields, with dazzling white buildings that seemed to hang from the mountainside. I fell in love with the place, and seriously began to wonder what life would be like if living there, in a non-English speaking environment, and if it would be possible to find work there. I realised that I'd had enough of England and I wanted to move to somewhere with character, with that atmosphere only time creates. I felt I needed to breathe an ancient culture in one of those aesthetically satisfying places where every day brings joy to the soul. Arcos had what I was searching for. Two-week annual holidays in a Mediterranean country just weren't enough for me any more.

For a while, Nicola shared my enthusiasm but her keenness soon faded and, practical as ever, she began to dismiss the topic as a vacuous adjunct to whatever conversation we were having at the time, but for months afterwards, a voice inside me continued to nag. "Go to Spain," it said, "you know you love it there."

But I needed Nicola's support and to be sure that she wanted to leave her native country behind. It had to be her decision and I knew I shouldn't, couldn't, browbeat her into making it, although I persisted with the subject. I felt that she was warming to the idea, but there still seemed to be something holding her back.

It was on one of those flat Sunday afternoons when nothing seemed to be happening that my frustration at not being able to emigrate to Spain, and in particular Arcos, blew up. "Why don't we give it a go and try living in Spain?" I cried out.

Nicola completely ignored me.

A few days later, there was a documentary about Salvador Dali on television and it included scenes of the Spanish countryside that had become so familiar to us. I wanted to be there, to experience the place once more. Nicola was in the kitchen, cooking when I blurted out, "Damn it, let's just pack up and go. What is there to lose?"

She made me apologise for my impromptu statement before she responded. "Am I supposed to guess what you mean?" She demanded, "I suppose you're talking about moving to Spain?"

When she followed it up by saying, "Okay, if that's what you want to do then let's do it! Why not? We only have one life!" I nearly kissed her. I was astonished. This was the sweetest music and I wanted her to repeat what she'd just said, many times over, to help alleviate my surprise.

"Yes!" she kept saying. "Yes! Yes! Yes! Yes! How many more times do you want to hear it? At least if I keep saying yes, it might stop you banging on about it whenever you get the chance."

"But I have to be sure we are both set on going to Arcos so we can start to make plans!" I answered.

"My concern," she countered, "is how we are going to find enough work to survive in such a tiny village when we don't speak any Spanish. I'm not sure you've thought it all through properly. And I'm not sure if it might be more practical to try an English speaking country, like Australia, or South Africa, or even America."

I agreed that it might be more practical, I told her but to me, living somewhere other than Spain where the quality of life wasn't as good wasn't a consideration.

"How do you know?" she countered, "You've never been to any of those countries. I just mentioned these places because we don't know what they're like. For all we know, their quality of life might be fantastic!"

Despite her finally agreeing to help me fulfil my dream, Nicola was still reacting cautiously by suggesting places to live I wasn't keen on. This perturbed me, so I tried to keep the focus on Spain by reminding her of what we would be missing.

"Do you remember," I said, "all that sunshine and all that wonderful food and wine we enjoyed so much on holiday? It's still there, waiting for us. When shall we go? In three months, two months, a month? When can you hand in your notice at work?"

She was in two minds about Spain, so to try to cast aside any conflict over our choice of country, I suggested that we should take a course of Spanish lessons.

"Absolutely!" came her reply. "If your intention is for us to move to Spain, then surely you don't think I'm going unprepared! Language lessons are the main priority!"

I saw her point, but to me, the priority was the cost of it all. We would need every penny we could raise to make the move and to survive when we got there until we found some work. Her precedent was to find a private language teacher and, depending on how soon we wanted to go, whether we needed to book an intensive course or not.

"It might cost a couple of thousand pounds, or maybe more," she said, "depending on how quickly we become proficient."

This was a lot more than I had envisaged paying, so as a

way of deferring the idea I suggested we wait until we arrived in Spain, but she frowned upon this.

"There is no way we are going to get out of it," she insisted, "If you really are set on going to Spain we will need to learn the language to at least an adequate standard, so we either pay over here or we pay over there. What's the difference?"

After that, each time we had discussions about moving to a new country, the subject of work raised its head immediately. Or to be more precise, giving up work in England; and it continued to do so. Nicola's contract of employment specified that she had only to give one month's notice, but she wanted to give her employers as long as possible to find a replacement for her. This was on Nicola's proviso we both learned Spanish properly before we moved, and she made it plain that she would monitor our progress and until she deemed we were competent enough she wasn't going to contemplate resigning.

For me, swapping countries wasn't as much of a concern as it was for Nicola, because with the way my work was, I had far less to lose: my situation couldn't have got much worse. But there was one vital thing we had to deal with before we undertook language lessons, or even looking after our own welfare, and that was what to do about Lucy, our beloved cat.

"When the time comes and if we haven't found a good home for her then I'm not going to Spain," Nicola said, "I hope you realise that."

I wanted to take Lucy with us, but Nicola put her foot down. "No," she stated, "we can't carry a cat around Europe with us. She'll be confused. Cats like stability and a set routine and if it doesn't work out for us, what then? We can't just bring her back into Britain and put her through the torment of six months' quarantine."

I sympathised with her point of view, but what were we to

do? Fortunately, Nicola had an answer.

"I'll ask my sister in Rugby if she'll have her," she said, "she's a cat lover and I know for certain she'll look after her as well as we do. That way, if we have to come back we can always have her back. In the meantime, I'm going to telephone Christine in Italy for a chat."

I thought it a bit strange to be talking about Spain, then cats, then her sister in Rugby and then suddenly switching to somebody in Italy called Christine with no connection whatsoever between what had been said previously, but who was I to argue?

"Who's this Christine?" I enquired, irritably.

"You know her," Nicola said, "Christine Masin in Moltrasio."

"Ah, that Christine," I mumbled, "How is she?"

"That's why I'm going to 'phone her, to find out."

Our first holiday together, six years previously, had been in Lombardy in Northern Italy, when we stayed in the medieval village of Moltrasio, on the western shore of Lake Como. Nicola knew the village well, because at the age of sixteen she had worked as an au pair for Christine, her husband, Giorgio, and their two children. During the eighteen months she spent there, she and Christine had become good friends, and they remained so, speaking regularly on the telephone. It was during one of these phone calls, that Nicola had arranged a twelve-day holiday for the two of us in Moltrasio. Christine told us that she could not put us up at her house, as she already had guests, but she arranged for us to stay with Boris, an expatriate Hungarian, a friend of hers. He owned the Palazzo Passalacqua, a forty-roomed, three-storey palace in the village and it was here that we would be staying.

Nicola was delighted by this news. "I first met Boris ten years ago," she said, "The palace is magnificent; wacky, but magnificent. Boris is rich, and completely crazy, but harmless."

Christine met us at Milan's Malpensa airport. To my surprise, she wasn't actually Italian, but a New Zealander of Dutch extraction who taught English in a Como language school. She was a large, blonde lady, a warm-hearted, energetic, Earth mother type who had that rare knack of making everyone who met her feel immediately at ease.

On the journey from the airport Christine and Nicola gave me a potted history of the Palazzo Passalacqua. Set in six acres of ground that slope gently down to the lake, it had been presented as a gift in the late eighteenth century to Count Andrea Passalacqua by a Papal family, and is typical of the Italian aristocracy's summer residences that were built when the region was part of the Austro-Hungarian Empire. During the holiday season, hundreds of guests, the women dressed in crinolines, the men in breeches and all in wigs and buckled shoes, would arrive by coach and, beside the most exclusive of all the Italian lakes, spend time being entertained by masked balls and magnificent banquets. Almost certainly they would have heard the music of one of Italy's great composers, Vincenzo Bellini, who was a friend of Count Passalacqua and a resident of Moltrasio. Here he wrote some of his most famous works, including *La Sonambula* and *La Straniera*, and had them performed at La Scala opera house in Milan.

The story of how Boris became the owner of the Passalacqua is less clear, but apparently, as a young man between the two World Wars he had worked there as a chauffeur and part-time gardener. He famously declared to the rest of the staff that one day he would return and buy the place. And in the middle of the nineteen-sixties, he did just that.

It appears he made a lot of money soon after the Second World War, and he was able to negotiate a price with the then proprietor, Baroness Nalder, to buy the palazzo.

Christine told us that Boris was away for a few days, and also not to expect too much of him when we did meet him, or indeed to expect much of his palace. Now in his mid seventies, Boris did not have anywhere near as much money as he used to have; in fact he always was less rich than he would have people believe. In latter years, many of his business plans had not produced the results he had dreamed of and in consequence he had not been able to maintain his palace to a reasonable standard. For the three years previous to our visit, he had been living in a camper van that he'd parked to one side of the palace, running a power cable and a water pipe to it because he found it more economical than heating the palace, especially in the wintertime. His wife, a powerful Russian lady, and their three daughters lived separately from him, in the lodge near to the lake.

"Don't worry," Christine said, "you'll be staying in the part Giorgio and I rented from him when we first came to Moltrasio. It's still in habitable condition. I still use it sometimes during the holiday months when our friends and family all want to stay at the same time."

Christine left us pondering about Boris and his situation as we passed through the busy town of Como, with its grey, slightly shabby stuccoed buildings and typically anarchic Italian drivers. Leaving the town behind, the road north along the western lake shore is cut into a narrow strip of flat land between the lake and the steep mountains. As we rounded the bend to follow the road, we could not have had a better impression of the area. There ahead of us was the magnificent Lake Como, bathed in the sunshine of an early September af-

ternoon. Tree-covered mountains rose steeply from the shores
and there was an almost mirror-like sheen to the water, disturbed only by the white ferryboats and the occasional water-
fowl.

A few kilometres along the lakeside road, we turned off
down a long, private driveway and caught our first sight of the
Palazzo. Its completely plain, stuccoed walls gave it a mono-
lithic appearance, and it still bore traces of its original, golden
yellow ochre wash known as *Giallo-Milano* – Milan yellow. At
the large wrought-iron gates to the side entrance of the
grounds of the Palazzo, we expected there to be some sort of
security system where we would announce ourselves via an in-
tercom and, in response, the gates would glide open to allow
us a smooth entrance up a wide driveway. Instead, Christine
got out of the car, took a key from her handbag and fitted it inside a badly rusted padlock that secured the gate. Struggling
with the lock, she asked me to give her a hand and together
we managed to unfasten it. I put my shoulder against the gate,
the hinges of which were as rusty as the lock, and, pushing
hard we managed to swing it open. Around the back of the
palace was a well-worn gravel courtyard, where horse drawn
carriages used to wait for their aristocratic passengers, and it
was here we unloaded our cases.

The palace appeared to be deserted. The shutters of almost all of the two-hundred-odd windows were closed, except
for those in the part on the ground floor where we were to stay.
Christine told us that because the weather had been so warm,
she had opened some of them to air our rooms. There was no
risk in leaving the windows open it seemed; Boris had sold off
so much of the palace's contents to cover his debts; there was
little of value left to steal.

Christine took us around to the front of the house via a

wide pathway, which was so dry that every footstep threw up a cloud of beige dust. Inside, Palazzo Passalacqua still possessed the grandeur and self-assurance of its era. There was an atmosphere of serenity, as if the rooms were relaxing in the shade, whilst outside everything was wilting in the heat, and a sense of permanence that was confirmed by the fact that all its features seemed to be untouched since the day it was built. Now these features, the columns and panels on the walls, the elaborate marble floors, were in need of repair, but at the same time the building's very presence suggested that it would be better to leave all as it stood.

The suite of rooms where we were to stay was on the ground floor. Once unmistakably grand, and now discoloured with age and grime, they were still in reasonably good condition. In the centre of the dining room was an enormous, dark mahogany table. Around it were thirty massive, studded leather chairs, blackened with age, each of which would require all of a person's strength to slide it away from the table. Set against the wall was a matching two-piece sideboard, with an immense mirror above. The dining room might once have been an anteroom, as it led through huge double doors into a much larger banqueting hall and beyond it were more sets of double doors, opening eventually onto a massive ballroom.

More heavy furniture filled our bedroom. There were two single beds, two bedside cupboards, a couple of upright chairs, another bulky table and another huge mahogany, mirrored sideboard. Around the entire room were dozens of wooden pegs, set just above head height and from these we guessed that the room's original purpose was as a guest cloakroom, or possibly a dressing room. Off the dining room, along a short corridor and through more double-doors was an en-suite kitchen. It stood silent and unused, but hanging from an armature of iron hooks, securely bolted to the ceiling joists, hung scores of great iron pots and deep copper pans. There were two wide, stone utility sinks, with immense white wood draining boards worn thin with bleaching and scrubbing. Oversized white ceramic tiles covered the walls from floor to ceiling. Here was a glimpse into what life must have been like, two centuries ago, when a battery of cooks slaved to feed the Palazzo's voraciously hungry guests. Christine informed us that our kitchen was the smallest of the three the palazzo possessed. Nicola's main concern was where to find pans small enough to be of any practical use that did not need two people to lift them.

That little problem aside, we already had the feeling that staying in the Palazzo Passalacqua was not going to be a hardship. In fact, our holiday would prove to be even more of a delight than we had hoped. Christine helped to make it so by introducing us to some of the locals in the village, and, one evening inviting us to dinner to meet her Italian friends that were staying at her house. It was then that I met Boris for the first time. He arrived dressed all in black, with a wide brimmed hat and an exaggerated cape made from heavy wool, which gave the impression that he was even larger than he already was. He was now seventy-five, still a robust man, full of energy, with a hearty laugh and a colourful demeanour and he scoffed his food as if he were starving. Even after an evening spent in his company I still had discovered little about him because most of the conversation around the dining table had been conducted in Italian. Certainly I got the impression that when Boris was around everybody seemed to know about it.

But that was all to come as Nicola and I began to find our way around Moltrasio and the leg of Lake Como where this little village is situated. Lake Como, like the other northern Italian lakes, was formed by glacial action and all are very deep, with steep mountains either side. Lake Como is in the shape of an inverted letter 'Y', with the town of Como at the bottom of the western fork and Moltrasio a little further north on the western shore of that fork. During the day we travelled up and down the lake, using the ferryboats that provide a regular and well used service, including a couple of charming old steam boats that originally replaced the large, covered rowing boats that acted as ferries until the late nineteenth century. We basked in the sunshine in Passalacqua's garden, cooked for ourselves in the ample kitchen and in the evenings, when the temperature had cooled somewhat, we sometimes rode to a bar in the next village on a couple of ancient bicycles we had found in an abandoned stable.

One Saturday night, for reasons unknown, we drank ten Sambuccas each and when the barman started to give hints he wanted to close up for the night we both realised that this was the first time either of us had been drunk in charge of bicycles. Outside in the street, as we tried to mount them, equilibrium deserted us, and attempting coordinated pedal rotation under the influence of a potent liqueur proved to be quite unfeasible. After several attempts to ride back to base we literally piled into each other, ending up spread-eagled across the main high street in a giggling heap, on top of a pile of tangled steel. It was then that the situation turned from laughter into a serious discussion about how to get back to our lodgings. Through our alcoholic haze we concluded that it was past midnight, we were too far away from Moltrasio to walk the distance required and we were incapable of riding bicycles. Besides which, some of the locals were beginning to gather around to watch the unorthodox spectacle of two floundering drunks trying to disentangle themselves from their bicycles. The sight of them brought Nicola's mind into focus, and she managed to raise herself upright, adjusted her clothing and made a vain attempt to walk in a straight line back to the bar we had just left, before the owner could pull the shutters together. There she rang for a taxi to take us back to the Palazzo Passalacqua. Surprisingly quickly, what must have been the only taxi in the whole of the Como region with a roof rack large enough for our bikes arrived and transported us away from an embarrassing situation. The next day, when our senses were reunited with rationality, Nicola thought that the only reason we got back to Moltrasio in the early hours at all was that when she mentioned the Palazzo Passalacqua, they must have thought we were VIPs of some sort.

The evening following our drunken adventure, two friends of Christine's, Enrico and Dina, invited Giorgio, Christine, Nicola and me to dinner. Enrico and Dina rented a small section of the converted stable block on the opposite side of the courtyard to where we were staying, which had previously been servants' quarters. On our arrival, Enrico, a man of average height with a stocky, muscular build and a large, square head devoid of any hair, opened the door to receive us. The four of us arrived reasonably well dressed for the occasion as guests with good manners are supposed to do, but we were surprised to see him dressed in a hole-ridden vest that had probably been clean at some time, but was now an indeterminable greyish pink colour. Dina, his wife, looked a lot better. She sported glossy, bright red lipstick, traditional Italian peasant costume with a full red taffeta skirt, a wide black belt, a short black embroidered bolero and a hairgrip decorated with green and white artificial flowers. Outside in daylight, it was a beautiful summer evening with the temperature around twenty-eight degrees Celsius, but inside it was dark, because the tiny windows kept daylight out and the room was lit only by candles. A log fire burned in the fireplace to keep the chill off the room; despite the temperature outside, the room was made comfortable because the sun's heat could not penetrate the thick stone walls.

We sat around the bare wooden table, with wooden plates in front of us. Bubbling away in a large blackened iron pot hanging on a hook over the fire was *polenta*, a kind of cornmeal porridge. It is a speciality of Lombardy and something I'd never even heard of, let alone had the chance to try. It is as much of a staple in the mountains as rice is in the rest of the north and pasta in central and southern Italy. It is cooked slowly for an hour, and cooking it in an iron pot over an open fire is the preferred method, which gives it a special roasted flavour.

For at least forty-five minutes after our arrival, Dina continued to stir the thick yellow mixture, whilst everyone else sat around drinking the local wine, a Barbera from Piemonte, and chatting mostly in Italian, but with the occasional translation from either Nicola or Christine so as not to leave me totally out of things. When the polenta was ready, Dina placed an oblong wooden board in the centre of the table. Enrico then lifted the heavy iron pot off the fire and poured its steaming contents onto the board. It was like watching hot lava flowing from the mouth of a volcano. Then he took a rack of beef from the oven, where it had been stewing in a sauce with porcini mushrooms. He removed all the bones from the beef, mixed it back into the sauce and took the whole to the table and tipped it into a well that Dina had made in the centre of the polenta. When he had mixed it all together into a scalding mass, each diner spooned as much as they wanted onto their wooden plates, washing it down with a few more litres of wine. When it was all eaten, Dina presented us with a delicious homemade tiramisu. All this demolished, we were served espresso coffee and brandy-filled chocolates.

When the meal was finished, we three men left the women to chat and sat on stiff, upright wooden benches each side of the Italian equivalent of an inglenook fireplace that had been blackened by centuries of heat and smoke. Enrico brought out at least twenty interestingly shaped bottles of grappa, an Italian *digestivo* and poured each one out, one at a time, for Giorgio and me to try, until we found one we could swallow without it taking the skin off the inside of our mouths. Of the samples we rejected, Enrico emptied onto the fire, the raw alcohol flaring up and lighting the dim room brilliantly for an instant.

I was surprised to wake early the next morning, considering our high alcohol intake during the two previous evenings. I swung open our bedroom window shutters, which opened on to the courtyard at the back of the palace. There, to my surprise, I saw Enrico, dressed immaculately in a light grey silky suit and seated in an equally immaculate silver five-litre Mercedes-Benz saloon, about to start it up and drive away. My impressions of the man were thrown into confusion: the night before we were in the company of what appeared to be a simple peasant, offering us a meal, wine and grappa that I would have thought cost much more than he could realistically afford. And here he was, sliding into the driving seat of a very expensive Mercedes. Did he own the car? Was he a chauffeur, or a bodyguard, about to pick up his boss? When I told Nicola what I'd seen, we went to ask Christine about him. It turned out that he had a very successful silk printing business in Como and he and Dina were very comfortably off, but at weekends they chose to discard the trappings of their modern way of life in their home in Como and decamp to the former stable block to celebrate an old style of living, and they liked to dress appropriately.

On the morning of our last day on holiday we wanted to thank Boris for letting us stay in his palace, and so we made our way to where his camper was parked. In the twelve days we had stayed on his premises we had only been to that part of the garden once before to visit him. His camper had been closed up then, but this was our final opportunity before we left for the airport, so we hoped he was there. From a distance we could see that the door and windows were wide open. We presumed there was a good chance he was at home, so we intentionally made as much noise as possible by talking loudly and stamping our feet on the dry impacted earth, to give him some advance warning of our visit. As we drew nearer, we saw that he had some time before removed the van's wheels and it was resting on piles of bricks. We hadn't noticed these bricks before, as the grass in the shaded area underneath was long and almost enveloped both the bricks and piles of discarded household objects he had obviously stuffed underneath the camper.

I knocked firmly on his caravan door, but the flimsy aluminium it was made of gave off more of a rattle. At first he didn't answer, but after Nicola called out his name, he came out and welcomed her warmly. When we told him we were about to leave Moltrasio for home, he reacted as if this was news to him, even though we had told him the date we were leaving the week before, at Christine's dinner party. I think that if I had visited him without Nicola's company he would not have known who I was. I think too that it was only because he had remembered Nicola from the time when she was the Masins' au pair, and from Christine's subsequent reintroduction he recalled that we had been staying on his property at all.

Nicola presented him with a litre bottle of gin and a large bag of mixed fruit as a thank you gesture, which he accepted graciously, spinning the top off the gin bottle within a matter of seconds. He then began rummaging in his kitchenette, presumably for a glass to pour it into. Unsuccessful in his search, he took a significant swig of it directly from the neck and then another. A brief glimpse into the inside of his caravan told us he wasn't the most domesticated of people, nor that he went overboard on cleanliness.

That visit to Italy left me with a deep impression. It was the first time I had been on holiday abroad and mixed in a non-English speaking environment with the people who actually lived in that country. It was also the first time I had been on holiday with Nicola. I had got to know her well but although I knew she had worked as an au pair in Italy, I had never once heard her speak a word of Italian. I thought, perhaps at best she would know a few words or some well-rehearsed stock phrases to get by on, but far from it. She was practically fluent. It was riveting watching her lips move, knowing the sound and tone of her voice well and all its intonations and yet not understanding a single word she said.

That experience in Italy had taken place in 1985, and now, six years later, I was sitting in our kitchen in Surrey, formulating plans for us to emigrate to Spain whilst Nicola chatted on the 'phone to her friend in another room. After a few minutes she called out for me to come into the living room and then told me what they had been discussing.

"Chris says that Giorgio has been transferred to an office in Rome," she said. "They are moving to the city centre in a couple of months' time, about the same time we plan to move to Spain and they want to rent out their house in Moltrasio."

I'd already guessed by the energised look on her face the plan that had sprung into her head. She didn't need to ask whether the same idea had entered my head as well. Forget Spain. It had to be Italy, and it had to be Moltrasio.

By the end of their conversation Nicola and Christine had come to an arrangement: We would take the house initially for one year, fully furnished, for a small rent. Both parties agreed on a year because neither could say what they would be doing beyond that. We knew that we could afford to spend a year without either of us working; we just hoped that we would find something to do to keep us going beyond the twelve months. Christine was happy with this arrangement, because if Giorgio's engagement in Rome didn't work out and they needed to return to Moltrasio, there would not be any complications. Also, she preferred people she knew to look after the house on a non-contractual basis and was not really interested in making a profit from the rental. And it meant that they could return from Rome to stay for holidays when they wanted. So, within twenty minutes, from a chatty 'phone call to tell Christine about our intended move to Spain, we had ended up making a firm commitment to fly to Italy the following April to take over a three-bedroomed house.

As soon as Nicola put the telephone receiver back in its place and turned round to face me she had a completely different expression in her eyes from the one she had a few minutes earlier.

"Now I'm much more confident our adventure will be a success," she said, "or at least more of a success than if we had decided on Arcos, because Christine can give us introductions to the right people in the Como area to find work."

For another twenty minutes we danced around the kitchen in delight. Italy or Spain, I wasn't too fussed about which one we went to. I think that both are fantastic countries and I was looking forward to the experience. Nicola was now in a position to hand in her notice at work.

"And as I am self employed," I said, "I shall go down to the pub and hand in my notice to myself."

A week later, a local friend and his girlfriend decided they would like to rent our house for the year we intended being away, with the possibility of an extension if we did not return. They were both looking to leave their parents' homes and set up house together and we tempted them to make the break by offering them the opportunity they had been seeking for some time at a rent they could afford. Rose, Nicola's sister, agreed to take our cat Lucy and we set up pet-insurance cover so she wouldn't be a burden to her if anything horrible should happen. Now the package was complete. All there was to do was work our time out and send some boxes ahead containing our heavier necessities, along with our bicycles. There were no other preparations to be made, apart from buying two return flight tickets to Milan from a travel agent. We bought return tickets, not because we lacked confidence in our commitment but because return tickets were cheaper than one-way tickets. And when the travel agent asked for our return date to the UK so she could issue the other half of the ticket, we answered, "None – we won't be coming back!"

For a brief moment after buying the tickets, I wondered what a person has to do to qualify to become an expatriate, apart from boarding an aeroplane and leaving his or her country of origin. Was there a statistics office we were supposed to report to prior to fleeing, to inform them of our intended whereabouts? Or to demonstrate to them in person that we weren't about to mysteriously disappear off their records?

There doesn't appear to be any legislation on this subject – one just departs. It's exactly like going on holiday, the only difference being, we did not intend to come back. At the airport I was half expecting to bump into some official form-filler waiting to foil our plans; after all, the UK authorities certainly want to know the whereabouts of their nationals when they live in their native country but when they are about to leave it, it seems they could not care less. Walking through the departure lounge at Gatwick for the last time as British residents, then stepping onto a plane knowing that in an hour or so we would be two of Britain's ex-pats gave us both an odd, empty feeling. For a moment I felt a pang of guilt at turning my back on a country that had on the whole been very good to me, but it didn't last. We were on our way, and to make matters easier, we were going to live in a fellow European Community country. There would be common rules and regulations regarding work permits, tax status and the like. Thanks to the EC, it was so easy for people to come to Britain to live and work and, if they wanted to, to stay permanently. Surely, we thought, it would be the same for us in Italy.

Oh, how wrong we were.

Chapter 2

Settling In

THE LARGE green, white and red sign opposite the exit doors of Malpensa airport that said 'Welcome to Italy' was looking very blurred. It took just a moment for us to see that it was pelting rain that caused the diffusion of the message. After running a dozen or so paces to a taxi we were pretty well soaked through. This was some welcome to our chosen country.

"Stazione Centrale per piacere," Nicola told the cab driver, as she slid into the back seat of his taxi.

"Certamente, Signora, subito, s'accomodi," he replied, "Di dov'è Lei?"

I had sat beside him and he was looking directly at me. "What?" I replied, smiling at him.

"Inghilterra," came the reply from over my shoulder.

"Mamma mia, Signora," he said, "mi dispiace molto per questo brutissimo maltempo. Questo è il secondo giorno d'acqua. Ma piove sempre in Inghilterra, no?"

"Ma stamattina in Inghilterra era bellissimo," Nicola said, "com'è la previsione qui?"

"Brutto, Signora, pioverà ancora domani, venerdì e la fine settimana e lunedì, speriamo che martedì sia bello di nuovo."

After we had left the taxi, I found out that this brief conversation that had taken place during the fifteen-minute ride to the Central railway station in Milan was simply about the in-

tensity of the rain, but my understanding of it was zilch. I had
not had any Italian lessons in England at all and had managed
to persuade Nicola that I would wait until we arrived to start
learning. She did not seem to be too concerned at what she
called my 'misguided logic', because she knew I had her to fall
back on, so the subject of an intensive language course had
faded for the moment.

"At least one of us can communicate when we get to Italy,"
she had kept saying before we left. "I think you're wrong not
to study the language, but that's up to you."

However, to help occupy the time on the plane from
Gatwick, I'd had a brief lesson in numbers, so when we landed
I had learnt to count from one to twenty in Italian both for-
wards and backwards without hesitancy.

From the station, we needed to take a train to Como, and
then another taxi to the house in Moltrasio where we were
about to start our new life. The unwelcoming weather still persisted, and according to the second taxi driver, torrential rain
was forecast for the next five days. We found the keys to the
house under a stone outside the back gate in an obvious 'secret' place Christine had prearranged with Vicenzo, her gardener and handyman. We had not much time to view the house
from the outside as we had to make a quick dash through the
back garden to avoid more soaking, but it seemed a lot taller
and narrower than I remembered from six years earlier and I
did not recall it being half-covered in Virginia creeper.

The house sat in a fork in the road on the southern outskirts of the village, acting as a landmark for local drivers. The
road to its left rose up to the centre of the village, half a kilometre away, whilst the road to the right hugged the contours of
the lake. The gardens, one at the back and one at the front,
were well stocked with flowers and plants, a shaded terrace

and a spectacular view across the lake to the ancient village of Torno. Arranged on four floors, the kitchen and dining room were on the ground floor, the bedrooms on the upper floors and a wide stone staircase with ornate wrought iron railings running from top to bottom.

Once inside, we could tour the place at our leisure. Nicola telephoned Christine and Giorgio in Rome to let them know that we'd taken a preliminary look around the house, that all was okay and we were already settling in. They had only moved out one month before, so there was none of that odour a building acquires when it has been closed for a long time.

The next day the rain subsided enough for us to venture to the shops in the centre of the village so we could shop for food before the downpour started again. As the bulk of our clothing wasn't due to arrive from the UK for another four days we had to borrow some plastic rainwear hanging in one of the wardrobes. Before we set off, Nicola gave me instructions that I must say 'buongiorno', which means good day, to everybody we came into contact with or to people we might pass in the street, so that the locals would begin to recognise and remember us.

And if we were out in the evenings, I was told to say, 'buonasera', which means good evening. 'Buonasera', I discovered, is used when dusk begins to fall. Nicola pointed out to me that there might be some confusion here, because some Italians, depending on the region they are from, prefer to say 'buonasera' in the daytime as well as in the evening. However, in practice it wasn't too difficult to get the hang of.

On this first visit to the shopping area, it wasn't really possible to say 'buongiorno' much, or to draw the attention of the locals to their new neighbours because in Italy, more than in most countries, it appears that the population tends to remain under cover when it rains, unless it is absolutely imperative to go out.

Consequently, the village was deserted and I had to wait indoors for another four days and for the weather to break into blazing sunshine for my inauguration. Then when the weather changed, I began happily strolling up and down the main street *buongiorno*-ing to every soul I saw. Before very long Nicola was telling me the complete opposite to what she had said on our first outing, that I had to regulate how many times I actually said '*buongiorno*', or at least remember who I had said it to and who I had not. She remarked that one old lady was looking completely bemused because I had said 'good-day' to her on four separate occasions.

Almost everyone in the village spoke only Italian, or at least that's how it was when we arrived in 1991. A few school children we met spoke a sentence or two of English but out of a population of nine hundred we came across only one older person who spoke any English, and he had once worked at the Savoy Hotel in London. Without a doubt, if Nicola had not been able to speak Italian to a good standard it would have been a pointless exercise choosing such a place, because communication would have been almost non-existent for a long time. Our original choice of destination, Arcos de la Frontera was of a similar size to Moltrasio, and very similar in its cultural make-up, so if we had gone there with neither of us speaking any usable Spanish it would have been very difficult, if not impossible, for us to have made any sort of life. At least here we could depend on Nicola's ability to speak Italian well.

I now realised just how completely unprepared I was. My only justification for this had been that I wanted to see if we really could settle in Italy before I committed myself to learning the language properly, but in the first few months of our settling in, I changed from being Nicola's middle-aged companion to the equivalent of her small child. I soon discovered, even after a few months of trying to communicate with the locals, that any Italian two-year old held a better grasp of the language than I did. If I had never felt like an encumbrance to her before, I did now.

At the start, whenever we went out shopping in the village, or on the days we spent exploring the area, I found that during a conversation with an Italian it felt more comfortable if I stood half a pace behind Nicola so I could hide behind her. Then, if somebody wanted to speak to me directly she could act as a kind of language deflector. On other occasions I found it helpful to stand to her side and watch her face intently for the appropriate expression to fit the subject being talked about and I would try to copy it agreeably, so as to appear as if I understood what was being said even though I hadn't a clue. Then, between pauses in the conversation, I would wait patiently for her to translate the general gist of what was going on.

Nicola is a very generous person and will help anybody as best she can over any issue and at the beginning she never criticised me for being slow to learn. "Just listen intently," she would say, "get your ear tuned to the different sounds and you'll soon pick it up."

She was now trying to encourage me by making it sound as if speaking a foreign language was as easy as falling off a log. That might be the case for some people, but not for me.

Our luggage and our bicycles were due to arrive any time in the next week or so, but without our bikes we were without our most reliable form of transport. Vicenzo, Christine and Giorgio's gardener-cum-handyman, and his wife, Adriana, came to our rescue; in fact they were to become indispensable to our survival during our initial weeks in Moltrasio. They were both small in stature but big in heart and were about as local to Moltrasio as you could get. Mainly by giving us lifts to the shops in their car, Vicenzo, whom everyone knew as Enzo, later introduced us into the local society. Recently retired, he had been a short-haul lorry driver and the work he did for the Masins topped up his pension. Adriana, known as Ada, did light domestic work for them. Neither Ada nor Enzo could speak a word of English, but somehow, with Nicola acting as my intermediary, we managed to communicate with each other. They were both exceedingly patient with me and my dependency on Nicola as a translator during those early days.

We think that Moltrasio is one of the prettiest villages of the many around Lake Como, if not the prettiest. It is situated in a man-made valley on the west side of the lake, nine kilometres north of Como town centre. It was once a Roman settlement: its ancient name is Monteraso, which means 'shaved mountain'. It is famous for its very hard, dark grey, almost black stone that was hand quarried and split into slabs to be used as steps or flooring. At three hundred metres above sea level, the village centre rests under the shadow of Monte Bisbino, a steep mountain of 1,325 metres (4,000 feet), which is regarded in these parts as a mere foothill compared with any of the neighbouring Swiss Alps. Two of Britain's highest peaks, Mount Snowdon and Scarfell Pike, are mere molehills by comparison. Without doubt, the view from the summit of Bisbino is spectacular and one can see more or less the entire panorama of the Swiss Alps, some thirty kilometres away to the north.

Although larger than most of the other lakeside villages, Moltrasio has a sleepy and relaxed atmosphere. The bottom of the village beside the lake has a completely different atmosphere from the older, upper part. It is very pretty and very exclusive, and it's where the well-heeled live and the smart tourists stop for a few days in one of the two hotels located in the village, either the smaller one by the lakeside, or the larger, half a kilometre from the lakeside in the village centre, with very few of them ever setting foot in the upper part, the *centro storico* - literally, the historical centre. Higher up a mountain pathway is where the food shops and the local bar, the Bar Centrale, are situated. Most of the older buildings in the *centro storico* are around the three hundred year old mark and are all built in the same style, being narrow and high with thick rendered stone walls, low pitched roofs with overhanging eaves and *tegole*, the traditional half-round clay tiles on top. The rooms are small – anything bigger than four by five metres is considered large – but all have high ceilings, sometimes with moulded plaster relief, and the ground floors are covered in either ceramic or marble tiles.

The reason houses here are narrow is that the flat bedrock on which the foundations were first laid had to be levelled by hand, and therefore land is at a premium. For the same reason, the lanes or passageways between the houses were built just wide enough for a laden mule to squeeze along. Moltrasio's Bar Centrale is in an elevated position, and to stand there, looking down on a patchwork of terracotta roofs, golden ochre walls and forest green shutters, bordered by the dense trees that envelope the mountains and beyond to the lake, is a memorable experience. It is all a happy composition of naturally aged buildings and streets where nothing is contrived or pretentious. Such an effect is indeed impossible to build at one go, from scratch. Although built by human hand, it appears to be completely natural. It is one of man's better achievements in a world full of planned and regimented townscapes.

Away from the village and further up the mountains there is another of man's collages on the landscape, the terracing of the mountainside. Used as grazing for cattle and goats, these terraces were made by building dry stone banks, filling the space behind them with earth and grassing them over. Nowadays, these examples of ingenuity and physical effort are mostly overgrown and difficult to identify underneath the foliage that has grown over them, but there are hundreds of kilometres of them running around the entire lake shore. The last of the herdsmen abandoned them and their animals during the middle years of the twentieth century. Italy's fascist dictator Benito Mussolini knew that Italy had not developed industrially like many other nations of Western Europe. To bring Italy into the industrial age, and to earn money from exports, he offered attractive financial incentives to the farmers and smallholders to move to the cities to take part in his public works schemes, turning Italy from a poor agricultural country into a prosperous industrial one. Now one legacy of that time can be seen in these abandoned terraces.

Three weeks after our arrival in Italy, our boxes of clothes and our bicycles finally caught up with us, two weeks late. We had soon found out that the house we had rented was in an isolated position, and without our bikes we had started to become reliant on Enzo and his car, an ancient, well-kept little Autobianchi to take us to a supermarket five kilometres away for the heavy foodstuffs. Nearly every time he passed by the house he would stop and kindly volunteer to drive us there. He told us it was no inconvenience at all, as he bought his petrol in Switzerland because it was cheaper than in Italy and he had to pass our house on his way there. Of course we could not let this go on forever, but without our own transport our opportunities to travel to outlying places were restricted.

I think Enzo enjoyed our trips to the supermarket and the occasional excursion he gave us to show us the local sights. I was bemused that he always wanted me to sit next to him in the front of the car, when I could hardly say anything comprehensible to him except basic greeting words and a few stock phrases that Nicola had been pumping into me. She would always sit alongside Ada in the back and the three of them were forever chatting, with Nicola constantly amusing them with news of our latest happenings as we tried to find our feet in a new environment.

And it was very new to me. Despite most aspects of the Italian way of life appearing similar to those in Britain, in practice many things are very different. For example, the names on hot and cold water taps gave me some sharp surprises. At first I decided that '*caldo*' meant 'cold', when in fact it means 'hot' (think of the word 'cauldron'). British Post Offices are open all day every weekday, whereas an Italian Post Office, the *ufficio postale*, closes at 1pm every day for the rest of the day. All local shops close on Monday afternoons. The rest of the week they all close at one o'clock for lunch, reopen at four in the afternoon and close in the evenings at seven. Throughout the whole of Italy, bus tickets are only sold at tobacconists' shops and bars and not on the buses as one might expect. And there are local oddities that confuse the issue still further. For instance, in Moltrasio you don't buy bus tickets in the bar. The local barber (who also closes all day on a Monday because it's against an ancient law to cut hair on that day) sells them, although the bar had done so until not long before our arrival. Industry and office workers have a two-hour lunch break, the majority of them going home for lunch and taking a half-hour nap before returning. This causes four rush hours per day instead of the two we are accustomed to in Britain.

All these things and more meant a different daily routine from what we'd had in England, and it took some getting used to; so much so, that on occasions I thought I was beginning to lose my faculties. A good example of this was when I stood pressing what I thought was a doorbell, fixed to the wall next to an apartment door in a condominium block. Beside the button was one of those plastic window tags that bear a resident's name. This one said 'LUCE', which I assumed was the name of the female occupant. After some time Nicola came along to rescue the situation and asked why I was standing in the hallway pressing the light switch on and off, illuminating all the corridors every ten seconds or so. I simply stared at her in amazement when she told me that '*luce*' in Italian means 'light'. This is the sort of thing I knew would get straight back to Enzo, which would amuse him the next time he took us on one of our shopping trips.

But I truly didn't mind Enzo laughing at things like this. To me, he is such a placid person, with an uncomplicated philosophy and he takes everything in his stride. I really felt I wanted to get to know him properly but it was still difficult for me to say anything of any significance to him or indeed to Ada. Trying to continue any sort of conversation with them without Nicola's aid was practically impossible, and if she had to leave our company for only a few seconds I was lost and we had to be content with smiling at each other, muttering 'ums' and 'ahs' or using sign language. If we had any of our new Italian friends as guests for a meal, be it Enzo and Ada or whoever, conversation just ground to a halt if Nicola wasn't close by or if she was slow in returning to the dining table for any reason. Pouring out some more wine, whilst we waited in embarrassed silence for her return, sometimes facilitated a mute situation, but if she took longer than I'd wanted I would have to take myself off to find her, exactly the same way a toddler does in those moments of desperate insecurity if its mother ever disappears out of sight. On other occasions she would often find me hanging onto her hand under the table, out of sight of our guests, which she soon understood to mean, 'for God's sake please don't abandon me at this particular moment'. Nicola also became a master at covering up for my deficiency in speaking Italian by talking 'at' me in Italian during some discourse or other to give people the impression that I understood what was being said. She cleverly angled the conversation so that it did not need a reply from me; at least I think that's what she did, because I still could not understand any more than the gist of what she was saying, if indeed I understood anything at all.

Nicola continued to amuse Enzo with more tales about the difficulties with the language and other peculiarities I was experiencing whilst living abroad. Although I soon worked out that if she had not informed him of the latest titbit about me to keep him amused, and if he felt like having a chuckle at my expense, he would ask her outright what I had been up to since we last met. I might have been a complete non-starter as far as speaking the lingo was concerned, but I wasn't a fool without sensibility or experience of life. At this stage in my development, that experience was about the only advantage I had over a two year old child.

I hadn't been wasting my time by not trying to learn Italian. On the contrary, I had got myself a book that promised me that I would learn the lingo quickly. By the end of the first month, according to the manual, I should have been on page twenty-five. When Enzo found out I had just turned to page three that morning, he started crying with laughter.

Just how quick is 'quickly' supposed to be, I wanted to know.

"In your case," Nicola said, "bloody slow."

I'd been hoping there might be an average time to learn a new language and that after a few weeks' study there was guaranteed proficiency. I was now beginning to feel humiliated, especially when I consulted the scale of competence on the latter pages of the textbook, only to discover I was evaluated as being irrefutably deficient. Somebody who wishes to live in a foreign country and is a bit overfull of pride, and does not speak the language of the country of his choice to an acceptable level will soon discover that his ego will take an awful battering. The longer the individual takes to learn the language, the more occasions will present themselves where he will begin to think he was born a complete buffoon. A lot of people can't hack the feeling of being dependent on somebody else to look after their welfare, even for a short a period of time. For the individual with a slow learning rate, permanently living abroad can severely rock his confidence. When it comes to learning a second language from scratch, it appears there is no definitive time span. It all depends on the capabilities of the person concerned, no matter how good the manual is. And if he doesn't learn it quickly enough to a satisfactory standard, then he will always be treated as a foreigner in his chosen country.

Nicola's excellent standard of Italian had been a great help to me in the early part of our residence, but it could also be a hindrance. Not only had she learnt Italian well, she had also picked up the mannerisms and gesticulations Italians are renowned for to good effect. Her membership of the Godalming Dramatic Society had stood her in good stead, because like an actor in character she knows when and how to

apply the correct gesture in any conversation so as to empha-
sise a particular point, so much so that she has continued to
fool many Italians into believing she is actually Italian. When
we first arrived in Moltrasio and we started to mix with our
new neighbours, they were eager to know what part of Italy we
had come from. But they found it confusing that she spoke
Italian fluently and I spoke it so appallingly. Nicola had a
tough time convincing people that she wasn't actually Italian
and had no parental attachment to the country at all. But when
I opened my mouth or attempted to use the correct hand and
facial gestures to accompany what I was trying to say, some of
the locals thought I was autistic, rather than artistic.

One such person who thought this was a local plumber,
whom we had called to fit some new taps in the kitchen. When
he had got to know us better he told us that when he first met
us in the village bar he thought Nicola was Italian and he could
not understand why an intelligent, elegant, woman in her late
twenties should want to shack up with an older Englishman
who was completely incoherent. Apparently he had got this
misapprehension about me when I was trying my best to communicate with everyone I came into contact with, trying to up-
date them with my latest progress in my attempts to learn the
language. At this stage I thought I was doing pretty well, because after about six weeks I had taught myself to count up to
a thousand without any hesitation and I was also learning how
to tell the time properly. I was pretty proud of that achieve-
ment, to the extent that one day in the Bar Centrale I tried to
inform this plumber and his mates, all of whom were slightly
intoxicated, with the sort of information a small child recites
to its parents. It wasn't surprising that he had formed this impression of me.

After several more weeks of self-tuition I was still at the

stage when, in common with most language students, I was beginning to feel inadequate. Some days were hard to get through and self-doubt was always to the forefront. According to the book I was using, this is the stage when the beginner considers giving the whole thing up as a bad job and even going back home. "Is it worth carrying on?" they ask themselves. "Isn't life difficult enough without adding more problems?"

I had read an article that said that when it comes to learning languages, acquiring a second language is the most difficult task. Learning a third is easier and the fourth and beyond are easier still. There is, it seems, an area of the brain that deals with learning languages, and if this area is re-awakened from years of inactivity its capability begins to increase. In my particular case, whoever it was who wrote the article had obviously assumed that that area of my brain actually exists! There are of course people who live abroad very happily in expat communities where they hang out with their own nationals, never needing to mix with the local community, and enjoy every day without ever needing to use a single word of the local lingo. Even asylum seekers have their needs taken care of through translators.

However, if there were any doubts I had done the wrong thing about moving abroad they were expelled very quickly when the month of June arrived. The summer was turning out to be blissful. Every day the sky was azure blue as far as the eye could see. The powerful scent of rosemary, jasmine and lilies wafted around village gardens. Lizards basked in the mid-morning sun as I lay next to them: my suntan was coming on a treat. A bottle of high-factor sun-protection lotion bought in England three years earlier that I had never had the opportunity to open, ran out in the first week. Nicola, forever the bookworm, relished wading through Christine's library between shopping trips and long afternoon siestas, whilst she left me to plod along slowly with my 'Learn Another Language Quickly' book.

In the evenings, we ate on the veranda in shirtsleeves, watching the sunset over the mountains while the lights from the houses on the opposite side of the lake began to wink at us. This was a period to savour, with every day a small adventure. Life was truly worth living. The weather, the food and the wine complemented each other perfectly and we kept saying the same thing to each other several times a day, that this was the life, and asked ourselves why we had not come to live here years before.

Every Saturday morning we bought bus tickets from the barber and took ourselves to the indoor food-market in the centre of Como. Anybody who likes food is mesmerised by this place and it's important to get there early to witness the most magnificent sight of fresh food in plenty before it's all sold. It's a gourmet's dream and he could go mad in there if left alone for too long. There is one particular stall that has continued to fascinate me to this day. It sells only one food product and would not look out of place as a living sculpture in Tate Modern or in the mollusc house of a zoo. It consists of a small kitchen table with a piece of that artificial grass that greengrocers use to cover their stalls. Placed on top of that is a bulging, hessian sack slightly smaller than the table top, weighing about fifteen kilos, with a knife slash running diagonally across it. As the morning progresses, big snails of the edible variety begin to creep out of the dark interior of the sack and eventually swarm over the entire table and down the sides of the artificial grass. Some of the more adventurous ones aim to cross the floor, inevitably meeting an early death when trodden on by the shoppers in the market.

After these trips to Como market we'd return home, enjoy a hearty lunch and then I'd sprawl out in the garden, rolling over occasionally like a well-basted piece of pork on a spit to even out my sun tan, letting ideas flit around my brain as I drifted in and out of a semi-conscious haze. Just about the biggest inconvenience I'd had to experience since arriving in Italy was having to move the sun-lounger from the front of the garden to the back in pursuit of the sun's orbit. Eating wonderful salads and enjoying the true taste of tomatoes was enlightening. Sipping light white wine under the shade of the fig tree was paradise. Being chauffeured around by Enzo and Ada and introduced to various parts of interest in the area that tourists hardly, if ever, see was inspiring. Enzo once took us to Lemna, the hamlet where he was born. Rustic in the extreme, it is in a completely unspoilt location. The houses are built entirely of stone that was rough-hewn out of the mountain and incorporate whole tree-trunks still with the bark left on for floor-joists and roof-trusses and the roofs are covered in stone slabs. If nothing else, it's a movie director's delight.

A day like this was typical of that first summer, an opportunity to recuperate from our previous, hectic, life in the UK. It took us a little while to be drawn into the sleepy pace of life in Moltrasio, but without any deliberate plan to do so, we began taking a one-hour siesta and we brought our bedtime forward by at least an hour. In a book I found on Christine's bookshelves I read how the lake area is supposed to have a soporific effect on the residents, and it would seem that since the Romans left, visitors have spent fortunes on building magnificent villas in which to reside, solely for the purpose of enjoying a good night's sleep. We had not been in Moltrasio long when we both noticed that once our heads hit our pillows we felt we could happily go on sleeping forever. We became aware of a blissful feeling that wafted over the senses, sapping all desire to stay awake, in the way it must have affected most lakeside residents over the centuries.

"Leave the real world on the Milano Autostrada," it seemed to say, "Relax and enjoy it while you can."

Slowly and unexpectedly, that attitude took us over. If the stock market had fallen 40% in the last two months, so what? The disasters that happen all over the globe, tragic as they are to those caught up in them, all seemed so unreal, so distant. How unnecessary worries seemed: they were for others. Moltrasio is a seductress who slowly draws out stress, replacing it with a feeling of contentment that soothes the mind. She can reverse age, ironing out the frown lines and crows feet on once care-worn faces. Even visitors from abroad remarked on how much younger we were looking since they last saw us. Peace and tranquillity reigned. Another day passes, another dollar is lost but there's no care. Here nothing seems to matter any longer.

However, we could not be idle for long. We had one year to prove to ourselves that swapping countries was a good idea. We were in no doubt that from the point of view of the quality of life we had done the right thing. It suited us perfectly, but could we find enough work to enable us to stay in Italy and enjoy more of the same? Were we living in fantasyland or in the real world? We were soon to get an opportunity to find out.

Chapter 3

Learning the Language

ONE EVENING we got a phone call from Christine in Rome, saying that she and Giorgio and the children would be coming up to Moltrasio for a week's holiday. Or longer, she suggested. They hadn't seen us since our holiday there six years ago, and she wanted to remind herself of what we looked like. She also wanted to help find me work. She told Nicola that she would organise a party at the house and invite some influential friends to view my portfolio. Hopefully, she said, that would do the trick.

Before the first day of their stay was over, Christine had telephoned so many of her friends that her social calendar and ours was full for the whole time she was in town, which had already expanded from one week to three.

"That's playtime sorted," she declared, "Now to find you some work."

Next, we sat down and talked about the plans I'd formulated whilst basking in the sun. I outlined how, when I lived in England and was first searching for work I had contacted all the architects and interior designers in the London area, and how it had paid dividends. Now, I hoped to use this method here in Italy.

"Looking at your portfolio, and from the quality of your

past work, you should find work here," Christine said, "but from my experience of living in this country, your method of cold calling simply won't work. Here, you have to know somebody or know somebody who knows somebody who will offer you work, especially with the client list you are going to be searching for. Frankly, without a contact base there is not much of a chance in this country, especially in the art world."

This left me a bit deflated, but she continued, "I have an idea. I have two good friends in Torno, on the opposite side of the lake, who have recently bought a large apartment in the Villa Taverna and they are in the process of doing it up." Holding up a photograph of one of my murals, she said, "They might go for something like this."

Within five minutes of telephoning them, she had persuaded them to take a look at my portfolio and arranged an appointment that same afternoon. Two hours later, I had a commission. Better still, they wanted me to start as soon as possible.

After the first day's work in their apartment, I announced to Nicola with some glee that to my relief they spoke English perfectly! When she heard this she looked daggers at me. I knew she had been waiting for the day when I landed my first job in Italy and had been intrigued to know how, with my miniscule vocabulary, I was going to cope in a work situation when she wasn't around to hold my hand.

"I'm glad you've found work," she said, "but these people are not going to do you any favours if they continue to speak English to you. All you are doing is postponing the inevitable. Either you learn the language properly, or we pack up and go back to England."

She also included Christine in this forceful assault against me, using the advantages of her friend's experience as a language teacher to reinforce her opinion against my evasive attitude to learning. She then followed it by saying to Christine, "I think he's beginning to believe he can exist here without ever speaking a word of Italian. He stubbornly refuses to take schooling, which is simply ridiculous."

Christine, sensibly, did not openly take sides, but I could still sense that there was an unspoken agreement between her and Nicola that I should be making better progress and that they would make an effort to ensure that I did.

Nicola voiced that consensus when she said, "I think it would be wise to do something about your inability to speak Italian sooner rather than later. You are lucky that communication with these clients is easy, but it might not be so easy with others."

I wanted to continue to live in Italy because I was in love with everything about the country, but I was afraid to admit to myself that I might never learn the lingo properly and thereby ruin my, and Nicola's, chance of staying here permanently. I also knew in my stomach that one-to-one lessons with a language teacher and learning against the clock would not work for me. Most things I had learned in life had been gained by my own endeavours in my own time and not by traditional learning methods, but I was very cautious, scared even, of telling Nicola about this particular aspect of the way I tick in case she flipped.

Learning Italian was definitely hard work for me, but considering their collective talents, Nicola and Christine could not have been less sympathetic. They understand the structure of language. They study grammar and literature for fun. When they are together, they talk about language, in the language of language. They talk about nouns and pronouns, verbs and adverbs, defining relative clauses, discuss prepositions and past participles (not forgetting the present reflexive and the imperfect), the conjunctions and the consonants. And who could forget demonstratives, possessives, and interrogatives, as well as the definite and indefinite article? Consequently, if they set out to learn a new language, they simply apply the same set of rules to it. It is the sensible way to go about it: it makes the learning process simpler, instead of a perpetual riddle. To them, learning a foreign language is a pleasurable experience that opens up new horizons. Languages allow the opportunity to travel and explore and to mix with people from different cultures.

Christine, the language teacher, and Nicola, whose knowledge of grammar was coupled with perfect pronunciation, were frankly baffled by me. What was foreign to them was that somebody should find learning a new language such an insufferable burden and they must have wondered how on earth they had become associated with such a numbskull as me.

Perhaps it was paranoia, but there appeared to be a noticeably stiff atmosphere when I was in their presence. They would sit next to each other, always watching me, with their legs crossed as tightly as could be. Christine would sit in her favourite upholstered Queen Anne lady's chair, with Nicola perched on the arm beside her, each with a glass of dry white wine in one hand and a cigarette in the other. Empty-handed, I would watch them and I could see their painted lips, whispering behind a hazy smoke screen. Their furtive eyes, almost lifeless, eerie and uncanny, weighed me up as if I were some sort of biological misfit. Muttering behind cupped hands, they assessed me ominously, as if deciding my fate. Occasionally they would indulge in a slow synchronised inhaling of tobacco smoke, callously exhaling it in my direction. If our eyes met, theirs would divert and focus elsewhere on nothing in particular. Their lips would curl downwards. Their bottoms would wriggle uncomfortably as they leant from side to side. Then, cigarettes exhausted, they would symbolically grind the stubs into the ashtray. Ashes to ashes, dust to dust.

Something had to be done. Since the moment we landed at Malpensa airport Nicola had become my protector, mentor and surrogate mother. At my insistence she took on the added role of teacher and sat me down with the intention of instructing me daily in our adopted language. She tried her very best to help. We began by spending two hours at a time of intense learning until she said her brain was beginning to hurt and I was too tired to think straight any more. The next day we started with revision from the previous day's work. For Nicola, retention of the previous day's work would be the proof of the pudding that her method was working.

The day after my first lesson her patience held up. The day after my second lesson it began to fray after only a few minutes. After day three it had deteriorated to the point where, scolding me like infant teachers used to do to their pupils, she took to corporal punishment, applying the edge of a ruler, the part that hurts, across my knuckles. Her exasperated conclusion was that I had the concentration powers of a flea and the retention capabilities of a demented geriatric.

It was clear early on that this exercise in home tuition wasn't working the way either of us had hoped it would and it was putting a great deal of stress on our personal relationship. After session four, our association nearly terminated altogether and I felt it wise never to ask her to teach me Italian ever again.

In the middle of one of these ill fated lessons Nicola described how ten years previously she had been through a similar encounter to the one I was experiencing, when she failed her driving test for the third time and could not afford any more private lessons to enable her to take it for a fourth. She then begged her father, a former driving instructor, to give her some free lessons. This, she said, ended in traumatic circumstances when she crashed his car into a traffic island. The moral of the story is, never ask relatives or partners to teach you to drive or to learn a language if living in acrimony is to be avoided.

Christine at least expressed some sympathy with my predicament, pointing out that as people age, the part of the brain that retains language has been scientifically proven to shrink in size if not used. If it is exercised regularly by the learning of new languages, the reverse can happen and it enlarges. Added to that, the older we get the more we lose the habit of learning and we forget how to do it. One reason that children are more receptive to learning than adults is because they are involved in the daily process of study at school and therefore the brain absorbs information with less effort than with an adult. However, all was not lost, Christine added, because it's quite possible that I was the type who picked language up in conversation, in contrast to others who learnt via the textbook in the traditional classroom method.

Nicola, now becoming really concerned about my inability to learn, decided to give this conversation method a try. In her mind the best place to pick up the language in all its forms and where there's always a plentiful supply of conversation about all matters under the sun is at the local bar.

"The next time we go shopping in the village," she declared, "and every time after that, we are going to stop off in the Bar Centrale and introduce you to the villagers. There is always somebody in there prepared to chat, especially if you're going to be buying the drinks."

A couple of days later, as promised I followed her to the village bar. Nicola was the only woman in there apart from the barmaid. Not to be deterred she soon got the ball rolling by ordering everybody a *bianco sporco con spruzzo*. This is white wine with a dash of Campari, topped up with soda water and a twist of lemon. It's a drink local to Moltrasio that's drunk by anybody who's a drinker. '*Bianco sporco*' means 'dirty white'. It's a peculiar name for a drink and ordering the same drink outside of the Moltrasio area, in Milan for instance, can cause offence if asked for without an explanation. A barperson might think it was a slur on the clarity of their wine or the cleanliness of their glasses.

We had, of course, visited the Bar Centrale previously on a few occasions but not for a long stay. A glass of wine each, a packet of cigarettes for Nicola, or the occasional coffee and a brioche in the morning, then we would be on our way. This time it was different. Because it was a sunny day, we decided to sit outside where there was more space to spread, well away from the smoke filled interior and at one of the well-worn tables on the terrace, next to the old men and the all-day card players. Here we joined a typical picture of life outside any bar, an essential feature in the heart of any village in a Mediterranean country where all the fit and early retired male pensioners and local tradesmen unite to pass the time. In fact they are more than just bars. They are the heart and soul of the community. For the folk of Moltrasio the sight of new people moving into their village is unusual. It's even more unusual when they are foreigners who wish to enter their daily ritual.

Foreigners who move into a village like Moltrasio rarely become involved in daily life. Almost all that move in are extremely rich and live in exclusive villas behind electronic gates and are certainly not inclined to mix in with the commoners in the local bar. They tend to remain standoffish and completely faceless all the time they are resident, so none of the locals would know who they are because they are unlikely to ever meet them. Nicola was keen to make sure that the locals knew we were not of this type, or that we had wandered into the bar by some error of judgment. She wanted to let them know we were not rich, nor were we renting a smart villa for the summer season. Most of the regulars at the Bar Centrale have known each other since childhood. One or two of them recognised us from our shopping trips to the food shops and already it was surprising after only a few weeks in the village how much information had filtered through about '*i due stranieri*', the two foreigners living down the road. Back in Surrey, Nicola's parents had run a bar for thirty years. It became famous for its village games and its vibrant atmosphere and ever since she was tall enough to reach up and pull a pint of beer she had learnt the practice of how to talk to people from every walk of life about nothing in particular and for all day long if necessary. A lover of people and social company, she is a good listener and an even better talker and she knows how to hold an audience.

So in the situation we had placed ourselves, almost akin to entering a members-only bar, Nicola was at her best. After I had bought everybody a drink she introduced the both of us to the entire clientele sitting on the shaded terrace outside. Most of regulars responded by pulling up their chairs around our table and welcoming us to their village. After that introduction, and every time that we walked into the bar we were greeted like old friends. A couple of the older men told her that they really enjoyed our visits, because it livened up the place and it gave them somebody new to talk about when we had gone.

So far as my learning Italian was concerned we had at least made a start. I had also begun to get some work, but I trusted Christine's assertion that I needed proper contacts in order to establish a reputation. One of the many social evenings that Christine had arranged was a dinner party for a lot of her rich and influential friends. If anything would get me work, she assured me, it would be this party.

For the fifteen guests Christine had invited, Nicola suggested I cook an Indian curry from a recipe I had practically bought from an Indian cook one evening in her parents' bar. I told him how I'd been trying to make a real curry for years, but they were a long way short of that magic touch I'd always enjoyed in a restaurant. We came to an arrangement whereby if I bought him drinks for the rest of the evening, he promised he would hand over the secrets behind Indian cuisine. We loved Italian food as much as we loved anything about the country, but every now and again we craved a curry. Unfortunately in Italy the chances of finding any type of cooking other than Italian are scarce and an Indian restaurant virtually nil, as Italians are conservative with a capital 'C' when it comes to eating other people's food. We did find a small Chinese restaurant in Como and visited it just once but, as we suspected, the Chinese proprietors had done what their compatriots do all over the world and had adapted their cooking to the palate of the host country. 'Italianised' Chinese food is bland, because northern Italians are extremely reluctant to try hot, spicy food –*piccante*, as they call it – and there is not much difference between it and Italian cuisine. The aromas and colours are different, but it contains lots of pasta, so the taste and texture are very similar. (To be fair to the Chinese, they did invent pasta centuries before Marco Polo is said to have discovered it during his travels to the Far East.)

Finding any foreign food products in Italy is a rare occurrence and so is finding food products made outside a particular region. Italy is composed of previously independent states
and to this day Italians identify themselves with their region
rather than their country, so cultural traditions in food run
deep. Thus Italians will stubbornly refuse to try anything new,
often deciding they don't like it before they've even tried it.
They are even likely to turn their noses up at Italian recipes
that are considered by the world at large to be one-hundred
per cent Italian but originate from a region other than their
own, so Nicola's suggestion of my making a massive chicken
curry served with basmati rice and side dishes, including mung
beans, pulses, mint potatoes in yoghurt and mango chutney,
and expecting Italians to eat it was taking a big risk. But Christine gave it the thumbs up, encouraging us by saying that the
crowd she had invited were a cosmopolitan lot whose culinary
tastes were not typically Italian. She added that she intended
preparing other things that she knew would be acceptable to
them in case the curry was frowned upon.

As it turned out there were no problems whatsoever. They
ate it all with great enthusiasm. Some even asked for seconds
and one Italian who lived just over the border in Switzerland
came back for thirds. I had intentionally made the dishes more
aromatic than hot, as most were tasting Indian food for the
first time. After it was all eaten, some of the guests wanted to
know the ingredients involved and, more importantly, the
methods I used. But when I started talking about ghee, ground
cumin and coriander, turmeric, sesame seeds, green car-
damoms, black mustard seeds, root ginger and grinding fresh
garam masala paste in a pestle and mortar, they started to look
a bit blank and tended to switch off. The general consensus
was that they had never heard of any such spices and doubted

their existence in Italy.

After the food, Christine cleared the table so that I could display my portfolio of photographs of contemporary Trompe l'Oeil murals I'd designed and painted and my unique Trompe l'Oeil painted furniture that I'd done over the years for clients in the UK and worldwide. It must have made an impression, as a Swedish friend of Christine's, married to an Italian businessman who was the best man at the wedding of Princess Caroline of Monaco, said her husband would organise a meeting with a famous architect in the Como area. Another guest knew the biggest firm of architects in the nearby Lombardian town of Monza and said she would also arrange a meeting. Not bad at all for an evening's work, and what's more, both introductions resulted in commissions for work.

A couple from Torno who were also at the party provided work that would last me ten months. The first phase was to paint a mural of a Japanese water garden in the mist in their oval dining room. They then commissioned one of my specialities for the end of their sitting room, a Trompe l'Oeil mural which represented an ornate wrought iron balcony overlooking the countryside of Brianza. Then they wanted one of their en-suite bathrooms painted as if it was a pergola covered in Japanese honeysuckle. In the cantina, the cellar where they kept their wine, I created the illusion of stone arches opening onto a view of Lake Como. It was a copy of the view they would have seen had there been a hole in the wall through to the lake. After that they asked me to colour wash their large office in eight overlaid pastel colours, creating the same hazy, sunlight effect I had achieved in their Japanese dining-room, with a flock of geese painted on the ceiling arriving back from migration.

The architects in Monza asked for a large Trompe l'Oeil

mirror to be painted in their showroom. The idea was to paint a series of shelves on the mirror with very expensive looking porcelain placed on them. A plain mirror the same size was then fitted on the facing wall to create the effect of the shelves and the porcelain pieces continuing into infinity. The Como architect, who was probably more famous as an Italian play-boy than as an architect, having married a succession of famous women and been a regular name in the magazine gossip columns, commissioned several projects that helped take the strain off our bank account.

I was certainly glad to have work coming in, but I soon found out that working for the Italians is not easy, because when they are paying for a project they tend to want to take complete control of it. On the surface, this might not sound unreasonable, and if I were an employee I should perhaps accept that they have an automatic right to exercise regulation, especially when it comes to having something added to their home that they are going to have to live with, day in and day out. But I'm not an employee, and although I am self-employed, I'm not a builder, and although my murals and Trompes l'Oeil might loosely be described as a form of interior decorating, I'm not an interior decorator in that sense. I am an artist with a particular talent for painting murals and the rules I follow are not those of a builder or a house painter, but I was often forced, and still am obliged, to make allowances for my client's lack of understanding.

At first I thought it just happened to be the caprice of the occasional client and that I'd been unlucky to have been chosen by one with a dictatorial nature, but I soon found out that they all behaved in the same way. It was most off-putting, and I kept hoping that I would find one that would be able to view the art work in progress from my point of view instead of their own and allow me to be the decision maker. But what I discovered was that when it comes to commissioning an artist they cannot, or refuse to, comprehend that there is a distinction between what I do and the work of, say, a cleaner.

It had become a case of the amateur dictating to the professional how he should be going about his business. It became so frustrating to deal with and yet I couldn't say anything in my defence because they were paying me for my skills. In general all the clients I work for are wealthy businessmen. They are the type of people who look into everything within their business and spend all their days ordering people about. They implement a technique for handling everything and every individual associated with their lives in the same way, so when I happen along I am treated the same as the next man. It is unlikely they will have employed a freelance artist before and so they don't know what to expect, how to handle me or what the outcome will be.

After I arrive at their house or villa, in general none of them has any idea at all of what they want and they will say that is why they are employing me, to give them some suggestions. I would in most cases come up with an idea or two of what I thought they should have painted on their walls or ceiling I would then return to my studio to prepare a design for them to consider, based on what we had arrived at, as a visual specification. It was also a guide towards payment based on the amount of time it was going to take to do.

If all is agreed and they like my suggestion, when the day arrives to start work, it can happen, depending on the attitude of the client, that he takes control of the project from there on in. It's a case of now he has been given the idea he begins to think he first thought of it and he knows it better than I do.

I describe what I do as 'artwork to order'. Generally, at

the end of every day's work I would be given the thumbs-up or down based on the client's opinion before I can progress. On several occasions I haven't had just the client to contend with. He will invite all his immediate family and maybe other relatives as well into the room I'm working in so they can make a joint decision about my work. It can be like battling against a storm. I might feel disillusioned by this, and although I might want to pull out, it is too late, because if I do I know it is unlikely I will get paid for what I've already done.

Since coming to Italy, most of the projects I have been asked to do have been for the nouveau riche in properties that are either new or have been extensively restored. These are generally people who have made enough money to set up their ideal home, but when they start, they find they are ignorant about what the construction process entails and normally the job ends up costing them a lot more than they anticipated. After the builders, plumbers and the like have left the site it is the time to furnish the place. That can include wall decoration, and that, to them can become more of a chore than a pleasure, because although they are probably very successful at what they do for a living, interior décor is a job for a specialist. Clients like these can and do make some awful errors of judgment, so much so they sometimes find they haven't got enough money to finish the job. I suffer from the effects more than a builder might, because the artist is the last of all the trades to be utilised and I've had some difficult moments at payment time because very little money, if any, remains in the pot. I've had a client who wanted to offer me a holiday in his family's mountain retreat as payment because his wife wanted a mural. I told him that I didn't want a holiday in the middle of the winter and I cannot ski. I've had one who wanted me to do a mural for free, on the proviso that it would be good publicity for me. I said, "I cannot do three weeks' work for nothing and besides who is going to see it in your bedroom?" I've had other ones who think that what I do for a living is just a bit of good fun and he said, "An artist doesn't need money because he gets satisfaction from what he does." I replied, "An artist has to eat and pay bills like everybody else has to."

I had another one who owned a massive chicken farm on the outskirts of Milan who packs and then distributes them to supermarkets. He is exorbitantly rich and his new villa was also exorbitant, yet when it came to payment time, he not only wanted a large *sconto* (discount), he wanted to pay some of my fee in frozen chickens, a huge rack of lamb and, as it was Easter, a couple of *capretti*, young goats. I told him he had to be joking, but it turned out he wasn't. I argued, but he wouldn't budge and so I was forced to load my car with his merchandise. Our poor freezer wouldn't hold even a quarter of what he'd dumped on me.

What happened after that added more insult to injury. As it was Easter, Nicola and I had been invited to a neighbour's house for lunch and I decided to deliver all the meat I'd been given to his house two days before, so he could prepare it for the feast. He was more than delighted with my contribution towards the proceedings because there was enough to feed all ten of his guests. When we arrived on the day there was hardly any of it served and all I got was a scrappy bit of goat. He had a large family of relatives scattered around the village who he said didn't have enough money to buy baby goat, which is not cheap. It transpired he'd cooked it all in his kitchen, then he'd distributed most of it to his family, so with the fruits of my labour, I ended up feeding a couple of dozen people I didn't even know!

With some work to get on with, there was a pressing need

to buy a car. Rolling up at a multi-millionaire's villa on a bi-cycle is good from a fitness angle but it's not very good for the image and the joke wears thin after a short time. Working in Torno, which is on the opposite side of the lake, had been no problem from a transport point of view. I took the ferryboat every morning through the most sensational landscape, re-turning the same way in the evening, which was more conven-ient than having to cycle 25 kilometres along the lakeside road. And if the owner was at home he brought me back in his pow-erful speedboat, which was so fast I felt like I'd got back to Moltrasio before we had even left Torno. We knew that buy-ing a car involved getting various documents processed, which would bring us sharply into contact with Italian bureaucracy. If we thought we knew something about the Italian way of life, we were in for quite a surprise.

Chapter 4

A Fight with Bureaucracy

THE FIRST DOCUMENT we as foreign residents needed in order to buy a car, or for that matter to make any other major purchase, was a work permit, a *permesso di soggiorno*, which also acts as both the permit required for residing in the country for longer than three months and the document required to get a *codice fiscale*, a fiscal code.

An occurrence during a village coach outing started us making comparisons between Italian and UK bureaucracy. During the trip, a young woman from Moltrasio by the name of Marina introduced herself and asked us if we had any contacts in Britain, because she wanted to go there to improve her spoken English and, hopefully, to find work. She was nervous about the bureaucracy involved and whether it was a tortuous business and, worse, would make her ambitions unfeasible. Within five minutes, Nicola had wiped away any fears this young woman had. Firstly, she told her she could stay with her mother at her bar in Surrey for free, probably on the proviso of offering a donation towards her food, until she was settled. Secondly, to find work, all she had to do was to go down any high street in any town and she would find a job centre, where she could register for work. There, she would be handed a list of available work and if she were prepared to do anything, she would probably find a job immediately. Thirdly, there is no additional layer of bureaucracy. Now we were all partners in the

European Union and as a European citizen Marina did not need any documentation or permissions. She could get on the next plane and start work in Britain the same day if she wanted to.

"It's that easy," Nicola told her, "the Job Centre will fill in any forms you need and your employer will fill in the rest, so you won't need to do anything. As a tourist, you will need a P11 form that covers you for a year for any medical requirements, or until you start work, and then National Insurance contributions will automatically be deducted from your wages."

The surprised look on the young woman's face was comical. She could hardly believe what she had just heard and she seemed to look to me to confirm what Nicola had said was the truth. A few weeks later, Marina did just as Nicola had suggested. She went to stay with Nicola's mother for a while, found work, moved on and we've never seen nor heard of her in Italy since.

In our case, a completely contrary chain of events was about to happen, and it was a period in our lives we will never forget, much as we might want to. We experienced restrictions, and the emotions that go with them, that people must have endured during the fascist regime. If you are familiar with the work of the Czech writer Franz Kafka you will recognise strong similarities between our experiences and the oppression and frustration that Kafka's characters suffer. The only difference between Kafka's fictional characters and us was we always had a choice. We could at any time use the 'get-out clause' of our UK citizenship and return to Britain if everything got too unbearable.

There are, however, certain groups of people exempt from these trials and tribulations. Foreigners, whether EU citizens

or not, who work for international or multinational companies and who are transferred to Italy for any length of time
will not have to face any of the problems we had to undergo.
The company they work for will take care of all their bureaucratic details. All their housing, taxes, medical insurances and
schooling for their kids in international schools will be taken
care of. Also, most of them will never need to learn a word of
Italian because their work colleagues will undoubtedly speak
their mother tongue or the accepted international language of
English.

Then there are the people, mainly the early retired, who
wish to move abroad to see out their twilight years in areas
like Tuscany, Umbria and the Veneto with secure private pen-
sions and other investment income and most likely private
medical insurance. Like the employees of the multinational
companies, these people will have little involvement with Italian bureaucracy because they don't require any involvement
with the state. They will have comparatively few forms to fill
in and will live more or less autonomous of the system. And if
they do, the areas where these ex-pats tend to congregate have
a host of agencies that can help them on matters such as land
and property purchase, as well as supply translators to take
the strain out of it all.

But it was very different for us; for instance, if Nicola
wanted to take a job with an Italian employer, or for me as a
self-employed artist looking to set up my own business in the
Como area and hoping to carry on as if I were still in opera-
tion back in the UK, or for either of us trying to buy a car or
open a bank account or make payment for any other major
transactions we were to be disillusioned, big time. The pitfalls
in Italy were cavernous and for us there was nobody to ask for
advice. We had come to Italy off our own bat and we did not

know anybody, or know of anybody, who had tried to set up a small business in this country.

So now we each had to get a *permesso di soggiorno*, and to make our applications we both had to go to the *Questura*, the main police station in Como, to register ourselves. Naively, we imagined that we would pop along with passports in hand to be met by an obliging policeman who would rubber-stamp a piece of paper for us, then say, "Here's your permit, sir, and yours, madam, all present and correct. Have a nice stay in our country."

So, off we went, one weekday morning, taking a bus ride to Como and a two-kilometre hike across town to the *Questura*. We arrived at 09:30, and the first error of judgment we made was to arrive at what turned out to be quite a late hour. Our second error, made immediately after, was to stroll casually into the building. As soon as we got inside, we were promptly ushered outside again, and told to join a queue of about fifty poor looking souls in the street who turned out to be a load of impoverished immigrants all wishing to live and work into Italy. From our position at the back of the queue, we could see that the doors to the room where the processing took place were open and it appeared to be packed to busting with another fifty or so people also waiting to have their documents processed. Nicola spoke to a man in blue, who was allowing two people in at a time.

"We are EU citizens, not aliens," she said, "Surely there's been some mistake?"

"There is no mistake," he informed her, "You have to wait here along with everybody else until I let you in."

Our turn to be admitted came after about two hours, and being squeezed into this very noisy processing room our concern was how to stay upright. The swell of people had not lessened any and we seemed to have one of two choices; either to get out of there and forget about applying for documents on this particular day or join the push and shove and ram our way further in, like everybody else was doing. In those few seconds our indecision about what to do for the best was decided for us by the people behind us. We could not have got out of there even if we had wanted to, because we were unceremoniously packed against jostling bodies of all races, colours, creeds and smells. There were no signs of any kind to divide EU citizens from non-EU citizens.

"Surely this is a mistake on the part of the immigration authorities," I yelled to Nicola above the din. "If it's not, then they must be blind or they're having a laugh at our expense. Haven't they noticed we are the only white faces in a sea of darker shades? Tell the policeman we are English and we are from one of the most civilised countries in the world and that we demand attention! Tell him, we don't have to be in this country and that we are here because we want to be here, not because we have to be! Tell him there's a difference between those who are desperate to get into Europe and those who are already here!"

"Tell who?" she snapped back. "I can't move to tell anybody anything!"

When I saw a tear welling in her eye and her despair under the weight of an ever-increasing swell of bodies in front of her and behind, my temper began to boil.

Nicola said that at the rate people were being dealt with, there was a good possibility of the office closing down for lunch and that we might have to repeat the entire travesty of a process all over again in the afternoon.

"No way," I retorted.

In a situation of injustice like this, my competitive instincts kick in and the British bulldog resolve comes to the forefront and dignity, good manners and respect for my neighbour's welfare go out of the window. Back in England I had played football to a semi-professional standard, and this was one of those occasions in life when my experience on the soccer field came in useful. Within a few seconds my adrenalin was pumping high and my self-control was threadbare. I used every ounce of weight, anger and brute force I possessed to bulldoze a passageway to the front of the mêlée and one minute later we were both in front of a wire mesh cage, and through it facing the one and only policeman doing the processing. Behind his protective screen, his mask-like expression made him appear to be totally immune from the pandemonium in the room.

Nicola, dishevelled, disturbed and very unhappy at having to fend for her own safety, handed both our passports over the counter, whilst I protected her back from the surging crowd behind. We watched his eyes for a glimmer of reaction but, without saying anything or raising his head, he lifted his left arm and waggled his hand about as if he had an agitated twitch in it. This was his way of indicating he wanted something in addition to what we'd already given him.

When Nicola managed to persuade him to actually tell us what he wanted, he said that we should have filled out and brought with us an application form each, a document of which we knew nothing, plus four passport photographs each and photocopies of every page of our passports.

The man was neither helpful nor unhelpful. He spoke in a muffled voice with a heavy southern accent that seemed to be intentionally inaudible, but when Nicola asked him as nicely as she could to repeat what he had said, he passed us a couple of application documents he needed us to complete, then he simply called out, "Il prossimo!" (the next one).

He then raised his left arm again, this time high above his head, and demonstrated an aggravated impatience at our presence by flicking his hand in a bombastic way, which was supposed to signal our dismissal. Then on the downward stroke of the same arm he bade the next in turn to replace us. Immediately the crowd behind us saw his signal, the sheer weight of numbers pressing against me in the surge to be 'il prossimo' forced us to one side.

Outside in the street once again, Nicola turned to me and said, "I don't know what we have to do. I am completely baffled and totally livid!"

After recovering somewhat from this completely unexpected trauma we had a serious discussion as to whether or not we pack up and go back to the UK. From this, Nicola came to a decision and said angrily, "This system is completely illegal and degrading and I intend defeating these authorities and this system, even if I die in the process!"

Before we trudged back to Moltrasio, Nicola suggested that we should get our passport photographs taken. We knew the Central Station at Como had the only public photo-booth in the whole town, and fortunately for us it was working, so at least the day was not a complete waste of time. The next day we went the Municipal Building in Moltrasio to get the photocopies we needed from the only public photocopying machine in the village and the day after that we returned to Como, arriving outside the Questura one hour before they opened the floodgates. This time we almost got to the caged-in counter first but made it in third place. That was acceptable, but further frustration and irritation was at hand, because we only had one photocopy each of our application forms instead of two each.

"Come back when you have them," said a tired looking officer.

Outside in the street once again, Nicola could not contain herself any longer and burst into tears of frustration, mixed with anger and despair. My fraying temper was willing me to physically destroy anything that came to hand, but I fought it and eventually it passed over. What really angered me was we had everything in order, apart from two photocopies. The policeman could easily have copied them to help us avoid any more anxiety, because behind him, no more than a couple of strides away we could see a photocopying machine and yet, when we asked him, he refused to do so.

I'm sure the only thing that got us through that morning was the relief of knowing all we had to do was get two more photocopies done and survive one more battle in the processing queue. If it had been more complicated than that, I think we would have said, 'forget trying to live in Italy!' Finally, the next day we got our hands on the necessary pink duplicated form that told us we should return in four to six weeks time to receive the documents we needed, duly processed.

Four weeks later, exactly to the day, Nicola telephoned the Questura's enquiries number to ask them if our papers had been processed. There was no answer, and she continued to phone several dozen times over the next two days in the hope that everything was ready, but she never did get through. We waited another week before we returned to Como central police station, in order to make sure there was more of a chance that our documents had been prepared. We remembered to set off at the crack of dawn to get to the front of the queue in front of those confounded doors. Finally, round one was over. 'Valid for one year only' said these primary documents that would allow us to obtain the rest of them.

Our anger was still festering inside. Nicola especially found the whole process humiliating and for members of the European Union she knew it to be illegal and unnecessary. She was so infuriated at the injustice of it all that for a while she intended to tackle the authorities at a higher level or to make a big noise in front of the European Council if necessary. For five weeks we had been marooned by officialdom. We could not buy a car, we could not open a current bank account and we could not, legally, work. The absence of any information or assistance was beyond reason. Even Nicola, who possessed a near-perfect command of the Italian language, with a well above-average intelligence and, having worked at a high level as a legal secretary in Britain for many years, with the professional ability to cope with complex officialdom and the law, could not make head nor tail of this system. What perplexed both of us was how on earth the unfortunates we had fought against in the processing queue, who were most probably illiterate and more than likely with none of Nicola's talents, cope with the system they and we had to undergo.

Soon after that never to be forgotten experience, we were passing the Questura one day when we spotted a couple of Asian gentlemen in a side street, using the bonnet of somebody's Fiat Uno as a desk. On closer inspection we saw they were doing a roaring trade, filling in application forms for a row of immigrants waiting to apply for their right-to-stay permits.

"So that's how it's done," Nicola said, "If only we'd known that, we could have paid them to take care of all the nonsense we had to suffer."

After this experience we became sure that it was obvious, even to someone with the dimmest spark of intelligence, that the Italian state doesn't want the foreigner working in Italy.

With millions of its own people out of work it doesn't need
visitors, EU citizens or otherwise, knocking on its door, making the situation even worse. Therefore the system is intentionally made as hard as possible to comprehend. It's only the
really determined that make it through the considerable dis-
comfort that's placed in front of them.

Round two was to obtain a residence certificate, a *permesso di residenza*. Even though we held the obligatory and hard
earned *permesso di soggiorno* it did not necessarily mean that
we were guaranteed residency. If we as foreigners were refused
this document we still would not be able to live in Italy officially. Christine's dinner party had resulted in more recommendations, which in turn provided a list of potential clients
all wanting my work, so to fulfil my commitments a car had
become essential. We found out from *il Municipio*, Moltrasio's Town Hall, that to obtain the *permesso di residenza* we
needed to make an appointment with our local village policeman, so he could verify that we were not undesirables.

In Moltrasio there is only one policeman, *il vigile*, and instead of a police station he has the use of a small office in the
Municipio. We needed to see him as soon as possible but we
discovered that before he could issue any documentation he
first had to visit the applicant's place of residence, to witness
for himself that they are who they say they are and that they
live where they say they are living. Therefore we set off in determined mood to find him. His office door was wide open.
The room was 'L' shaped, with walls of a drab, nicotine colour
and there was a battered old desk in the corner with piles of
unfiled papers scattered about on top of it. A strong smell of
stale tobacco lingered in the air and there were two ashtrays on
the desk with the stub-ends of at least two packets of cigarettes forcefully stumped out in them. Well above head height

were two windows, firmly closed and my impulse was to open them to let in some fresh air. *Il vigile* himself was nowhere to be seen, but there was one cigarette end still smouldering in the ashtray and this suggested that he could not be very far away. The question was, should we wait for him or should we go?

We decided to ask where he might be, and returning to the ground floor, we found a middle-aged lady sitting at an ancient typewriter in the general office.

We asked her if she knew where *il vigile* was. She glanced at a massive wall clock, then suggested we try the Bar Centrale. "It's ten thirty," she said, "so it's his coffee time."

At the Bar Centrale, a short walk away, we asked the owner if *il vigile* was there. "No," the owner told us, "he's not here. You've missed him by a second."

"Great!" Nicola responded, "we might as well have a coffee ourselves whilst we decide what to do next."

Coffee duly drunk, we returned to the Municipio to find his office door firmly locked. On it was a sign we had not seen before, showing his hours of duty. 10:00 to 12:30 and 14:30 to 17:30, it proclaimed. The time was a little after 11:30. Downstairs again in the general office, the lady at the typewriter said she did not know where he was if he wasn't in the bar or in his office, and suggested we telephone him between the hours written on his door to make an appointment. She then wrote down his telephone number for us.

That same afternoon, Nicola telephoned his office several times but there was no answer. The following day I had to return to Torno to continue working. I could not have another day off wandering around in search of an elusive policeman. But the next day Nicola did manage to speak to him on the telephone and arranged an appointment for 10:00, two days hence, on a Saturday morning.

Half an hour before our appointment with the policeman we set off from the house. Already the temperature was at twenty-eight degrees Celsius, so the trek had to be done in shirtsleeves and taken at a relaxed pace.

It was almost a replication of three days ago. His door was wide open, the lights were on and a cigarette was balancing on the edge of an ash-tray, with a thin line of blue smoke spiralling from it, towards one of the closed windows above.

"Would you believe it?" Nicola said to the lady behind the typewriter. "We have an appointment right now with the *vigile* and he's not in his office."

Just then, a young lad passed by carrying a plastic beaker of coffee. Nicola asked him if by any chance he had seen the *vigile*.

"Si, Signora," he replied, "I've just come from the bar and he's in there."

We thanked him then rushed to the bar as fast as we could. A quick glance inside and around it and we could not see him.

Nicola stood in the centre of the bar and addressed a question to everyone present. "Where is the *vigile* now?"

"He's just gone," somebody replied.

"He's in the toilet," somebody else added.

There was a bit more discourse between some of the other customers and their consensus was that he must be in the toilet because he always relieves himself at 10:00 every morning.

Hot and sweaty, we decided to join our new-found friends on the bar terrace for a chat and to cool down, at the same time keeping a close eye on the toilet door. In the meantime Nicola entertained the locals by telling them the trouble we were having tracking down our elusive Mister Policeman.

One old boy's advice to us was to take it easy and don't fret. "If you need him," he said, "it's best to wait for him here and that way he will come to you, instead of you having to go to him. After all, he's only in his office for an hour a day and for the rest of it he's in here on bar-duty drinking grappa or cognac, or he's in the *gabinetto* (the toilet) getting rid of all the crap he's so full of."

Some of the locals told us he possessed a police-issue bicycle, but he had not been seen on it for at least a decade because he was carrying so much lard around his waist that it was impossible for him to lift his leg over the crossbar. They continued to reinforce their opinion that it would be better for us to wait in the bar until he arrived for his morning coffee, and then, if we bought him a large cognac to go with it he would sign anything put in front of him.

Ten minutes later there was still no sign of the *vigile* leaving the toilet, but the old boy who commiserated with our plight was having a great time slagging off his local cop, suggesting all sorts of things he might be doing behind the closed door and calling him a *terrone*, which literally means 'person of the earth' but it is a discriminatory and disparaging term the northern Italian often uses to describe southerners.

Suddenly, in the middle of his discourse Nicola sprang from the table and pointed towards the street. "There he is!" she declared spontaneously, "in the blue short-sleeved shirt. Let's run after him before we lose him again!"

It was then everybody in the bar turned their attentions from the toilet door and focused them onto the village copper apparently heading in the direction of the town hall.

I had never seen this *vigile* before; in fact, thinking of it, it was the first time I had ever seen a policeman in Moltrasio at all. On first impression he reminded me of a heavily set, suntanned Rod Steiger, when he played the role of the local slob cop in the film *The Heat of the Night*, which was set in a southern US hick town. I could never imagine this figure walking the half kilometre distance to visit our house in the heat of the day to issue us with the correct documentation and then back again unless we were prepared to carry him there.

"Oh, by the way," Nicola asked the onlookers as she rushed to exit, "What is mister policeman's name?"

"Pompino," was their collective response.

"Signor Pompino!" she shouted to the man in blue, "un'attimo per favore!" "Please wait a moment!"

As she shouted his name I leapt to my feet and was a few paces behind her when she shouted out his name for a second time.

"Signor Pompino! Per favore!"

It was then I happened to turn and look back at the customers in the bar and saw them rising in unison to their feet, all drawing in their breath rather like everyone in a football crowd does when the ball is nearing the goal.

"Signor Pompino!" she continued, "Fermi!" "Stop!"

But the man kept on walking. After a few more paces she caught him up and ran around his corpulent figure, standing in front of him and blocking his path.

"Signor Pompino," she continued, "I'm very glad to see you. My name is Nicola and if you remember, I telephoned you the other day for an appointment in your office this morning. I arrived with my companion at ten o'clock but obviously you must have had more urgent things to attend to and you were not there. Please, Signor Pompino, I need you to come to my house as soon as you can, that is, when your busy schedule allows you to do so, if that's agreeable to you, because we need our *permesso di residenza* documents as soon as possible."

On closer inspection of the *vigile* as I stood near him I saw that he was sweating profusely and, judging by the stink of his extremely overweight body, decidedly unwashed. But worse was to come. He had a startled, bewildered expression about his face that didn't look wholly receptive to her request.

"Who are you talking to?" he said gruffly, as if he was shaken by her approach.

Nicola held out her hand with the intention of once again introducing herself, but he just looked at it disconsolately and brushed it aside, turning his enormous belly away from her. He then snarled, curled his nose up at her as if she were omitting a peculiar smell, stepped around her coldly and started on his way again.

"No! No!" Nicola appealed. "Signor Pompino, I think you've misunderstood! We need to speak to you as a matter of some urgency about getting our papers in order."

But he continued to walk on, unheeding of her pleas. Once again she caught up with the corpulent figure, ran around him and spread her arms apart to bar him from moving any further. The look on his face now turned from a disgruntled frown into one of horror, as if he had been stung on his backside by a persistent bee. Then curiously, he slowly raised his upper torso to its full bloated height (which wasn't actually very high) while at the same time breathing in a load of air to his over-proportioned chest. And then, in a display of agitation, he spun his gun holster around his ample waist at least three times as if preparing to draw his pistol on her. In the same instance, like an angry bull, he expelled the air from his lungs, directly into her face. She recoiled from the stench of alcohol, second-hand cigarette smoke and strong coffee. It was at that moment, we heard a spontaneous, roar of laughter coming from the direction of the bar.

The laughter from the bar grew as more people arrived to watch what was, as far as we were concerned, a rather unspectacular spectacle. One burst seemed to cause *vigile* Pompino to turn one hundred and eighty degrees to face everybody on the bar terrace. Then as if to display his contempt he stuck out his chin, narrowed his eyes, grimaced repugnantly, flared his nostrils yet again, like a fierce prehistoric beast, opened his mouth wide, gasped, then let out a perceptible roar. He then put his hands on his hips, tucking his thumbs inside his straining leather belt and stamped his feet as he spread his legs wide apart, which changed his character from that of a local copper into an officious parody of Mussolini.

At this point, Nicola stepped around him, her back to the crowd, to confront him once more. She tried a slightly different tack, asking the man if he had a few minutes to spare from his very busy and important schedule and inviting him to share a coffee, or something a bit stronger in the bar. The expression on his face changed once again: he raised his eyebrows and widened his eyes, as if deliberately trying to make himself look half crazed. Then he raised his arms to the sky, then, slowly and melodramatically he moved them out to the sides as if he had been impaled on a cross. Suddenly, and without warning, he grabbed Nicola around the waist and thrust his great big stomach against her as if imitating a form of sexual intercourse. At the same instant, with a lecherous grin on his face he whispered something into her ear, which changed her expression from one of bemusement to one of shock. She had to make an instantaneous decision about what to do for the best: whether to court this man and allow him his moment of indulgence or push him away, thereby signalling unfriendliness and rejection. She seemed to have arrived at a point where she was asking, in fact almost begging, him to do us a favour when it was supposed to be part of the job he was paid to do. The whole episode seemed to have turned into a fiasco, especially when he began laying on a show for the benefit of the spectators at the bar by gyrating his hips in such a sensual manner that Nicola was left not knowing what to do.

Finally when enough was more than enough and his audience was beginning to disperse he did say he would visit our house but he did not ask for the address or fix a date or a time. She thanked him for his attention at the same time skilfully slipping his grasp. He went on his way, still looking very disgruntled, in the direction of the Municipio, at the same time flicking the underneath of his chin with the back of his hand in an exaggerated manner, which, in Italy, signifies to all and sundry, 'I don't give a toss'.

Nicola walked in the opposite direction with me in tow.

"What on earth was that pantomime all about?" I asked her.

"The man's mental," she snapped. "I don't think he understood a word I was saying. How we are going to lay our hands on this tiresome piece of paper now is anyone's guess. Let's go back to the bar. After that ridiculous episode I need a stiff drink."

Our faces must have looked very glum as we approached the steps of the bar terrace. By contrast, the faces of our drinking chums, whom we had come to know and love, were the picture of happiness. They broke into rapturous applause, with Nicola being hugged and kissed by just about everybody.

"Cosa state facendo?" "What are you doing?" she wanted to know. "Why are you all laughing so much?"

One of the locals asked her what the *vigile* had whispered in her ear, but she replied, "It was too disgusting to repeat." She said, "I'm completely bemused. I know my Italian's not perfect but surely *vigile* Pompino can understand a simple request for a residential certificate?"

Finally, somebody explained it all to us. He had been the village copper for over twenty years and his real name was not 'Pompino' but 'Pompeo'. 'Pompino' was a nickname the villagers used behind his back. He had just three months to go before the moment he had been longing for, when he could draw his pension and return to his beloved south, never to be seen nor heard in Moltrasio ever again. Until that day, he hadn't known that he had a nickname. Then a couple of foreigners, complete strangers to him, revealed the villagers' little secret to him. *Pompino* is Italian slang for fellatio.

Eventually we got our *permesso di residenza*, but not from *vigile* Pompeo. We made sure we kept out of his sight until he retired from the service. Then, to get it, we simply went and asked nicely at the Mayor's office.

Chapter 5

Down to Business

THE NEXT important step for us was to register me as a business as soon as possible, which had to be done at the Chamber of Commerce in Como. Our recent experience at the Questura had already made us somewhat cynical, so to avoid any unforeseen difficulties we rose early allowing ourselves plenty of time to get everything done and dusted before the office closed for lunch. Astonishingly, on this particular occasion the Chamber of Commerce office turned out to be eerily quiet and we were seen more or less straight away, but sadly, not without being confronted by the mysteries of Italian bureaucracy.

Nicola explained to the young lad seated behind a glass-panelled counter why we had come, and held out my documents to show him I had come some way in completing the pile of paperwork the state demanded. He photocopied the documents, then in silence and for what seemed like an eternity read the copies, as if he didn't trust what was on the originals. After he had finished, he began to look unsure and said something about my being a foreigner, and that he did not know what to do with my papers or with me. A few moments later he disappeared into another office for what seemed like another eternity. Eventually he came back with two others who looked to be about the same age. They then ushered us into a fish tank of an office, the sort of room with four glass walls that passers-by look into to see if they recognise anybody in them. The tallest of the trio, who told us he was the senior clerk, said that they were having difficulty locating the correct papers that dealt with a foreigner registering a business in Italy.

For about fifteen minutes, they and Nicola studied a weighty manual, and then filled out some alternative forms on my behalf, while I sat there, drinking machine coffee. They were, they said, not the correct forms. Apparently they had so few foreigners wishing to set up business in Italy that the incorrect forms would have to do because they did not have any others.

At first, I think they thought I was about to register a mega-manufacturing business, something that would be useful to the Italian economy, but then they discovered it was just me, a one-man-band, and that I was an artist. When we got to the part of the form that asked how much I expected to earn per annum, I replied that I did not know because so far it was only an experiment to see if I could exist to work in Italy, and that I would be happy to earn enough to get by. As if they were puppets joined together by one single string, the three of them slowly raised their heads from what they were doing and gave me a quizzical, almost disappointed look, followed seconds later by deeply gouged frowns, then looks of suspicion as if I'd been sent to them by some practical joker for their first appointment on a miserable Monday morning. When they saw that my face had not broken into a smile of recognition, or that Nicola had not confessed to being part of a conspiracy to wind them up, one of them asked an apparently sensible question: why did I want to register a business without having a business to register?

"Ah!" said Nicola, "we want to do it properly, so that when he does have a business he will be ready to do business.

We need to register him so he is able to pay his IMPS (the equivalent of National Insurance contributions) when the time arises. That is how it's done in Britain. Isn't that the way it's done here?"

"Ah!" said their spokesman, "That's another office, not this one."

With that said, they all rose up as one, apparently relieved that they had found a reason to get rid of us. The first lad we had met was about to hold out his hand to salute me goodbye, but he soon discovered that was being a little premature when Nicola told him she needed this form urgently so as to be able to register me as an Italian taxpayer. With that, they then turned their faces away, huddling close together and mumbling something to each other behind the cover of a clipboard, presumably to avoid us reading their lips. Then, the most senior official surprised Nicola by turning to her and asking her if I was mad.

After more lengthy exchanges we all sat down again and I was told to sign along at least fifteen dotted lines, pressing as hard as I could through dozens of layers of pink carbonised paper. My signature on the bottom few layers must have been so indistinct it could have been anybody's mark. To cap it all, I needed to pay a fee of 200,000 lire, about £80, for the privilege of registering.

With that office out of the way, we had enough time left to run across town and register at the National Insurance office before they closed at 12:00pm for the rest of the day. Almost unbelievably, our business here was completed with no problems whatsoever.

At the end of the morning we congratulated ourselves on having got two more offices crossed off our list of imperatives and all done in one stint. We had only four more to go: the

Agenzia delle Entrate for my fiscal code number, the IVA office to register my projected business for the Italian equivalent of the British VAT and the *Camera di Commercio Industria ed Artigianato*, a sort of craftsman's union where I also had to sign a document declaring I would never work for the Mafia. After that, we needed to find a commercialista, an accountant, to explain it all to us. Having accomplished all this could have led us to believe we were at last getting to grips with Italian bureaucracy. Of course we knew we would have to return to all the offices we had visited over the forthcoming weeks and queue for the accustomed perpetuity to pick up the processed papers, but that was only to be expected. Nicola's suggestion of asking all the various official bodies we encountered to use the postal service was dismissed as foolhardy. "Forget that," they told us, "your documents will never arrive."

We discovered there were very few small businesses run by non-Italians that were legally registered in Italy. Only the multi-national companies registered. People like myself who arrived and attempted to start up a small business were practically unheard of in 1991, hence the problem of finding the correct documents to complete. There were two main reasons for this; the first, and the obvious one, was, and still is to many, the language barrier and second were difficulties with the bureaucracy, which seemed to be set up intentionally to discourage the foreign entrepreneur. At the time, Italy, it would seem, wanted to keep competition out by making it difficult for the foreigner to get a foothold. The ordinary Italian appeared to have nothing against the foreigner setting up in business and more than likely he would be hospitable towards such a person: it was the policy of the state not to make it easy! Italy is a founder member of the European Common Market, what is now the European Union, where freedom of movement is supposed to be what it says. Italy acknowledged this as one of the agreements to joining the EU but it didn't stand by the accord it signed. It still put mountains in the way of anybody who tried to settle in the country. This balking policy was very successful and the potential foreign businessman soon became so frustrated he packed up and went home, or tried his luck in a country where the bureaucracy is less intimidating. Italy appeared to be happy to shoot itself in the foot, stifling creativity and fresh ideas by placing a brick wall in front of anybody who tried to offer fresh ideas to a country that needed the lifeblood of the entrepreneur more than most. For the ones who did try, they were confronted by a web of red tape that was so confusing and expensive in fines if they got it wrong, they either curled-up and withered like a dried out leaf, or they left Italy altogether.

After examining the situation that existed at the time we were struggling to achieve legal status, I concluded that there were three degrees of difficulty for anyone who wanted to work in Italy. One, it was not easy for Italian citizens to work in Italy. Every Italian we know, told us that many times over. Two, for a member of the European Union it was very difficult to work in Italy, and three, for the non-EU person arriving in Italy it was virtually impossible. It would seem that foreigners, either EU or non-EU members who are not Italian citizens but who ran a business in Italy, generally operated illegally in the black economy because it was both less complicated and cheaper.

Why the man in the Chamber of Commerce had questioned my sanity preoccupied me for some weeks. It seemed a little odd that a person in an official capacity should come out with a phrase like that when all I wanted to do was register myself for business. But after living and working in the country for some months it dawned on me that as a single operator, not intending to grow into an SpA, a public company, what he had been really trying to say was why didn't I do what other foreigners do in Italy and operate outside the law? Of course, he wasn't allowed to tell me that in so many words. Then after I became involved in the system and I'd tried to pay my dues I realised, by the Italian standards of the time, I probably was a bit crazy and it might have been a lot easier and worth chancing arrest to operate in the black economy.

However, I didn't choose to work in the black economy and for the first two years I did the proper thing as best I could. Trying to understand the rigmarole involved was daunting and I had to make several visits to my *commercialista*, my accountant's office, to help me understand what it was all about. On one of those visits, to my horror, I discovered a large percentage of what I had earned in that time had to be paid back in contributions and taxes, so to continue to exist I had to take the veiled advice the Chamber of Commerce official had given me and liquidate my company. On occasions, my working for cash-only payments in a country that distributes stiff fines like handfuls of confetti at a wedding caused arguments between Nicola and me. She, with her background of legal work, said I'd most certainly be liable for such a fine if I were to be discovered. My only consolation was the advice given to us by local Italian residents: "do it and don't worry about it". According to them the risk of being caught was low because there are some very big fish working inside the black economy, so for sure the *Guardia di Finanza* (finance police) have their hands full trying to identify them and they are not interested in small fry. This eased our sleepless nights somewhat but for an honest Brit who had played by the rules for most of his life and kept up to date with all his tax and National Insurance payments it took some getting used to. If the *Guardia di Fi-*

nanze or someone with a grudge had seen me carrying cans of paint, paintbrushes and ladders et cetera in the car we eventually bought, I could have been leaving myself open to prosecution. Many's the time I saw a *Guardia di Finanza* roadblock ahead, searching for people such as me, and I did a U-turn to find a different route. Also there is the confidential 'green line' that encourages people to 'squeal' if they suspect somebody is on the fiddle. Hardly anybody uses it because most think it might draw the attention of the authorities, who would then start questioning the caller about their own affairs.

The famous architect that Christine's friend introduced me to was a sometimes good and sometimes bad provider of work. Despite the advice of local tradesmen not to touch him with a barge pole, I gave the man a try and I worked for him on several occasions, painting murals in the homes of some of Italy's wealthiest people. At the beginning of our working relationship he was fine, and I was glad to find the sort of work I'd been privileged to enjoy in the UK. But later he became scornful and began paying me what he felt like paying after the price had been agreed. It was like working for an agent who retains anything from ten to sixty per cent whenever he felt like it, but until the job was finished there was never any certainty as to what I would actually end up with in my pocket. When one is not able to present an official *fattura* (a registered invoice) this seems to give the employer *carte blanche* to treat the employee like something stuck to the sole of their shoe, because they know immediately the employee is working unlawfully! To the employer this often hands him the opportunity to treat his employee however he likes and generally he treats him poorly! This particular architect was the type of person who did not get to the top of his tree by being nice to people. He had a reputation throughout the region not just as an architect and a rich playboy but also as a complete swine! My making a commotion about what I regarded as an injustice would not have been worth the consideration because the man was so powerful with friends in high places, that if he felt like it he could finish me as easily as squashing a pestilent insect. On some of the occasions I worked for him I had done so at a financial loss, but I stuck with him for a couple of years because of his importance and the size of the projects he gave me.

But he was not alone in acting in this way. To the Italian, the exploitation of the foreigner working 'in the black' is part and parcel of everyday life, because they have a deep-seated belief that any foreigner seeking work in Italy must be in a desperate situation. As history has shown, the downtrodden and the destitute have always sought work beyond their own shores and the Italians tend to think this is how it is for everybody, even after having signed up to the European Union treaty that allows freedom of movement to work. It seemed the EU *modus operandi* was completely disregarded by the Italian employer, who continued merrily along as he always had and probably always will, because that was how it had always been. Trying to inform the employer that some of us are not desperate and that we are forced to work 'in the black' because the Italian system makes us do so is like talking to them in Chinese.

Besides that, they looked at me as if they thought I was completely nuts when I said I worked because I liked to work. According to the Italian mindset, nobody works because they like to work; they only work because they have to. Here, the work ethic comes way down the list of life's priorities, because there are far more pleasurable pastimes to experience in a country rich in leisurely activities.

There have also been private clients of mine who are of

the same mentality as the Como architect, who employ 'black' labour because it is classified as cheap labour and they know it gives them the upper hand to help themselves to a *sconto* (a cash discount) out of the final payment. In Italy, *sconto* is one of the most familiar and most popular words. A large proportion of businesses in Italy, legal or otherwise, load their prices intentionally so that when the client asks for *uno sconto* they have a margin to be flexible with, but for the person working in the black with no documentation to back it up they can easily be abused.

Another disadvantage for an individual working in the black is that they cannot advertise themselves or their business. Also, because they will not be paying IMPS, they have no medical cover and will not be eligible for a pension.

Now we had all our papers in order we went in search of a car, and in so doing we visited a truly enormous Lancia showroom on the outskirts of Como. There were at least a thousand cars for sale, all neatly lined up in rows. We asked the lone salesman to direct us to a price range we could afford and he courteously escorted us past the latest range of new, bright red models that looked more like racing cars than anything I had seen on the highway. They were fabulous things, there to be admired rather than driven and all far too expensive and impractical for us. Without my realising, Nicola and the salesman had moved on ahead and left me behind, daydreaming, but I caught them up. They were somewhere in the middle of the vast place, looking at plain, domestic cars, all a lot less impressive than the exotic Lancias but far more familiar. The salesman left us to browse, telling us that if we saw something, he would look up the details on his file. Within a few minutes, two scruffy looking guys arrived and started to examine the same car that we were considering buying, which I thought was an odd coincidence. With such a huge choice available, what was so interesting about this very ordinary, low-value car? They looked under it, over it, inside it and all around it, as if in a hurry, until I began to think that perhaps there was something special about this particular vehicle that wasn't obvious. When they had left we found out that it wasn't the car they were interested in, but lifting Nicola's purse from her pocket. I ran in all directions looking for them but they had found enough cover amongst all the cars to hide and eventually get away. She lost around 500,000 lire (then the equivalent of £200) plus her driving licence.

On the way home, after we had both recovered somewhat from the ordeal, we went to a police station near to Como town centre, where Nicola attempted to report the theft. A police officer who appeared to be no more than twelve years old got half way through taking her statement and then told her that he could not deal with the matter as the theft had taken place outside their particular jurisdiction.

The next day she took a two-hour journey by bus and train to the police station nearest to where the theft had occurred. There she found the officer loath to incur any paperwork and he tried to persuade her not to report the incident officially as, in his opinion, such a small amount of money had been taken and that she was unlikely to ever see it again. It was only when she insisted that she might require a document to prove her driving licence was missing that he felt inclined to complete the forms. When he arrived at the part that required details of her relationship status and she told him she was single, he entered the word *nubile*, but he did look at her in a very dubious way when she told him the meaning of the English word 'nubile'.

A couple of days later, Enzo gave us a lift to the Lancia dealership and we bought a car. I was now in a position to go food shopping on my own without having to rely on his kind assistance. From here on in our living and domestic arrangements soon took on a pattern.

My part of the household chores involved driving to the supermarket for foodstuffs, and Nicola did most of the cooking and the cleaning. After a few weeks of this arrangement she began to show displeasure at my approach to shopping. Part of her disapproval stemmed from her dislike of supermarkets. She was and still is suspicious about the long-term health and safety aspects of consuming mass-produced food and she steadfastly refuses to go anywhere near the stuff, almost to the point of it becoming a phobia. In Italy, fresh food looks to be of a much better quality than it does in the UK and it is supposed to contain fewer pesticides and chemicals, but to her if it's sold in a supermarket, Italian or otherwise she's not happy consuming it. Of course without the specific scientific equipment and a degree in chemistry it is impossible for the mere consumer to prove the truth of this. Hence, she refuses to shop in any of the mass-market food chains, regardless of country, that sell what she calls 'disgusting food', even if she were starving to death.

Her remedy was to insist that I buy all our food in the local shops and to forget that supermarkets exist. "That way," she said, "we will know where the food has come from because it is all grown locally. Even the butcher manages his own organic farm and he assures me all his meat and poultry are fed properly and are not pumped full of growth hormones.

"I know you continue to use the supermarkets because you think they are cheaper," she added, "but in the long term this will prove to be a false economy. When you are too ill to work because you've been poisoned and you have to pay out a fortune in medical bills it will be too late to say I was right."

But there was more to this than the quality of the food, and I should have seen it coming.

"I know what your other little game is," she declared. "If you shop at the supermarket you don't have to ask for anything by name. You can pick the article off the shelf by looking at the picture on the packaging, and you don't have to have contact with anybody or speak a word of Italian."

I'd been sussed. She was correct on both issues. In the village not only did I have to come face to face with the proprietor of each shop and ask him or her for each item by name, but the rest of the customers lining up to be served expected me to converse with them. Nicola had been responsible for pushing me more and more into the places where the locals congregated and therefore they had become accustomed to seeing my face and had begun to treat me like one of their own. When out shopping, my concern at this stage of my linguistic development was coping on my own without my personal interpreter. My conversational abilities at this stage were still, disappointingly, practically nil.

When any individual enters a small country shop in any village anywhere in the world, the locals are naturally curious to see who it is and Moltrasio is no exception. To help me overcome my inability to learn Italian quickly, Nicola started to write notes for me to take with me when I went shopping in the village. The notes contained more than just a list of food and household items. They also contained lines of basic conversation, not unlike an actor's script, with spaces between the lines where an anticipated reply might fit. The script idea worked in principle as long as I could keep people to it. Almost inevitably, what often happened was that the shopkeepers and customers would listen intently to what this newcomer had to say, and from it they became encouraged by what they thought was a sudden improvement in my capacity to speak their language. Then, they started to say all sorts of things that had not been accounted for in the script. When that happened, I would make a discreet escape so as not to appear to be a complete muttonhead. Sadly, after making such a promising start the script idea had to be abandoned.

These crib sheets aside, I thought I was managing to communicate reasonably well with everybody in the local shops and I had understood perhaps twenty-five per cent of what was going on. That is, until I had to pay. Getting to grips with having to fork out thousands upon thousands of lire for a few articles wasn't the main problem; it was when the lady on the till asked for payment, I could not comprehend requests like "Diciassettemilacinquecentosei lire", which could have been said in Chinese for all I could understand it. So much for me learning to count up to a twenty on the plane over from Gatwick. If there was a pencil to hand she would write down the amount on a scrap of paper, and if not I would tip the contents of my wallet onto the counter and let her sort it out for herself. Something else that I found confusing at first was, if I was in the alimentare, the grocery store, and if she did not have the right change in the till she would often give me telephone tokens or a small piece of cheese in compensation. This is not as bizarre as it sounds. These were the days before mobile phones became commonplace and people used to use public phonebooths. Small denomination lira coins were virtually worthless and often shopkeepers would give telephone tokens, which were also accepted as general currency, or sweets as change.

Eventually, after a lot of practice, I could handle basic greetings without any problems and could even ask and answer simple questions. I had mastered weights and measures in kilogrammes and knew the names and recognised the shapes of all the basic and some of the not so basic food products. I was also learning to fit names to faces and faces to names of the folk I came into contact with and even who they were related to. This last task is very complex even for the locals, because in Moltrasio there are five large, predominant families and they have been intermixing for generations, and most of the village's nine hundred or so residents are related to more than one of these families.

During the first few weeks of our arrival in the village, word got around there were two English people living in their midst. The villagers we had not already met, who were generally the older women who did not frequent the Bar Centrale, kept asking us the same questions over and over again, about who we were and why we where there.

Moltrasio is the type of place where everybody knows everybody else and most of their personal business as well. Italians are a gregarious lot and will generally tell you all about themselves upon first introduction, but of course in fair exchange for similar information. If strangers intend to linger in their village, the villagers will very quickly want to know all about them and a cross–examination can be expected. If he or she (in this case us) wants to live in their society, then somebody, if not all of the villagers, will ask outright what it is they want to know. This process of indoctrination went on for some weeks and Nicola became slightly jaded at being asked the same questions by each individual we met. Her response was often determined by her mood and by her assessment of the merits of the inquisitor, yet it would have been obtuse of her not to concede to the naturalness of the inquiry or adopt an evasive strategy. At one time she jokingly suggested that she should prepare a written statement, get some photocopies printed and hand them out like a press release. She therefore formulated a story ready for when she was next examined, so she didn't have to keep expiring energy thinking of something different to say each time. It became like filling in the same questionnaire half a dozen times a day and if we had written out that questionnaire, it would have looked something like this:

Q1. Why did you choose to live in Moltrasio?

A1. We came here because, seventeen years ago, I had been an au pair for the Masin family and I always said to myself that one day I would come back because I fell in love with the village. Now I have and I've brought Paul with me.

(To some extent, this was true: if it had not been for the opportunity to rent the Masins' house, we most probably would have been living in Spain.)

Q2. But why Moltrasio in particular?

A2. Because it is so beautiful here, because of the atmosphere and of course the temperate climate.

(But this is not enough to satisfy them. None of the questions have been answered specifically, particularly what it is about Moltrasio that has drawn us to the place. Hence question 3.)

Q3. But what brings two young foreigners to Moltrasio when there is nothing to do here? There isn't any work here, there's nothing to see and it's full of old people. Why haven't you chosen Tuscany, where all the English reside?

A3. For the very reason there *is* nothing here to see or do. If there were, it would become like so many other places, full of souvenir shops and overrun with tourists. We are here because there is none of that and the reason we haven't chosen Tuscany, or 'Chiantishire' as it's now called, is because it is heaving with Brits and we prefer to be the only Brits in the area.

This seemed to appease them slightly and they were pleased to hear about the appeal of their village. However they were still unsure about our intent and spoke of how their children left the village years ago and sought a life of capital gain in a modern environment to raise their families. Nicola would then speak for us both and tell them that we are tired with that sort of life and that the pendulum was beginning to swing back the other way, with people wanting to return to country places like Moltrasio to live the sort of life people are meant to live.

From Nicola's point of view, if we decided we wanted to stay in Moltrasio on a permanent basis it was good to meet as many of the locals as possible and inform them of our position in their society and show them we had nothing to hide that could make them suspicious about us. If we intend to reside here, she said, we must be their equals and not some aloof interlopers they are mistrustful of. What's more, it is very important in a close community to be known as *bravi* ('good people') and not *stronzi* ('shits').

Nicola also wanted us to join in the activities of the village on a daily basis, with the aim of becoming as local as the locals.

"It's up to us, not them," she kept telling me. "They did not ask us to come and live in their village. Either we choose to be bravi and join in or we remain distant and closed. If we choose to be stronzi it will invite them to talk about us behind our backs and invent whatever mischief people invent about people when they don't like them. If, in the future, we need their help or assistance with something, as we surely will, it is of the utmost importance, especially in Italy, to connect with the community. If we choose to remain outsiders then we haven't got a prayer and we might as well pack up and go back to England right now."

There would be several opportunities for us to join in the many activities held in Moltrasio throughout the year, and in the coming summer we would meet one truly unforgettable character, the man behind them all.

Chapter 6

Stagione Estiva - the Summer Season

IN AND AROUND the towns and villages of Italy, July is *festa*, or party time, and Moltrasio is no exception. *Festa* is the opening event of the summer holiday, when the country closes down for the whole of August and virtually the entire population transfers itself to the coastal resorts to seek the mandatory suntan. July evenings in Italy are beautifully hot, and come the festa season everyone is in a happy mood, looking forward to their annual vacation. Moltrasio's own *festa* was one of the biggest events on the lake and was held every Friday, Saturday and Sunday throughout the month on the *campo sportivo*, the sportsground. Seating for three hundred was set up around the campo, as well as a stage for live traditional music, plus an enormous dance floor and barbeques of industrial proportions. Wine and beer tents also helped transform the sports ground into a people's theatre.

Eating, drinking and chatting are extremely important at the *festa*, as they are in any Italian social event, but the main reason folk take part is to show off their skill at dancing. Be they young, old, or middle-aged, the Italians go in for social dancing in a big way and they cannot wait for the season to start. We were dab hands at eating and drinking, but our problem was that, when it came to dancing, we were woeful at it, and we knew it. I hadn't been to a Saturday night dance since I was a teenager in my home town of Formby on Merseyside, and in those times, the British male's attitude to dancing was a complete contrast to that of the Italian. English lads like me were completely reluctant to dance, preferring to stay in the bar until the last waltz, when we'd venture out to ask the girl we'd been fancying all night to dance, by which time we were too drunk to make any sort of decent impression. Nicola, being a few years younger than me, grew up when ballroom dancing had gone out of style, so neither of us had had any formal dance experience, let alone instruction. We realised that if we wanted to enjoy the *festa* to its utmost with our friends, we had better learn to dance. Soon after we had made this resolution, we saw a poster stuck to the outside wall of the community centre advertising *un corso di ballo*, dancing lessons. With *festa* in mind, we vowed then and there to do something about our inability and enrolled for a course of ten two-hour lessons in the hope that, come July, we would be there gliding around the dance floor as smoothly as everybody else.

There were about twenty beginners who started the dance classes. All of them were Italian apart from us and as soon as the music started it became obvious that none of them needed the tuition as emphatically as we Brits did. I am sure the dancing course was excellent. I am sure the instructors knew their stuff, but when it came to our turn to show what we were made of, oh dear!

It wasn't that we were physically handicapped, or that we were inhibited or dim-witted. As an ex-footballer I had reasonable control over my feet. Nicola, who is a music aficionado, knows all about timing and rhythm and so, with the idea that all we needed was a bit of tuition to make us presentable, we started the lessons.

Individually, in the safety of our instructors' arms, we were not that bad, but when they went away and left us to it –

forget it! Whoever said that dancing was like making love set to music was way off beam when it came to our turn. To give us encouragement during the preliminary stage the instructors assured us they had an excellent track record of turning students with questionable capabilities into good dancers and that by lesson ten we would have learnt ten dances.

We looked again at the tuition programme Blu-tacked to the blackboard: week one, the mazurka; week two, the salsa merengue; week three, the waltza; week four, the bachata; week five, the valeta; week six, the tango; week seven, Latino Americano; week eight, the cha cha cha; week nine, the paso doble and, for the finalé, week ten, the highly charged, sexy lambada, where the man is allowed to dance very close to the woman, with the top of his thigh pressed against her groin throughout the entire dance. If that wasn't inspiration enough to become a competent dancer then I don't know what is.

So, we got started. We went every week, and every week we tried our hardest. During the mazurka we had a laugh. Learning the waltza brought tears to the eyes. The bachata brought pain to our feet. To dance the valeta we tried; we really tried. Attempting the tango, we fell to pieces, and in the middle of the Latino Americano we gave up and went back to the mazurka. We both realised we were a dead loss, although we found it hard to come to terms with finding the whole experience completely mystifying. Bravely, the instructors battled along with us and they referred to a time, several years earlier, when they had successfully taught a couple worse than us! What they did not tell us was how many courses they must have perspired through to achieve the result. In the end, our one definitive dance out of six of the ten lessons we attended was the mazurka. When the rest of our class had moved on to the cha cha cha (or maybe it was the Latino Americano), we were tactfully led into a dusty storeroom, provided with our own cassette player and an endless tape that kept repeating the mazurka over and over and told to practise until we finally got it. For anybody who doesn't know the mazurka, the female has to move backwards throughout its entirety, having to trust implicitly upon her male partner to steer her through the quagmire of bodies behind her without bumping into them. It was all very well practising in a storeroom with only a few cardboard boxes to out-manoeuvre, but the question was, how would we fare by July?

The answer was, not bad at all! This was more than surprising, it was staggeringly, gob-smackingly amazing! Admittedly, on the first Saturday night we had downed a couple of plastic beakers of vino beforehand, which was to bring out the British courage in us, but as soon as the band struck up, the brain connected to the legs, which in turn got the feet to do some bewitching stuff and impulsively, we were out there sliding around the dance floor as if we had been programmed. Suddenly, we found that the mazurka was now a piece of cake and when Ada saw us she bounded onto the floor and split us apart. She arranged a partner for Nicola and took me off to a corner of the floor to keep me for herself. How this metamorphosis happened during the long winter months was a mystery, but our performance on the dance floor was suddenly plausible and nobody seemed to be giving us furtive glances from behind their partner's shoulders. We seemed to be fooling everybody and getting away with it. After the mazurka was over, Ada must have been so encouraged by our progress that she began passing us around to her mates for them to have a go. The ladies I was assigned to were all well into their sixties, of differing heights, widths and graces. They were not what I'd envisaged as ideal partners, but, without wishing to sound unkind, were useful to practice on. Nicola, likewise, was passed between their husbands, brothers and cousins, but we coped, and, astonishingly they came back for more.

When it came to dancing, Umberto, the blacksmith, and his beautiful wife, Dona, were Moltrasio's star performers. Umberto was transformed from the burly, lumbering type into a veritable Fred Astaire when he put on his dancing pumps and together they became a smooth, efficient machine, moving with an effortless synchronisation and a magnetism that made them fascinating to watch. They were, in our opinion, at least good enough to be professionals, way beyond what we could ever aspire to, even in our wildest dreams.

As the night wore on, a personal little fillip made all the suffering we went through in the dance school weeks before seem worthwhile. It was when I danced the lambada with Dona. When she first came over to me and asked me to dance, my heart sank. "What now?" it asked. Not only was she an excellent dancer, she was also the best looker in the village, with a body that all the men had noticed at some time or another. "My God," I thought, as my heart rose again, "if Dona is asking me to take the floor, that really is a compliment to my dancing prowess." Plus I thought totally without shame that I'd get to hold her close and press my thigh against her more intimate parts. After my plausibly good performance with Ada, who was a roly-poly, five foot nothing with her shoes on, and her best mate, Sonia, who was even shorter and another two sizes wider around the midriff, my performance with the tall, slender Dona was, to say the least, somewhat erratic. Suddenly, to be thrust against this gorgeously bronzed, twenty-five year old athlete with her sensual coaxing jolted my sensibilities. Any complacency I'd been experiencing about my newfound abilities ought to have diminished rapidly, but when

I should have given my best performance of the evening, I could hardly get a single step right. When I had the opportunity to show her my credentials, my sense of rhythm evaporated. After such a good start to the *festa* season I could not get to grips with the lambada, or with the gorgeous Dona. It ended with me letting her and myself down badly.

When I returned to my seat next to Nicola I was feeling impotent and belittled, and when I looked to her for solace and maybe some sympathy, all I received was a rather narrow-eyed look of disdain.

"Well?" she enquired dryly, "Did you enjoy dancing with Dona?"

Of course I had, every second of it, despite my dancing being a total disaster, but I wasn't going to tell Nicola that! To the discerning observer, my dancing may have been useless, but what she had done for my inner man had been totally exhilarating.

"Shame about my dancing," I reflected. "I think I need some more lessons."

"That's what I thought," Nicola retorted. "Still, if you want to dance with Dona again, she should be all the incentive you need to improve your pitiful technique."

There was one patriarchal figure in the village whom the hypnotic effect of the village could not penetrate and even to this day is unlikely ever to do so. We were warned that at some point during our stay that we were bound to meet him. We had seen him at the *festa*, because he had organised it, but there, his presence seemed somewhat low-key compared with what Enzo and Ada told us about. He cannot be ignored, they told us. He was the self-appointed pulse of Moltrasio.

His name was Riccardo Del Meglio.

He was at the same time the most popular and unpopular character in Moltrasio. He either made people smile or made them grimace. He was a short, stout figure with a big, booming voice and when we first met him he was in his late forties. His energy was extraordinary. He was the president of every society and committee in the village. Most people have met someone like him at least once in their lives: he was the organiser, the prime mover, the mainspring, the fixer, the getter of things done; the sort who won't take no for an answer. Size didn't matter to him. Big people that should have been able to protect themselves would fall like mighty oaks at his feet. People would complain and moan bitterly about him but when he snapped his fingers they came under his spell and would follow this bundle of nuisance to the end of the earth if he demanded it.

Yet somehow this corpulent little fellow still found time to be a dedicated family man. He had a wife and four sons, the eldest then eighteen years, the youngest eighteen months. He had a full time job as a manager of a silk printing factory in Como but his spare time was enthusiastically dedicated to all the seasonal activities he himself had created, for the good of the village and for every resident to participate in.

One either respected Del Meglio for his efforts or one didn't. Those that were for him said that he was good for the community, that he brought people together, that out of the goodness of his heart he created special occasions when otherwise there would be nothing to enjoy, and for little cost. In the opposite camp there were those who said he should let a sleepy village lie and not pester people into becoming involved in projects that he invented for his own self-gratification, and that he held a sadistic pleasure in forcing gentlefolk to respond to his authority. Whichever way, he didn't care a damn what people thought. He refused to be ignored; he had a skin as thick as a rhinoceros's and was deaf to any criticism. If he needed a particular person with a particular skill that he could use for the benefit of village activities, then that individual had no chance to say no. If Del Meglio decided this person was the one for the job, he wouldn't let go until he got his way and the only way to have an easy life was to do what he wanted.

Del Meglio's particular passion was Moltrasio's own *Palio*. The word conjures up images of the magnificent, historical horse race that is held in Siena twice every summer; the breathtaking, highly colourful event where each of the ten *Contrade*, or city wards, enters a horse and jockey to ride bareback around the main piazza of the city. The prize is the prestigious *Palio*, a colourful banner, the holding of which bestows great prestige.

Moltrasio's own *Palio*, it has to be said, was nothing like Siena's. For one, it was not a horse race, and if it wasn't for the different colours of bunting hanging across breathless streets and narrow passageways that marked the boundaries of the five contesting zones, the locals could well have forgotten that their harmonious little village was about to be carved up into groups of fanatical teams.

The event took place during the public holiday weekend of *Ferragosto*, an annual festival traditionally held to mark the end of the year's labour in the fields, and Riccardo Del Meglio decided that once a year this village was going to get shaken into life, and until the event had been organised, run and won and he, the elected President, handed over the banner to the glorious victors, nobody, but nobody, was allowed a moment's peace. If he had been low-key at the *festa*, he was in full song for *il Palio*. Where the *festa* had been going on long before Del Meglio got involved, the *Palio* was his baby.

For Riccardo the best, and probably the only, place to hold
il Palio di Moltrasio was at the *campo sportivo*, the sports
ground. Virtually every village in Italy will have its own, a
sports ground used for outdoor public and social events.
Moltrasio's is about half the size of a soccer pitch and is covered in fine shale, which is fine for football. It is the only level
piece of ground in the village, a platform supported on enormous concrete piles driven into the mountainside.

One hot Saturday afternoon in the August of our first
year, we took our customary half a kilometre stroll to the village centre especially to see this 'President of Everything' for
ourselves, in action, running the whole shebang. As we approached the *campo* we could see banners and streamers
everywhere and the colours of all the different factions of the
village involved, and hear the roar of everyone in village, there,
probably, at Del Meglio's insistence.

The *campo* was divided into various courses or lanes with
coloured ribbons for various physical sporting events. At each
end there were refreshment tents and changing room areas and
in the middle, dominating the arena, was a substantial rostrum
with steps up each side. When we made our first visit there,
we saw, on top of it, shielded from the sun by an enormous
canopy, a small, stocky man with a big, booming voice. We
knew, without asking any of the spectators, that he must be
the famous Riccardo Del Meglio.

The activities staged in the campo were mainly for the village children and were supervised on the ground by volunteer
stewards, all smartly dressed in red overalls. The individual
games were the universal sort: the egg and spoon race, the
fifty-metre dash, the one legged race (run blindfolded), the
sack race, the low hurdle race, the wheelbarrow race, the 'carrying buckets of water over obstacles without spilling any' race

and another fifty-metre dash, this time with the contestants running backwards. For the toddlers, there was a tricycle race. No one managed to finish it this particular year, we were told, because the course was too long for the poor little mites. This confirmed in the minds of Del Meglio's antagonists that he was a sadistic swine, expecting tiny kids to compete in the blistering mid-afternoon sun when their little legs were too tired to pedal.

In the evening, when the temperature dropped, everyone moved down to the lakeside to watch the events for the adults. The first was the pillow fight. In this, one member from each team sat on a revolving drum hanging over the quayside of the deepest lake in Europe and tried to knock his opponent around the head with a weighted sack and plunge him into the drink. For the next event, four of the strongest men from each team had to push a saloon car eighty metres up a mountain path. It was almost as torturous to watch as it was to take part in.

The following day, the Sunday, the finals and prize giving were held, and as we approached the sports ground the noise was deafening and excitement almost tangible. Del Meglio was in his usual fine form, expounding as much energy from his raised platform as any of the competitors at ground level, and possibly more. As the afternoon progressed and the moment of the award ceremony drew closer, his gesticulating became so pronounced we began to fear for his safety, as it looked is if he might fall off the podium at any moment.

After the *Ferragosto* weekend, the Italian national holiday starts and the entire country closes down for the rest of the month. The weather in August is hot, very hot, and humid, so closing industry down and giving office staff a well-deserved break from commuting into the even hotter cities makes sense, and most of the population heads for the coast.

This is also the time when the majority of foreign tourists arrive, only to discover that many of the tourist attractions, especially in provincial towns and villages, will be open for only part of the day, or closed completely because the staff will have already gone away for their own holidays. To perplex the visitors further, public transport will have been cut by a third, especially during the middle of the day, because there is hardly anybody working or out shopping to make it worthwhile operating. In fact, apart from hotels, restaurants and banks, there is hardly anything else open and the tourist has to wait until the first Tuesday in September before things start to get back to normal.

During our first summer, we used the scorching heat as an excuse to do even less work and more sleeping in the garden. Right outside the back entrance of the house was a large fig tree, conveniently shading the bench where we would sit. I think it was the first fig tree I had ever seen and its fruit was the small red variety, not the larger, purplish-green kind you see in British shops. This year there was a bumper crop and they were just about ready to fall. Enzo advised us to leave the figs on the tree for as long as possible, even up to the stage when they have become shrivelled and unpalatable looking, then they would be at their sweetest and best to eat. However, we soon found out there was competition for the fruit and as if to be bloody-minded, the birds arrived first and pecked single holes in as many figs as they could. We would of course have preferred them to peck as many holes as they could in just one fig, but, oh, no. Then, the wasps arrived, burrowing into the holes the birds had pecked and filled themselves so full of the fermenting fruit that they became too intoxicated to fly. These half-eaten figs were now left dangling on the branches, dripping sticky syrup onto the path leading to the house, and it needed regular washing down with soapy water to prevent anyone slipping on it.

We considered whether, if we were to stay in the house for another year, we should pick the figs early on, when they were not at their sweetest, or leave them for as long as possible when they were undoubtedly more delicious. If we did the latter it would mean we would have to mop the pathway at least once a day. Having no heritage in fig picking in England, this was another section of our learning curve, but perhaps one of the sweeter ones.

The birds and wasps weren't the figs' only predators. I was lying semi-comatose on the sun-lounger in the garden, topping up my suntan, when I noticed that the branches of the fig tree started to sway alarmingly. Its deep green leaves, the size of dinner plates began thrashing around, which was a surprise because there was not a breath of wind. I leapt to my feet in alarm, my imagination playing all sorts of tricks. Maybe, I thought, there was a bird inside the foliage, but to cause such commotion it would have to be massive, or perhaps be fighting for its life with a cat. I gingerly drew closer to try and discover the cause of the tumult, and I could see, through the mass of fig leaves and the adjacent hawthorn hedge, the outline of an orange bus. Then I saw the bus driver, leaning out of his cab, gathering in handfuls of ripe figs.

When I next saw Enzo and I told him what had happened (I had by this time learned enough Italian to do that on my own) he told me that at harvest time it was common for bus drivers in the area to stop outside gardens where fruit trees overhung the road, and even for them to climb onto the bus roof to reach the sweeter fruits at the top of the tree.

By this time, we had really begun to settle into the village and had made some firm friends, but there were a couple of incidents where we truly came a cropper, and one of them was because of that damned fig tree. One summer day, when both Nicola and I were melting in the sun, Ada called by with her sister and brother-in-law, Louisa and Sergio. They lived somewhere near Como town centre, and Ada had been promising Nicola for some time that she would bring them to see us, as Sergio spoke English. We guessed she thought we would have some common ground to communicate upon and we didn't want to tell her we weren't particularly fussed if the man spoke English or not, because she might have translated it as being a sign of unfriendliness.

Sergio was a jolly chap with cheeks of a red colour not unlike one of our over-ripe figs. He told us he had visited England as a younger man and could recite all the names of the places he had visited and their related locality to each other without the use of a road map. His spoken English, he said, had been quite good at one time but through lack of practice over the years he had forgotten most of it. For the first ten minutes of his visit, we communicated in a kind of pidgin English when, sure enough, he began to prove his obsessive claim of being able to pronounce the name of every principal city and most of the secondary ones in the whole of Britain and the distances in miles – he stressed 'miles' and not kilometres – between their respective positions. I suspected he was trying to impress Ada and Louisa with his geographic and linguistic knowledge, but soon we all started to very become bored with this, especially Ada and Louisa, who went off to a shady corner of the garden and skulked until Sergio had grown tired of his own discourse, and they could return to have a good gossip with Nicola in a language they could understand.

Nicola, sensing Ada and Louisa's tactics, began to angle

the conversation back into Italian as much to save Sergio all the endeavour he was putting himself through as to talk about less tedious subjects. Because the fig tree was in such magnificent form it caught every visitor's attention and naturally the subject swung towards how delicious the figs tasted. The word for fig in Italian is 'fico', the 'o' on the end distinguishing it as a masculine noun, which is very unusual as the names of almost all fruits in Italian are feminine. Nicola, however, despite the exacting linguistic demands she had placed on herself since arriving in Italy, made the mistake of giving the Italian word for fig the feminine gender, and used the word *fica*.

What she was unaware of, despite her having previously lived in Italy for a year and half, was that *fica* is Italian slang for the most private part of a woman's body.

She began enthusing to Sergio and the two women who had now returned to the conversation about how her *fica* had blossomed this year and how lots of people had enjoyed sampling her *fica* and would he like to try, because if it wasn't plucked when it was at its ripest, wasps get inside and cause it to drip sweet, sticky juice all over the stone pathway to the house.

"Have you ever tried to get rid of sticky *fica* juice with a bucket of hot soapy water and a mop?" she said, "It's not very easy believe me, because it stains the stone. Also, if you are not careful, an over-ripe *fica* can drip on your head as you pass under it and you can end up with sticky *fica* juice in your hair."

Sergio and I could see that Ada and Louisa were looking very uncomfortable, but I had no idea why. Neither had Nicola, and she continued with her story, telling them about how the local bus driver is a very cheeky chap and he likes his fair share of a nice ripe *fica* and he often stops his bus outside her house to help himself.

"In some ways," she said, "he's been of great assistance to me this year because he's been very greedy but at least it saves me having to wash away the sticky *fica* juice every day."

Finally when she had come to the end of her account, there had been nothing in the way of a verbal response from our visitors, and then in what I thought was a rather outlandish manner, Ada and Louisa once again turned heel and made a retreat to the same shaded part of the garden where they had been a minute or so before, but with their backs turned.

Neither Nicola nor I had any inkling of why Ada and Louisa behaved like this, but, thankfully, before our visitors left, Sergio, very much the gentleman, led Nicola by the elbow to the opposite side of the garden from where his wife and sister-in-law were sitting and told her that she was causing herself, and the other ladies, deep embarrassment. He must have thought he had better do her a favour and correct her error, in case she made the same mistake in company that really would have taken offence.

We never saw Sergio again after that episode, not because of the fig *faux pas*, but because we heard from Ada about six weeks after his and Louisa's visit to our house that he had suddenly died. However, we did meet Louisa again a couple of months after his death in more unfortunate circumstances.

Ada and Enzo continued to treat us as if our welfare was their personal responsibility and continued to offer us lifts, even though we now had our own car. We came to the conclusion that Christine must have been instrumental in this before leaving for Rome by asking Enzo and Ada to "look after them" and as her former employees they had obviously taken her instructions a little too literally. Ada and Enzo are two of the sweetest, caring people anybody could have the good fortune to meet and they lavished attention on us, which was immensely kind of them and much appreciated at the very beginning of our stay, but after a few months it became an encumbrance, but we let it continue and anticipated that at some point they would probably realise that we were independent enough to cope on our own.

One example of their kindness arose after Sergio had passed away, when Ada brought a large bag of his clothes and shoes especially for me. She said they were much too big for Enzo and far too good to burn and seeing as I was about the same size as her sister's recently departed, she thought I would appreciate them. I wasn't too impressed with his taste in clothes and certainly not in his shoes and I was about to open my big mouth and say "thanks, but no thanks" when Nicola, always the tactician, and realising that Ada had walked the kilometre from the opposite side of the village with this bag, stepped between us and turned her back on me. I knew this meant "shut up!"

"Paul thanks you with all sincerity for carrying this heavy bag all this way." She said, "It's very kind of you and he will make good use of the unfortunate Sergio's things. What would we do without your and Vicenzo's kind consideration?"

I thought that this was just a bit too much kindness, and as soon as Ada had gone I asked Nicola not to encourage her or Enzo to believe we could not survive without them. We enjoyed their company a lot but I just wanted to spare two ageing people all their hard work. However, we began sorting through the clothes, and although they were of undoubtedly good quality, they simply did not suit me. One pair of light tan shoes, a pair of cream corduroy trousers and two pink pin-stripe shirts with white collars were the sort of things my grandfather would have worn. I wanted Nicola to ask some of the older men in the village if they might be interested in taking them, but appearance and style is of crucial importance to the Italian man. Passing second-hand clothes can cause offence, as he might think you regard him as either needing better clothes or that you think he cannot afford to buy them for himself. It made me wonder in what category Ada might have included me. Passing goods over to a thrift or charity shop was not an option, as in Italy they don't exist, so unfortunately we had to dump almost all of them in the rubbish bin.

There was one item we saved; a lightweight, grey cotton pullover with a distinctive Alpine pattern across the shoulders and this resulted in the second of our 'clangers'. I had adopted part of the house close to the back door for my painting. The light was good, especially when the French windows were wide open and the embroidered lace curtains were tied back. Regular visitors to the house knew that we never locked the iron gate at the bottom of the garden, always leaving it on the catch. On this particular occasion I had my head down over a watercolour design for the Monza architects, when a shadow from behind came to rest in the middle of what I was doing. Naturally, I turned to see who had cast it, and there, facing me, were Ada and Louisa, who had arrived completely unannounced.

When Ada had first told us of Sergio's unexpected demise, Nicola obtained Louisa's address and wrote her a note, sending our deepest sympathy. Ada, in her wisdom, had decided to escort her grieving sister to visit all the people in Moltrasio who had sent their condolences after Sergio's "departure to a better place", as Ada put it. It was hard to imagine where a 'better place' than this part of Lombardy could be. To me, the Lake Como area is already paradise on earth, but she obviously had other ideas.

The shock of Sergio's sudden death had shaken Louisa badly and this was her first venture out of the house since the day of the funeral. Ada had telephoned us several times since then, often saying how her sister was faring, how she had been a long time in mourning and that her recuperation from the bereavement was very slow. Louisa, it transpired, was a Moltrasina by birth and she wanted to pay a visit to all the people she and her husband had known in the village for many years and to the ones who had sent their respects by post. Rather surprisingly we were on this list of bosom friends and this was our personal visit from her. Unfortunately, on the day she chose to visit, there I was wearing her husband's grey pullover with the distinctive alpine design. Mouths gaped simultaneously, both theirs and mine. We all looked at each other as if the three of us had been knifed between the shoulder blades. Faces flushed, lips quivered, words failed. I wanted to pretend that this embarrassing reunion was not taking place. I turned and ran upstairs as fast as my legs would carry me. On the third floor, in my haste to lock myself away in the box-room, I bumped into Nicola on her way down.

"You won't believe it," I gasped, "but Ada and her sister are here! They've arrived without warning and seen me wearing hubby's jumper and the sight of me in it has sent Louisa into a state of shock! What should I do?"

"Shit!" she exclaimed. "Put something else on and I'll go and talk to them."

I sat on the edge of the bed, intending to wait until they had gone and the coast was clear to return downstairs. I tried to hear what was being said downstairs, but they had all transferred to the garden, so I couldn't hear anything apart from the pop of a cork. I was cursing myself because being stuck in the bedroom meant I wasn't getting any work done and I knew from past visits that when Ada visits, she visits. It's never a case of 'popping in and popping out'; she stays for hours and makes an opera of it. After a decent spell of time I found, amongst my range of four sweaters, a plain grey one and changed into it. That way, maybe there was a slight hope that when I reappeared they may think they had been mistaken in what they saw. Running away without speaking was going to be harder to explain, but if the worst came to the worst I could tell them I was taken short. Better still, if I could swing the conversation around to bowel pains or intestinal illnesses, always one of Ada's favourite subjects, then, that way they might forget about the sweater altogether.

I adopted a tragic face which I thought was fitting in such circumstances and gingerly made my appearance. The bottle of wine they had opened earlier had been consumed and so I opened another one and refilled their glasses. There had not been a glass put out for me, so I did not bother looking for one. I thought it better to sit down quietly and unobtrusively for a minute or so and then perhaps ease my way into their conversation, or preferably, ease away unnoticed and return to work. As it was, nobody paid the slightest heed to my being there. If I had walked in stark naked I don't think anybody would have taken any notice of me.

Meanwhile Louisa was completely engrossed, talking about Sergio's family and how six of his able-bodied cousins carried the coffin at shoulder height in a long procession all the way to the church from their house, about who had (and who had not) attended the actual church service and how many were actually in the church. She then described how the cortège moved on, this time with Sergio's coffin carried in a hearse, for a further service at the crematorium, recounting in fine detail how the undertakers embalm a body in preparation for the cremation ceremony and how the furnace has to be heated to the required temperature by law, so as to reduce a corpse to ash.

I did my bit by nodding agreeably to everything she was saying, and probably overdid the deep sighing and expressions of sympathy. But then, this is Italy and such behaviour is expected here. Here, the dead are as important as the living, if not more, and to some people heavy mourning is compulsory. Then, when the second bottle of wine was empty they upped and left to continue their journey to visit every one of the locals they knew in the village.

We have never seen Ada's sister since that day, nor have we ever heard her name mentioned. After my pullover howler I guess we had been well and truly struck off her list of people to visit.

Chapter 7

Natale - Christmastime

ITALIANS LOVE festivals and parties at any time of year, and Christmas and New Year give them plenty of opportunity to celebrate. Although Nicola had lived in Italy for eighteen months as an au pair, she had no idea how the Italians celebrated Christmas, because she had returned to England to enjoy that time with her family. I, of course, having spent only a few months in the country, hadn't a clue, but in early December I would quickly find out, as Enzo, a keen participant in village activities, had plans for me and my artistic skills.

Christmas is known in Italy as *natale*, which means 'birth', so for part of the celebrations, the artisans in Moltrasio constructed an annual nativity scene, known as *il presepio*, and it is different each year. Anybody who earns a living by using his hands or has any practical qualification is seconded to work on its construction. It's always been in Nicola's nature to be willing and helpful when it comes to a good cause, and I knew that sooner rather than later she would volunteer me to help with anything to do with the village. Nicola had told Enzo on several occasions that I would be willing to assist in village activities, and it must have been during one of his visits to our house, at a moment when I was out of earshot, that he asked Nicola if I would be interested in helping with the *presepio*. By now, my Italian wasn't as bad as Nicola thought it was. Sometimes I understood more than was convenient for her and what I hadn't understood of what was actually said I made up for by intuition. From their furtive glances and body language I knew they were planning something that might involve me, without consulting me first.

The night before the initial creative meeting for the *presepio*, Nicola let me into her and Enzo's little plan. They reckoned that, as well as it being important that both of us should include ourselves in village life and the social scene, it would be good for my spoken Italian to work alongside other Italians in a practical way.

"They're depending on you," she told me, playing on my compassionate side, "they need your guidance. Of course if you're not interested, I shall go by myself. I want to be involved in what's going on in the village, even if you don't."

Putting it like that, she made it plain that I didn't have a choice, unless I wanted to be regarded as a miserable so-and-so for the rest of our life together.

The preliminary meeting was held at Umberto the blacksmith's forge and we arrived at the stroke of ten on a cold, moonless December night. A heavy metal door led into the forge and we slid it partially open and squeezed through the gap. Everyone there was standing around the glowing embers of the forge, which was the best place to be on such a chilly evening. When Enzo saw us, he stepped forward smiling broadly, closely followed by Riccardo Del Meglio, who would preside over the meeting. Although of course we had seen him on several occasions, this was the first time we had actually met him and, as anticipated, he turned out to be as charismatic as our initial impressions led us to believe him to be.

He introduced Nicola and me to the rest of the assembly, about fifteen people in all. Some we recognised immediately as fellow members of what Nicola had dubbed the Bar Centrale's '*bianco sporco* drinking club'. There was Umberto the blacksmith, with his father, a man of eighty who, although very small by comparison with his burly son, was still doing a full day's work as the senior smith of the village. Next were Fillipo, the local builder and his crew, Roberto the electrician and his mate, Ovidio the carpenter and his assistant, and many more, whose faces we did not know and whose names we did not catch. Like Enzo, some of these men had retired, but were still willing and able to give their support to a village cause.

We soon discovered that everyone there was extremely well rehearsed from past years, especially Ovidio the carpenter. He had done more *presepi* than he could remember and had already produced a basic design, which helped the craftsmen estimate what materials were required and gave the rest of us a visual idea of what we were doing and who would do what, where and when.

The proceedings commenced calmly enough, but as we later found out after attending quite a few of these meetings it doesn't take long after a glass or two of wine has been drunk in conjunction with a couple of shots of someone's homemade grappa, for the blood to heat up, temperament to take over and common sense to be lost. Soon, everybody was talking above each other, with conversations crossing over conversations, until the whole thing became a wall of noise, spoken Italian degenerated into dialect and from there on in neither Nicola nor I could fathom a word of what was being said.

We found out later that a lot of the commotion was repartee between old friends, with one teasing another in front of an audience until familiarisation began to spill over into sensitive territory. But here, on our first appearance it did give us a few worries, especially when one of the older volunteers became very sonorous and appeared to be upset at one of the comments made directly to him. It took Riccardo, who naturally had the loudest voice in the workshop, to persuade him to accept an apology from his antagonist.

Another calming influence was Enzo, who toasted thick slices of panettone (a leavened fruit cake that is nowadays recognised as the Italian Christmas cake) on a wire mesh grill over the dying embers of the forge. These, spread with butter, plus roast chestnuts and other nibbles that had been laid on provided a break from the discussions and helped absorb some of the alcohol in people's systems, restoring order to the meeting. In the end the whole atmosphere was not threatening as it first appeared to be, but one of general banter amongst a bunch of good mates. It was like gate-crashing a working men's club, somewhere to escape and have a good natter, a social drink and get away from their wives and families for a few hours.

The *Comune*, the local council, provided a small budget to buy basic materials for the *presepio* and a lot of unofficial refreshments to keep the workers' enthusiasm going. The rest was up to the lads themselves, but at the end of it all, there was one thing for sure, it would be provided from the goodness of their hearts for the rest of the community to share. Nicola described them as "the salt of the earth; genuine folk who work hard all their lives for little reward". I was happy to agree with her, especially when she added that they deserved our support. It is the same story worldwide at any meeting of this sort; the only difference with Moltrasio's is that they took place around the smithy's forge where everyone in attendance had a good feed and a drink. So good, in fact that they didn't finish until two o'clock the following morning.

Our call to assist came three nights before Christmas Day. The *presepio* is usually unveiled a week before Christmas, so it was almost a week behind schedule. My task, making the figures and painting them, was going to be a last minute rush. Umberto the blacksmith had welded together the metal armature bases of the figures into recognisable positions and Ovidio the carpenter had covered them in chicken wire to form the basic shapes. My job was to dip pieces of calico into modelling plaster to form the heads and faces of the represented characters, shape the folds of their garments and paint them. With Nicola's help, I set to work. As soon as we had covered a figure in plaster we painted it and as a kind of reward and an encouragement to start another, stopped in between each one for a brief wine break. It would take us two long evenings and an all night session to get them done and around midnight on the final evening, when it was certain that we would be working through the night, Dona the blacksmith's wife came into the forge and offered us the choice of a drink from one of two bottles of red wine. Never one to miss a chance for refreshment, Nicola thanked Dona and then said, "We'll drink one bottle first, then we'll have the other."

When Dona turned up the next morning to see if we needed any breakfast, Nicola handed her back two empty bottles and said, "The same again please."

The rest of the crew had also worked throughout the night in the smithy's garden, toiling under floodlights, to build an enormous stable, large enough to accommodate ten life-size figures, including various shepherds and villagers. Roberto the electrician threw the switch that turned on the lights that brought the scene to life, revealing that every one of the figures bore some similarity to the people who were actually working on the construction itself. To christen the *presepio*, the crew popped a good few bottles of Prosecco, followed by enough grappa to sink a ship and a couple of large panettone.

After we'd all congratulated each other on our respective efforts we all went home to get some well-earned sleep, before returning for the official unveiling.

The opening ceremony of the *presepio* took place as soon as it was dark, some twelve hours after we had finally finished it. In front of the artisans involved, including their wives and families and the mayor, the priest blessed it and the church choir sang carols. Riccardo Del Meglio opened the show on time, thanking and congratulating everybody by name for working together for the benefit of everybody else. He emphasised that the creation of *il presepio* had meant asking everyone, after a hard day's physical labour to donate a bit more during the cold December evenings and produce, not just a setting from scratch, but something new and different, instead of regurgitating the same old scene from the previous year. I could not help wondering who would thank Riccardo. Now Nicola was getting to know him better he was, in her eyes, beginning to change from an ogre into a star. She, and I for that matter, had realised that not only did he provide boundless energy and organisational ability, he also drummed up all the sponsorship to enable it to happen, solely for the benefit of the citizens of Moltrasio.

At the end of his speech, Riccardo singled out Nicola and I, '*i due stranieri*', the two newcomers, who willingly gave up their time to help, which signalled a huge round of applause from all the onlookers, coupled with more shoulder hugging and kissing. Then, to our complete surprise, he and the crew presented us with the biggest food hamper imaginable. Tears ran down Nicola's face and I of course, being the resolute Englishman, fought them back so nobody could see them, but they were forming nonetheless. Enzo cried like a baby. All the crew, including Fillipo, his wife, Valeria, Ovidio, Dona the blacksmith's wife, in fact everyone, was in tears. We knew for certain then that we were in the company of firm friends.

We now possessed an enormous food hamper with enough food to feed about eight people over Christmas but we had no plans arranged for what we would actually do on Christmas Day. We had worked closely alongside Ovidio the carpenter on the construction of the Nativity scene and thought about inviting him over to celebrate Christmas Day with us, English style. We didn't know much about this very sweet and loveable guy except that he was a divorcee and we assumed that he might be spending Christmas Day on his own and he would be lonely. When, on Christmas Eve Nicola asked him if he wanted to join us, he said that, funnily enough, he had intended asking us to his place. He then gave her a complicated verbal description of where he lived, a place that could only be reached on foot. She said "yes, please" to his invitation, which really meant "maybe" but then confessed to me that she didn't think we could go because she thought that we'd never find his house. On Christmas morning he telephoned, insisting we turn up at his house at one o'clock and gave us much clearer directions of how to find it.

When we got there, we discovered that he was anything but lonely, or even alone, for sitting at the dining table waiting to welcome us was his large, friendly family and about eight of his closest friends. We were late and so we started to tuck in straight away. The atmosphere was fabulous, and so was the food; there was lobster, sliced cold meats, salami, cured and cooked prosciutto, mortadella, home made duck pâté, pickles and anchovies, then fresh ravioli, stuffed with porcini mushrooms in brodo (broth). The main course was roast pheasant, duck and beef accompanied by a selection of roasted vegetables. The roast meats were not carved at the table but pre-cut,

the beef cut into chunks and the birds cut into pieces with se-
cateurs. It was served with *mostardo*, which is mixed fruit,
pickled in a sweet mustard syrup. Then in true Italian style
there was a green salad to help digest what we had consumed
so far. Later, after a wine break, we had the traditional Pan
d'Oro as dessert, served with a rich Marsala sauce and other
various sweets, nuts and fruit, plus litres of Prosecco and more
wine, followed by a dozen different cheeses, coffee and a choice
of bottles of the inevitable grappa. We were eating for four
hours solid and in the evening more people arrived bringing
more food. At ten-thirty we eventually staggered home, swearing never to eat another thing, ever again.

The next day was the feast of San Stefano and we took up
an invitation to go to Enzo and Ada's for another blowout
lunch, after which I went to sleep on their divan. Then we remembered that I had left my jumper at Ovidio's house the previous day and had to go back to collect it. Amazingly, when
we arrived, we found the same people from the day before, all
sitting at the table in exactly the same positions we had left
them in fifteen hours earlier. They were deep in discussion over
the break up of communism in the USSR and what the long
term effects would do to Italy, and more particularly to the left
wing PDS (the Socialist Democratic Party). The Italians, like
the French and totally unlike the English, are a very politically
minded people and such discussions actually unite them,
rather than create the sort of embarrassing divide that occurs
when politics is discussed in company in England. Ovidio
found my lost jumper and insisted we stay for more wine and
grappa and more food. A couple of hours later we returned to
Enzo and Ada's for even more food. We then went home for
some respite, where Nicola crashed out on the bed, saying that
she felt like a snake trying to digest a hippopotamus.

The tradition in the north, if not in the whole of Italy, is to spend New Year's Eve eating in restaurants and *trattorie* with large groups of family and friends. These places will be booked up weeks before the event, serving food and drink well after the midnight celebrations. Enzo's daughter is married to the owner of a restaurant in Como and we were invited to join them, along with a big group of our fellow Moltrasini, for the celebrations. The food included four courses of sea-food, plus litres of wine and the inevitable Prosecco.

If food is one of the two things all Italians consider paramount in their lives, the other is how they look, and New Year's Eve gives them the opportunity to dress up in their best. And it's not only the outer clothes that matter. It is a tradition for men to buy their wives and girlfriends red underwear. It has to be red and it's more appreciated if it is a bit raunchy. At this New Year party, after a few glasses of the red stuff had been drunk it was interesting to see some of the ladies present flashing a quick glimpse of their loved ones' gifts.

As midnight approached, everyone in the restaurant went outside to the main piazza, down by the lake shore to join with just about every other Comascan of every age who was in town to celebrate. Along with many of the villages dotted around the perimeter of the lake, the city had laid on its customary firework display. For almost a half an hour the displays lit the entire sky with colour. When at last it had died down we returned to the restaurant and, in true Italian fashion carried on eating until the small hours of the morning.

For lunch on New Year's Day, called *pranzo di capodanno* (which literally means 'lunch at the point of the year') the food and drink is equally copious as it is during Christmas Day and the *Festa Di San Stefano* and Nicola and I were invited to join in once more, this time in a different house, but with all the same people in attendance. The traditional New Year's day fare for northern Italians, be it in the evening or in the daytime, is lenticche and pork, particularly *zampone* (pigs' trotters). *Lenticche*, the Italian brown lentils that soften when cooked but do not break down to a mush, are emblematic of good fortune for the coming year and the fat from the trotters represents a healthy, prosperous year ahead. Despite her trying to hide it, I could see Nicola's disgust at the thought of eating a pig's trotter, but she wasn't allowed to escape, as everybody in the room stood over her to make sure she placed at least a symbolic piece of trotter in her mouth and made sure she swallowed it. After that was over we had risotto Milanese, cooked with saffron and served with fillets of perch from the lake. These tiny fillets, no more than about five centimetres long, are fried until the outer coating is crisp and laid on top of the risotto. Like much freshwater fish, they have a delicate flavour, which is complemented beautifully by the saffron in the rice. This was followed by a vegetable soup with more lentils, then even more lentils with mashed potatoes, carrots and, for even more good luck the favourite *cotechino*, a large spicy pork sausage made with Romano cheese cut into slices, accompanied by veal *scallopini* and spinach.

For dessert we had Pan d'Oro with a sugar icing and something like eight bottles of Prosecco between us to toast the New Year. Then we sampled a large trifle, together with a selection of *canoncini* (literally 'little cannons'), which are small pastries with a chocolate cream and hazelnut nut filling and a glass or two of Manzocco dessert wine. Then to finish us off completely, out came the predetermined selection of grappa, mixed with *caffé espresso*.

It did not take us long to realise that this was the best Christmas and New Year we had ever had and, should fate allow it, we were already looking forward to the next one in the company of the same people. Nicola's insistence that we should join in village activities had more than reaped its reward and because of our involvement we had met many more people than we might have done otherwise, who through their generosity helped make us feel we had truly arrived.

Chapter 8

Carnevale - Carnival Time

IT SEEMED no time at all after New Year that February was upon us, and in Italy February is carnival, or *carnevale* time. Throughout the length and breadth of the country, the seasonal activities are taken very seriously and no more so than in Moltrasio. Once again the village was decked out in the individual colours of the five contesting factions of Niasce, Bella Ghita, Tosnacco, Molino and Borgo. And once more the competitive spirit in the village came to the fore, with the added incentive of prizes to be won. There was a plaque for best costumes, another for the best float and a third for the best performance. The winning entry would go forward to the regional final, held in Como city centre, with the opportunity of winning more honours.

The boundary lines of each of Moltrasio's factions had all been mapped out years ago by Riccardo Del Meglio, and in the run-up to the *carnevale* were clearly defined by the different colours he had presented to each one. He arranged for each of the five factions to organise a committee, then to contact all the residents who live within the boundaries of their colours to find willing volunteers to make the float and costumes for the parade. We happened to live in Niasce, which was given the colour purple. Enzo and Ada, Umberto and Dona, Fillipo, Ovidio and many more of our best friends all lived in the yellow faction, La Bella Ghita, which is Comascan for 'the beautiful girl'.

We realised then just how crafty Enzo had been. He had done a very good job in patiently courting us, involving us in all the social gatherings and the inside workings of the Bella Ghita, without our being aware of his intentions. When we went to watch our first *Palio* at the sports ground we sat with the Bella Ghita supporters' group. In November we went to the *castagnata festa*, the chestnut festival in the Bella Ghita area, where we drank plenty of red wine punch and ate too many hot roast chestnuts. The *presepio* is sited right in the centre of Bella Ghita territory and the blacksmith's workshop where most of its operations are constructed is the hub of Bella Ghita activities. It was all beginning to make sense. Enzo and all our friends, the same ones who had made generous contributions to our Christmas hamper, were all members of the Bella Ghita. Even Del Meglio himself lived in the Bella Ghita zone. Although we lived in the Niasce zone, we had become so involved in all the village activities that the thought of having to break away from our new pals and change allegiance to Niasce and to turn aside our connection to the Bella Ghita was unthinkable, especially when it would mean competing against our friends. After all, when we attended a Bella Ghita *riunione*, as the Italians call any gathering, and stood to attention with our right arms crossing our chests and sang umpteen choruses of "Viva Bella Ghita!" at the top of our voices, how could it be possible for us to be so disloyal?

Enzo had realised before anybody else, particularly the Niasce committee, that having me, a professional artist, on side could result in a sizeable coup for the Bella Ghita. He knew very well that none of the other entrants had even one amateur artist between them, never mind a professional. Unbeknown to us at the time, he made sure we were kept in the dark about the rules and regulations of the competition. To us, as outsiders, we thought *carnevale* was just a bit of fun, but to Enzo it was a serious business and he had worked out long before anybody else that having us two on board as part of the Bella Ghita team meant that the prize, for that year at least, was as good as in the bag.

We reckoned that Enzo must have figured that we, as residents but not Italian citizens, might be classified as neutrals and the Bella Ghita faction could be immune from any sanction by the ruling body as a result of this piece of naughtiness. Added to that, as we were the first ever foreigners to be involved in the Moltrasio carnival, the other factions might not realise or question that there was any wrongdoing. He probably thought there might be a clause that could be bent to serve his purpose, but for sure he wasn't going to draw their attention to our involvement unless he had to. However, if Enzo were to be called to task by the ruling body, which was made up of two representatives from each faction, to explain how two members of one faction ended up working for one of the others when they shouldn't have, his task of answering the charge would be pretty unenviable.

Bella Ghita's committee announced that they had chosen 'Robin Hood' as the theme for their entry in the carnival parade. It seemed to us slightly incongruous, not to say somewhat coincidental that for our very first involvement with carnival in Italy the selected theme should be a legendary Englishman. The outlaw had been chosen, we were informed, not because they had an English couple in the team, but because of the much acclaimed success of the Kevin Costner film that was doing the rounds of the cinemas. Still, whatever the reason, we knew that should it be asked for, we were the most likely people to ensure any kind of authenticity to the display.

The first production meeting was held four weeks prior to

the start of the carnival parade. The committee decided that I was the obvious candidate to paint the float, after the technical members of the crew, who were more or less, man for man, the same ones who had built the *presepio* two months earlier, had completed its construction. Their idea was that the float, built on a large trailer, should represent a castle, complete with a mechanised drawbridge and a staircase inside the keep that ran up to the battlements. It would be pulled by a builder's tractor, camouflaged to look like part of the castle ramparts.

Ovidio's pre-prepared design for the float had been accepted without argument, and the next item on the agenda was to decide who would design and make the costumes. No one was more surprised than me when Nicola volunteered to design and make most of them. Some of the wives offered to work in conjunction with her, making the tunics for Robin's Merry Men, the tabards for the Sheriff's men, plus costumes for the various attendants and maids in waiting as well as all the props. On our way home from the meeting, Nicola was regretting that she hadn't sat on her hands or kept her mouth shut, as she realised that she was now not only designer and costumier in chief, but that she had also agreed to play one of the principal roles in the carnival parade – the 'Prince of Thieves' himself. To add to her misgivings, Maid Marian was to be played by Carlo, an escalator repair mechanic by trade. Nicola's task of making Carlo's 'Maid Marian' costume was probably her biggest challenge, because Carlo was short, plump, very hairy and possessed a large red 'whisky' nose. But Nicola is nothing if not resourceful, so to make Maid Marian look as beautiful and alluring as possible, she designed a costume of pink and white layered voile and a white cowl for his face. As a contrast, she then made the costumes for the evil King John and his accomplice, the detestable Sheriff of Nottingham, in sombre colours and as heavy as possible.

It was no surprise that, three weeks later at the run-through, we found out that we were the only participants with any historical understanding on how to direct this epic. As Nicola was involved in the actual performance, she was obliged to volunteer herself to direct and choreograph every-one's performance. She decided that the Sheriff's men, all eleven-year-olds, both boys and girls, would be inside the cas-tle holding Maid Marian hostage as bait to try to attract Robin to attempt her rescue. The Sheriff's men were supposed to fight to the death with wooden swords and plastic bows and arrows in her defence. In the meantime Robin and 'his' men, all dressed in the famous Lincoln Green (some of them disguised as trees), were to sneak up to the castle structure built on the tractor trailer, climb onto it, scale the walls, kill all of the Sher-iff's men guarding the battlements, open the drawbridge and allow the rest of Robin's men (all twelve-year-olds) to pour in and rescue Marian from the loathsome Sheriff's grasp, hope-fully before his guards twigged what was happening. That was the plot; in practice, however, the Sheriff's men were outnum-bered two to one by Robin's men, which probably wasn't his-torically correct, but Nicola was finding it difficult to recruit soldiers to hold the castle intact, because everybody knew the inevitable outcome and not many of the participants were will-ing to be killed fighting for a lost cause, trying to keep the in-domitable Robin away from his beloved Marian.

The dress rehearsal was held the day after the run-through, and the day prior to carnival itself. As Nicola drummed into everyone taking part, Robin and her Merry Men would follow the castle on foot, concealed by other par-ticipants dressed as trees, until the Sheriff's men had consumed enough wine (which was actually water with red food colour-

ing) to become inebriated. Then they were to leave the cover of
the trees, leap onto the float as silently as possible and over-
power the Sheriff's men. A small contingency of servants
would trawl the float looking for loose arrows, to be returned
and reused for a repeat attack as the parade moved along, and
if a few arrows went astray and hit innocent bystanders, that
was tough luck. After each performance everybody old enough
would take a quick break for some real wine, especially Robin,
who estimated he/she would be exhausted from designing and
making costumes and stage managing everything as well as
performing the part of the famous outlaw. When everybody
involved understood their roles, she told her spare Merry Men
and Women to induce some audience participation. This
would take the form of harassing the spectators who lined the
route, in true Sherwood Forest tradition, as if 'robbing the rich'
and giving the spoils to the poor. Next on her agenda would be
the award ceremony from the balcony above the Bar Centrale,
where Riccardo Del Meglio would announce the winners and,
we hoped, hand over the trophies to the Bella Ghita faction.

This was her (and Enzo's) cunning plan.

The costumes were fitted and completed two days before
the day of the carnival, but the float was still way behind schedule, because the electric drawbridge was causing all sorts of
problems. This prevented me from getting on with my task of
painting the float. As time was running ridiculously short I decided I would have to work around the technicians and make
a start painting on the Saturday afternoon, twenty-four hours
before the parade began, and work through until some time
the next day. Theoretically this was the best thing to do, but the
paint on the ramparts was still wet when the float set out from
the assembly point at two-thirty the following afternoon.

I was shattered after working for twenty hours non-stop,

painting as fast as I had ever done. Nicola had some five hours to spare on the Sunday morning before the carnival was due to set off and as there were still a few of the props left to do, volunteered to lend me a hand with the painting. I set her up with an industrial paint compressor, gave her fifteen litres of Lincoln Green latex paint and told her to point the spray gun in the direction of piles of tree branches her band of followers were about to carry as camouflage for the advance on Nottingham Castle. After she had finished she told her waiting Merry Men that she knew Robin Hood was supposed to wear Lincoln Green but hands, face and hair covered in green make-up was going a bit far!

The starting point of the parade was in the village of Tosnacco, higher up the mountain from Moltrasio centre, and as the floats started to roll forward, an immense cheer went up from the multitude of spectators. For the people of the five factions who had worked tirelessly to put their creations on the road, their work was complete. They could now stand aside with their family and friends and enjoy the parade as it went past. Not so for the performers. Their contribution was just beginning, and no one was more energised than Nicola. She was performing her heart out, leading her band of boys and girls into battle against the younger ones valiantly holding the castle.

There were, as might be expected, some unplanned incidents. On the first corner of the route down the mountain road was a hairpin bend and here, in an awkward manoeuvre, the Borgo float, which was behind the Bella Ghita float, nearly mowed Robin down as she was about to run one of the Sheriff's men through the heart with her sword. Each performance took about half an hour, provided the Sheriff's men didn't fight back too enthusiastically or surrender too easily. Then after a welcome wine break, the whole routine was repeated over and over again until our finishing point, the Piazza San Martino, came into sight.

At the end of the afternoon the judges made their decisions as to who would receive the prizes for the best float, the best costumes and the best performance routine. We were all delighted that Bella Ghita won all three prizes, none more so than Enzo, who gave me a knowing wink as Fillipo the builder, and the chairman of our faction, stepped forward onto the balcony above the Bar Centrale to take the trophy from Presidente Del Meglio.

The local television station had been present throughout the carnival and the next evening as we sat at home watching the television, we knew that everybody in the village who had taken part in the carnival would be doing likewise, trying to spot themselves on the screen. After a short interview with the mayor the item included a great shot of Robin menacing an irate motorist by pointing her sword at his throat, demanding he hand over all his gold before allowing him to pass. Judging by the look on his face, the motorist had not entered into the spirit of carnival and he was shown arduously insisting that the pesky yokels move to one side of the road so he could drive through.

The following Sunday, the Bella Ghita faction's float and all the participants represented Moltrasio in Como, along with the winners of some fifty other village carnivals, in the traditional regional carnival procession. The weekend after that, the Como contingent moved to Chiasso on the Swiss border to make up an even bigger carnival parade that included floats from villages within the Italian–Swiss Canton. Towards the end of this parade, according to Nicola, matters became a little fraught and cracks began to appear amongst her band of

Merry Men and Women. It started when one of the girls complained to Nicola that her friend had nicer arrows than she had and another girl complained that her friend had a nicer frock, and it was made of a softer material that did not rub uncomfortably against her. Some of the technical staff working the gadgetry inside the castle began to argue over the problematic drawbridge. Umberto and Enzo, who had been friends for a long time, fell out with one another when the drawbridge jammed once again at a vital time in the siege, and Umberto accused Enzo of being drunk in charge of the electrics. As producer, director and leader of the band of outlaws, Nicola was brought into the argument to sort it out, but because they ranted at each other in dialect she couldn't understand a word and had to call upon Fillipo, the chairman of the Bella Ghita and a leading figure in Moltrasio society, to help sort it all out. Finally, with patience, they did resolve it and the drawbridge problem and from that moment on, Nicola told me, Fillipo started to treat her as his equal. Probably, she said, it was because she was bossier than he was.

Sadly, Moltrasio's float did not receive any awards in either the Como parade or the regional one in Chiasso, but two weekends after the carnival in Chiasso was over, all the members of the five factions who had taken part in the Moltrasio carnival packed themselves into the village community centre for a huge, free, celebratory dinner. The Mayor gave congratulatory speeches and later presented Nicola with an engraved silver plaque commemorating her work as the representative for the victorious Bella Ghita.

Chapter 9

Il Torneo di Calcio –
the Football Tournament

MY FATHER introduced me to football when I was three, and the only thing I was missing in our new life was not having the opportunity to kick a football around with any intent. I was born in Formby, a small coastal village in Lancashire, just north of Liverpool, where everyone is crazy about the game. Most males there are fervent supporters of one of the two top Merseyside clubs, Liverpool and Everton, but I was more than a supporter, because my father taught me to play and for my whole life in England I played regularly. I started with my school team, graduating to the local semi-professional team, Formby FC, who were affiliated to the Liverpool County Combination League. I was the league's highest goal scorer for two seasons running, and I played with or against some current and former professional players. From there I had extensive trial periods with Blackburn Rovers and Burnley, two Football League clubs in the north of England, which, sadly, didn't result in my playing for them, but later I signed senior professional forms for Cheltenham Town FC.

Although it was some time since I had played seriously, I reckoned I still had something to offer, and I had been keeping half an eye out for an eleven-a-side team in the area in which I might be able to play, even on an occasional basis. In a country as football mad as Italy, I imagined there would be an abundance of football pitches, with a choice of teams to play for on a weekend afternoon, but I had not seen nor heard of one, which I found both baffling and disappointing.

June is football tournament time in Italy and I wanted to play in one, if only I could find a club to play for. In the spring of our second year of residence, I saw a poster from Gruppo Sportivo di Moltrasio in the window of the village newsagent advertising a *Torneo di Calcio*, a football tournament. I begged Nicola to find out more. She told me that I ought to be able to find out about that sort of thing by myself by now, without having to rely on her. She was quite obstinate about it. Finding work contacts for me was one thing, but satisfying my needs for a hobby was another, and this, she insisted was a golden opportunity to do something off my own back.

She had a point, but even though I had worked on my Italian, and had used it as best I could when working with the local artisans on the *presepio* and in the *carnevale*, I wasn't sure if my language skills had improved any. Nicola kept telling me that I would be surprised how much I was absorbing and retaining without being conscious of it. For sure, I had picked up a few words of Comascan, the local dialect, and it had become a standing joke amongst the locals in the Bar Centrale that my dialect was definitely better than my Italian and that my *parolaccie*, my swearing, was even better than my dialect! It gave Nicola the impression that her intention of my learning pure Italian through conversation could backfire on her, and she certainly didn't want me learning a language that was of no use outside of the Como area!

Despite building some good friendships with a lot of people in the village, I still hadn't gained enough confidence to converse unaided, so I crawled a bit harder, even offering to go down on my knees and beg. "Just get me started," I pleaded, "and I promise I will do the rest for myself."

Thankfully, she agreed to do this much, and the next time we were in the Bar Centrale, she asked a few of the locals if they knew anything about the tournament. Oddly, nobody in the area seemed to know anything about football, so we decided to ask our friends. First, we went to see Fillipo the builder in his workshop. He said he wasn't a football fan and didn't know anything. We then visited Umberto the blacksmith, who said he had heard that they played seven-a-side, known as *calcetto* at the sports ground, but did not field an eleven-a-side team because the campo sportivo was too small. Then at the baker's shop we met Ovidio's son, who told us he had heard that GS Moltrasio played eleven-a-side football but they did not play in Moltrasio because finding a plot of land flat enough and big enough to play football on in the foothills of the Swiss Alps was out of the question. Our next stop was Enzo's house. He said he had not seen the poster and knew nothing about the tournament, but the best person to ask about anything to do with football would be the president and manager of the GS Moltrasio football team. We asked him who that was.

"Riccardo Del Meglio," he said, "The man is football crazy."

Nicola and I looked at each other in utter amazement. Why didn't we think of him in the first place? Who else would run the local football team but Riccardo Del Meglio?

We had not seen Riccardo since the carnival presentation in February, but the next time we went shopping in the village, we happened to bump into him. He told us that the soccer club had two eleven-a-side squads that played in the junior leagues – a schoolboys' under-fourteen team and a middle team with an average age of eighteen – but, as we had already discovered, neither played in Moltrasio. There had been a very good men's team but it had been disbanded two seasons earlier because of a lack of sponsorship. However, a mixed team of young and old players from the village competed in an annual knockout competition against other teams from the Lombardy region. It took place in Inverigo, a town to the east of Milan and about thirty kilometres from Moltrasio. As the GS Moltrasio poster said, the tournament was to be held in June and Del Meglio told us that training for it was about to begin at the campo the following week. There would be two sessions per week for one month prior to the tournament, and if I wanted to turn up to see how I fared, he said I would be welcome. If I did okay, I would be considered for selection to play in the *torneo*. This was music to my ears, and to cap it all, Nicola offered to go with me to the first training session to assist with translating.

As the players began arriving on the following Tuesday evening, it was plain to see that everybody knew each other very well and there was the atmosphere of a reunion. The regular football season had only just finished, and so some of the players appeared to be in good physical shape, with most wearing the latest Italian Lycra sportswear which complemented their male model physiques. Size-wise, I was about average, being neither too fat nor too thin. I was wearing an Internazionale Milan shirt I had found in the back of Christine's son's wardrobe, and when Del Meglio introduced me to the players and committee members prior to the warm up the shirt, with its black and azure-blue stripes, earned me a few pats on the back. Inter Milan are one of the biggest clubs in *Il Scudetto*, the Italian professional soccer league, and most of the men in Moltrasio supported the club, over and above the other two giants of Italian soccer, AC Milan and Juventus of Turin.

I was introduced to Pepe, who was GS Moltrasio's trainer.

He was one of Del Meglio's colleagues and committee members and probably his greatest friend. He was an amiable sort, always smoking a pipe, and possessed an unquestioning willingness to serve both the local community and be involved in Del Meglio's various exploits. After Pepe had put us through a few light stretching exercises and a bit of sprinting up and down the pitch, we waited for Del Meglio to divide everyone into two teams for the trial game. Traditionally, footballers are not the most conscientious of athletes and exercising is regarded as a chore rather than a necessity. We were all there for just one reason, to play football.

Supporting football is not Nicola's favourite pastime. She has always said that she can make better use of her spare time than standing freezing on the touchline of a soccer pitch. On this occasion, however, the evening temperature was beautifully warm. This was more encouragement for her to watch me play than she had had for many years, but it was less to do with the climate and more to do with my willingness to mix with Italians on a social basis. From her point of view this could be the severing of the umbilical cord of language support.

"I am not interested in football enough to have to travel around the countryside in pursuit of your passion solely to do your communicating for you," she told me, "and I don't believe the rest of the players would take too kindly to having a female translator sitting in the middle of their dressing room!"

I told her that she obviously didn't know footballers, and in particular, Italian footballers, very well.

She had made it plain that she was supporting me at this first training session to help me get accustomed to the various instructions and phraseology used during a game, and for no other reason. I knew she would be laughing up her sleeve, because she knew that if I wanted to play football I would have to get rid of my stubborn resistance to speak Italian.

For the first training game, Del Meglio put me in a defensive role on the left side of the team. Surprisingly, after thirteen months without a game, my fitness level did not seem too bad. I felt a lack of match practice but I managed to hide this from any onlooker by playing the ball in simple passing moves and not keeping possession for long periods. I also limited the amount of running around that I had to do by marking my opposite number very tightly, restricting his movement and concentrating on dispossessing him of the ball at every opportunity. It was what's known in the game as 'playing it safe', not being too adventurous, but more importantly, not making too many blunders. It was the stock stuff that any player with experience would know about. I was impressed by the high standard of play by the rest of the players during the game. Fitness levels were good, but what really caught my eye was the individual balance and the quality of close control when in possession of the ball that Italians are famous for, as well as their confidence as players, regardless of their role or position in the team. I was also impressed by their accuracy when shooting at goal from distance. For some reason unknown to me, players in Britain are taught to be cautious when shooting from a long range, in case they miss.

But for me, it was not the players who were the most impressive that night. It was Nicola. She put far more effort into the game than anyone on the pitch. Moltrasio's campo is surrounded by a net fence about eight metres high, which is designed to help keep the ball in play and prevent it from rolling down the mountainside into the lake, to be lost forever. Spectators have to remain outside the wire perimeter fencing and most of them tend to hang on to the netting by their fingertips, peering through the mesh.

Having been placed on the left side of the campo for the first half turned out to be a very convenient position for both Nicola and myself. It meant that I was no more than a few feet away from her as I ran up and down the pitch when in possession of the ball and she could run up and down, level with me, translating and dispatching instructions from the manager and my team-mates. By half time, Nicola was exhausted and she needed to switch tactics. For the second half, she'd worked it out that if she stood behind our goal she would not have to run about too much, because the majority of the comments aimed at me were coming from our own goalkeeper and she could relay messages from him to me during the second half without having to break sweat. By the end of the game there was only one winner for my money, and that was Nicola. She had put in a tremendous performance.

On our way back to the house later that evening, she told me that if I wanted to continue to play football in Italy there were a few essential footballing terms and phrases I would have to become familiar with before the next game. For example, I had cleared the ball down the pitch twice, when the goalkeeper was right behind me, shouting "LASCIA-STARE!", which meant he wanted me to leave it alone. Another time, I had left the ball for him to pick it up when he was screaming "LAN-CIA-LUNGO!", which meant 'kick it as far away as possible'. Even more dangerously, I had headed the ball over our own crossbar for a corner when he was right behind me waiting to catch it.

"By some of the language the goalkeeper was directing at you," she told me, "I don't think your playing style impressed him greatly."

She also reminded me that next time she wouldn't be with

me and she didn't want to hear that I had been responsible for the outbreak of World War Three. She also hinted that it would perhaps be prudent to buy our goalkeeper a bottle of wine the next time I saw him, to keep him sweet.

Four weeks and seven training sessions later, on a glorious summer evening in the middle of the week, a fleet of cars left Moltrasio for the thirty kilometre drive to Inverigo to play in our first game of the soccer tournament. Tension was high, grown men returned to being little boys and we talked a lot of gibberish throughout the journey. Remaining dignified while nervous isn't easy.

The tournament was scheduled to run for the next three weeks and was organised in the same way that FIFA, soccer's world governing body, uses for the World Cup. The sixteen competing teams are divided into four mini-leagues of four teams. Each team plays the other three teams in its group once, with three points awarded for a win and one point to each team for a draw. The top two teams from each of the four groups qualify to go forward to the next round, creating two groups of four teams, and the process is repeated. The top two teams from these two groups then go forward to the semi-finals, the winners of each semi-final going forward to the final. The worst a team can do is to be knocked out after the initial three games. The best of course is to win the final, having played eight games over the twenty-one days of the tournament.

I was pleasantly surprised to discover that the Inverigo ground was a small stadium, with a capacity of four thousand seats. There were covered stands around three sides of the playing area, but running the entire length of one of the ends was a wall of ugly permanent hoardings, about four metres in height, which blocked out what would have been a pleasing view of the Brianza countryside and the city of Bergamo in the distance. It also of course left no space for spectators.

Best of all, the pitch was real grass, the proper green stuff instead of the campo's shale surface. We were like junkies for grass; not the kind to smoke, of course, but the buzz was the same. An hour and a half before the kick-off we had the chance to make a close examination of the playing surface, which seemed to be in fairly good condition apart from the central area due to the fact that the regular league season had only just finished, but it was good enough for us.

After examining the pitch, the twenty members of our squad settled in to our dressing room, where the Inverigo groundsman introduced himself. He told us that the worn areas of the pitch were to be re-turfed after our tournament was over and made ready for the start of the next league campaign in late September. When I heard him mention the league, my heart jumped. If only the clock could be put back a few years, I thought, then I would be able to play every week. But then reality checked in very quickly. The spirit was willing, even the flesh was willing, but unfortunately the people who ran football teams were not. They consider that a player of twenty-six has only a few more years left in him. A player of thirty-six they class as a veteran. A player of forty-six who still tries to play football they consider should be certified.

The dressing room in the Inverigo stadium was much more luxurious than the ones you'd find at UK amateur level standards. For one, it was twice as large. It had air conditioning, individual showers with sliding doors, three massage tables, fresh towels galore, hair-dryers, mirrors, a wall safe to lock away personal valuables, a refrigerator packed with high-energy drinks and a freezer with plastic bags full of crushed ice ready to wrap around any potential injuries. The match kit for each of the players had already been folded and neatly laid out, with the player's shirt, socks, shorts and shin pads in his place, with another shirt hung on the peg above accompanied by an extra pair of shorts and a track suit top. I asked Lelle, one of the players I had formed a bond with over the training period in Moltrasio and who spoke a few words of English, why there were two shirts and an extra pair of shorts for each player. He told me they were for the pre-match warm-up. This was luxury indeed.

We were all anxious to be selected to play in the first game. Del Meglio had promised everyone who had done the training back in Moltrasio that they would get at least one game in the competition, which lessened the tensions somewhat, but nevertheless, everybody wanted to play in all the games, as any footballer does. If he didn't, you'd think there was something wrong with him. Now we were excitedly waiting for Del Meglio to come from the manager's room with his team selection. The tension was almost unbearable. "Where is he?' we asked each other, "Why is he taking so long?"

I suspected that Del Meglio knew the team he wanted to play right from the beginning. I'd been told by one of the regular squad members that for this tournament he always used the same nucleus of players, but this year there were a few places up for grabs, due either to injuries sustained in training or others not being available on the night. I was as anxious as the rest to see if my name was on the team sheet for one of the available positions and when he pinned it onto the notice board I was so disappointed not to see my name. Then I saw the name of a player whose name I didn't recognise, who had been selected to play in my position. 'Writ Powl', it said, playing at left fullback. Then I realised that it was me! I would be playing in the first game!

A separate piece of paper from the team sheet listed the five players per team allowed by FIFA as substitutes. One of the names was 'Del Meglio Riccardo'. At first I thought it must be a joke, but when I looked around at other team members' faces in the room, nobody seemed to be finding it amusing. Certainly there was no shortage of bodies hanging around waiting for selection and all of them were a lot younger than he was, so why had he put his own name forward? I asked Lelle why Del Meglio had included himself as one of the substitutes when there where five players out of the original twenty not even required to get changed. To my surprise, Lelle told me that Del Meglio had played as a professional in the Swiss B Series for many years and he was still a strong and aggressive striker.

Each player selected to play took his position beside the kit that corresponded to the number Del Meglio had written on the team sheet, which was now pinned to the notice board. With the announcement of the team, the atmosphere in the dressing room had become more serious. Del Meglio became more animated in his gestures, and curt with everybody. He cleared the dressing room of people not required to play, leaving the eleven players and five substitutes to change into a warm-up kit. From here on in the system became a completely new experience for me. This was the very first occasion I had been in any foreign dressing room, let alone an Italian one, before a competitive match and it was a lot different from anything I had been accustomed to in the UK. Fortunately, Lelle was sensitive enough to realise that I, even with hundreds of semi-professional games behind me, was unsure about what was going on, and that everything about playing the game here was that bit different. I felt a bit like a motorist driving a car on the right-hand side of the road for the first time. Everything can look familiar, the road surface, the road markings, the signposts and even most of the cars, but even after any amount of homework he can be nervous and uncertain, and there will almost inevitably come the moment when he finds himself on the wrong side of the road, with every other road user coming straight at him with their horns blaring. I hoped I wouldn't find myself in a comparable position at any time during the tournament.

When we had all changed into the warm-up kit and put on our GS Moltrasio track-suit tops, we went outside, with me following Lelle, making sure I did not get separated from him because I had no idea where we were going or what was supposed to happen next. We walked around the back of the stadium to a caged, shale pitch just like the one back in Moltrasio. Pepe was already there, waiting to put us through our paces. Some fifty metres away in another caged area the opposition were already well into their warm-up, working hard, sprinting, running backwards, stopping and starting and touching toes. As if Pepe wanted to demonstrate to them that we were no soft touch, he made us do everything they were doing, only in a different order. After ten minutes of this, we were transferred to another training area covered in artificial grass, with goals at each end for shooting practice and a general kick-about to get our eye in. This went on for about another ten minutes, and then we filed back into the dressing room.

Once there, Lelle disrobed and showered. Some of the team did the same, whilst others towelled themselves dry, some applied all-over perfumed deodorants or talcum powder to themselves and the inside of their socks and boots and some applied hair-gel. Some drank water, some drank trendy energy drinks, some drank Fanta and some drank milk. Two players even ate ice cream.

Everybody dumped his pre-match kit on the floor in a big heap, which was then gathered up by the kit-man and stuffed in a black bin-liner. I sat, watching, trying to get an idea of what I should do next. Pepe began massaging some players' legs on one of the padded tables. Other players massaged their own limbs, or each other's, and others lifted light dumbbells to avoid stiffening up. Whatever their particular preference, everybody seemed to be busy doing something to themselves as a part of their pre-match preparation: all except me, that is. By now, the Riccardo Del Meglio I had seen and heard many times before, the cheerleader, the heart and soul of the occasion, had come alive. He had changed from his daywear into a club tracksuit and was pacing the room, talking to everyone in turn, asking each one how they felt and if they were in form and looking closely into anyone's eyes to see if he could see any doubt. And if he did see even a trace, he would expel it by telling them what it was they were going out on that pitch to do. To players he already knew, who didn't need to be gee'd up, he'd speak softly and then, turning to the rest of us, at the top of his voice, he would shout, "Ragazzi! (Boys!) Forza Moltrasio! (Strong Moltrasio!) Grande ragazzi! Voi grandissimi Moltrasini!"

Everyone joined in. It was the noisiest dressing room I'd ever been in and Del Meglio was out-shouting everyone. When it was my turn to receive his personal attention, he put his hand on my shoulder and with the other he put some liniment in the palm of his hand and began massaging the nape of my neck, the spot where tension builds up and said, "Grande Powl, Grande Moltrasino. Come on, boy!"

These last three words were the only English he knew and he repeated them every time he looked in my direction, laughing and hugging me every time he circled the dressing room throughout the gearing up process, as if I were one of his favourite sons. This boisterous, stocky, human dynamo was only three years older than me, but he was like a father figure.

"Grande Riccardo!" I replied. "Viva Moltrasio!"

Why anybody should knock this guy – and there were plenty in the village that did – was a mystery to me. Here, this evening, he gave us all the feeling that we were the best, doing what a manager is supposed to do by bringing us together, and he did it with a big heart.

"Whatever the outcome of this tournament," he told us, "we are going to enjoy it. If nothing else the boys of Moltrasio are going to have a great time."

In my and Nicola's opinion, his standing amongst the Moltrasini residents was immense. He was not only a star: he was a hero.

When everybody had changed into the match kit, Pepe told us to place our ID documents on the corner of the massage table. Any players over the age of thirty-five selected to play had to produce a separate private medical insurance document as well as his state medical card, plus a doctor's recent examination report. This is because a person over thirty-five who plays a sport is classified as a high risk and the state doesn't want to be involved with having to pick up the tab for any infirmity. Pepe's demand brought a derisory cheer from the younger players, eager to get one over on the senior ones. When Pepe asked where my documents were, I did not understand what he was talking about. I thought it was something that applied to the Italian players only. Never in my soccer career had I ever been asked to produce identification papers and medical documents moments before the kick-off.

"Mamma mia!" Pepe said, to the whole room. "Powl doesn't have his documents."

"Porco Dio!" said Del Meglio.

"Merda!" said Lelle. "Do you have your passport?"

I admitted that I didn't.

"Powl, this is real problem," Del Meglio said, peppering his statement with a lot of other stuff that implied that some very unsavoury acts were taking place between the holiest of holies.

In Italy, everybody has to carry their ID card at all times and the police authorities have a right to ask to see them. ID cards are not issued by the UK government, and British citizens are not in the habit of carrying other forms of identification. As a non-Italian citizen living in Italy I do not need an ID card but I am supposed to carry my passport at all times. Those in the UK who possess a passport usually put it in a drawer at home for safekeeping, only to pull it out ten minutes before leaving to go on holiday abroad.

Del Meglio stood over me, red in the face. He then raised his eyes, maybe to the heavens and pleaded, "What am I going to do?"

There was no time to discuss it any longer as the dressing room door sprang open and in strode the referee, followed by his two linesmen. They had an air about them of officiousness or, maybe, intimidation that told us that they weren't there to waste time. In the UK, when, or if, the referee enters the dressing room, and he generally does it alone, most players try to pretend he's invisible. Nobody is actually rude to him, but nobody really acknowledges his presence or listens to what he has to say and there is always an atmosphere of 'him versus us'. Some referees like to inform players that they expect good behaviour on the pitch and some might lay down the law about what particular offence he finds intolerable. When he's gone, somebody might enquire, "Who was that strange person wearing the kinky black gear?" or "What was he gabbing on about?"

In Italy, all three officials enter the dressing room together, and when they do the general chatter and preparation that goes on before a game comes to an abrupt halt. On this occasion, complete silence reigned. Del Meglio insisted upon it. Those sitting by their clothes hooks stood up. Those already standing made their way to their position and stood in front of it, facing the referee. All of us, including me, almost stood to attention. It seemed to be the thing to do. My initial thought was that the ref would do what a British ref would do and tell us all the usual stuff about being good boys, not pulling opponent's shirts or showing dissent and certainly not swearing at him during the course of the match. He would then check the undersides of all our boots to see if there were any broken studs or sharp edges that could cause injury to an opponent, and to make sure that all jewellery was removed, especially necklaces, which can swing around and take an opponent's eye out when running at speed. This particular referee and his two assistants did all of that and much more.

But their presence in our dressing room signalled the end of the match for me before I'd even set foot on the pitch, let alone kicked a ball in anger for GS Moltrasio. It began when the referee took out the Moltrasio team sheet, which Del Meglio had given him and checked the name of all the selected players on it, to ensure that it corresponded with the name on the player's ID card, his face matched the photograph pasted inside it and the number on the back of his shirt matched the number on the team sheet. Then he inspected each player's state medical card and the additional medical cards carried by all players over thirty-five years of age. These were then checked against the players' ID card numbers to show they belonged to each particular individual and that the dates were current. If all certification was in order, then that player was allowed to play.

I had none of these papers. Nobody had thought to tell me I needed them, and as I was completely unaware of this procedure, it had not occurred to me to ask. My team mates and the officials probably assumed that the way a player's identity was checked in Italy was exactly the same way as in the UK and that I would know all about it already.

Del Meglio tried his best, almost grovelling in his attempt to convince the officials that I was who he said I was, that I was a stranger in their midst and that it was an oversight, but the referee was having none of it. I knew immediately I saw the authoritarian way he conducted himself and the look of complete disbelief on his face when he called out my name and number from the team sheet – he pronounced it 'Vrite Powul, numero tre' (number three) – and found there was no documentation provided for him to check, that my luck was out. He then spun on his heel, scowled a horrible face in my direction and then reprimanded me in front of the whole dressing room. He probably said something like,

"Never in the history of our glorious Italian Football Federation has such an act of insubordination ever been attempted like this before, and if I showed a chink of understanding or humanity to allow this 'foreign thing' to play football it would undermine my authority and it would make me the laughing stock of all my fellow referees and their assistants in our union. Not only that, but GS Moltrasio can count themselves very lucky I am not recommending that they be thrown out of the competition forthwith."

Whatever he said, I could only gather from the tone of his voice that I was being well and truly castigated, because I couldn't understand a word of it. But even before he had finished I had already pulled my shirt off and handed it to one of the chosen substitutes.

Lelle then turned to me and in broken English said, "I sorry for you. Next time we do it."

Still, looking at it from a positive angle it enabled me to watch the match, and the opening procedure from the stand, alongside the rest of our supporters – all six of them and all female – who had turned up to see their boyfriends in action. It also allowed me to assess Moltrasio's performance, and the very different procedure the Italians go through, even in an amateur tournament.

In the UK, at amateur level, players tend to take to the field as individuals. When a player has changed into his kit he might stroll on to the pitch or even jog. Some enter chatting with a group of friends who have turned up to support them and it's not unknown for a player to leave the dressing-room smoking a cigarette and even a pint of lager in his hand.

At professional level, as in the English Premier League, the two teams enter the pitch side by side. As soon as they set foot on the turf they separate and go to their respective ends of the pitch to salute their own supporters and perform the traditional 'kick-in' before the referee calls them to their positions for the kick-off. In international football the players walk into the arena in two orderly lines behind the referee and his line assistants. When they arrive in the middle of the pitch, they stand side by side while the national anthems of both teams are played as a prelude to the game.

The process at Inverigo was far more involved than any of that, and pretty typical of Italian amateur tournaments. Five minutes before kick-off, a distorted recording of a brass band started up over the loud speaker and played about forty bars of the Italian National Anthem. As it was playing, the referee entered the arena, carrying the match ball on the flat of his hand and his whistle already in his mouth. On either side of him were his two linesmen, each with their coloured flags rolled as tight as possible and carried under their armpits, just like a pair of sergeant-majors carrying their batons. This threesome fairly sprang onto the pitch in what can only be described as a comic, stylised, jogging motion, lifting their knees to waist height as they went, reminding me of a team of Hackney horses. They were followed by the two teams in single file trying to keep up with the three men in black, although, it must be said, stepping with less enthusiasm than the three officials. As soon as the whole entourage, officials and players, had reached the white markings in the centre of the pitch and had organised themselves into a neat, straight line facing the fans, the Anthem stopped abruptly.

With everyone in line, the referee sounded his whistle and each player's name was read out by a crackly voice over the Tannoy system at such a fast pace that it was impossible to tell who was who and who played for which team. Announcements duly made, the ref blew his whistle again and to a man all players raised their right arms in a regimental salute to the crowd. First, they faced the main stand, where there were about fifty people in attendance. Then they turned to the left and did the same to the ten or so spectators standing behind the goal. Then they made a third quarter-turn to salute the advertisement hoardings, where there were no spectators at all, and lastly to the goal to the right, where there were about twenty people. Another sharp blast on the referee's whistle brought the same crackled voice from the Tannoy, this time to announce what it was we were about to see and a brief history of the *Torneo di Calcio Maurizio Bugada*, which was named after a local businessman who was its sponsor. This was followed by twenty or so bars of a march played by a brass band, a tune probably known to the spectators but new to me. With all that over, the referee gave another blast on his whistle and the players dispersed to their respective positions without having any 'kick-in'. The two captains then tossed a coin to decide who would kick off and seconds later the game started, seemingly catching the spectators by surprise.

As it turned out, the game itself was disjointed. There were too many fouls and stoppages for either team to get into a rhythm for more than a brief spell, as the referee was far too whistle-happy. In a virtually empty stadium the shrill blast of his whistle echoed around the back wall of the stadium and publicity hoardings, which served to exaggerate his presence on the field. By far the most interesting part of the game was during the last twenty minutes of the second half. We were 2-0 down when Del Meglio put himself on the field, swapping places with the centre forward in the number nine shirt, taking on the role of the leader of the attack. Of course, it stood to reason that this would be Del Meglio's natural position and when he stepped on to the pitch he lifted the team's mood from one of complete gloom brought about by the 2-0 deficit, bringing them back into life. The six female supporters Moltrasio had brought with them also sprang into life when they saw him take to the pitch as if they had been charged by some electric force. Standing up simultaneously, they started to chant his name: "Ricco, Ricco, Ricco!"

I had no idea what to expect from him, this balding dynamo with bandy legs and a belly overhanging his waistband, as I had never ever seen him kick a football, never mind take part in a proper game. Obviously the girls had, and in the few remaining minutes left on the clock they seemed to be antici-

pating a world-class performance from him, expecting him to
turn the game around in Moltrasio' favour. He responded to
their enthusiastic support. I was amazed at his pace and agility.
He was nearly fifty years old, but he reminded me of that instant when a dog owner unleashes his pet at the gates to the
local park and it shoots off like a rocket. He seemed to cover
every blade of grass on the sparse pitch with so much passion
and fervour it was a delight to see him.

The girls agreed. "Del Meglio, Del Meglio, Del Meglio,"
they chanted, giving it their all. By now, so was I and everybody else involved with the club who were sitting on the bench
beside the pitch, such was the infectiousness of Del Meglio's
performance. He was everywhere at once, running continuously at full pelt, chasing and harassing the opposition, tack-
ling them, antagonising them, berating them, generally doing
anything he could to make them lose concentration. The op-
posing team's complacent attitude quickly changed, for within
minutes of his arrival on the pitch, they had started to wonder
where the hell this little bundle of nuisance had sprung from.

The six girls were by now standing on the wooden seats
and were in danger of wrecking them, stamping as hard as
they could, to the rhythm of their chanting: "Vai Ri-ccar-do!
Vai Ri-ccar-do! Vai Ri-ccar-do!"

There was no doubt that Del Meglio lifted a drab game
into a different realm by giving the opposition's defence all
sorts of worries, but within barely five minutes of his arrival on
the pitch, the referee stopped the game dead. Then, walking
over to Del Meglio in an artificially calm, autocratic way he
gave him a stern, almost hysterical finger-wagging lecture,
right into his face. Two minutes later, not to be outdone by
this, Del Meglio was giving the referee a stern fist-wagging lecture in return, about a decision that had gone against him. A

few minutes after that he let fly an amazing shot, sending the ball fizzing across the face of the opposition's goal. We all thought it was in the back of the net, but it flew inches wide. After that, he out-headed the centre-back, who was at least eight inches taller than he was, and again the ball went narrowly wide of the goal. Such was the self-belief of the little man that he could raise himself off the ground higher than somebody who was over six feet tall. Two minutes later he was back in defence, clearing a situation and denying the opponents their third goal. Seconds after that he did a spectacular, overhead scissors kick, but again the ball went narrowly wide of the goal. This resulted in his receiving treatment for a bruised backside from his best mate, Pepe, who without hesitation pulled down Del Meglio's shorts and applied an ice-pack to the painful part. A minute or so later, he was seen displaying threatening behaviour to the opponents' goalkeeper, receiving a yellow card for his effort. Not content with the referee's decision, Del Meglio followed him closely, pointing at the back of his head with his forefinger and thumb, as if imitating firing a bullet into the ref's brain. A short while after that incident the final whistle sounded and our first game in the tournament was over. It was a bad start for the boys in the pale blue shirts of GS Moltrasio, despite Riccardo Del Meglio's valiant attempt to swing the result our way.

The next evening, I was the first in my GP's waiting room to get my over thirty-fives' medical certificate. After the examination the doctor said that I was in excellent shape for my age, but forty-six was pushing the limit to play in a lengthy soccer tournament in the summer heat, and he wavered for a second or two before signing the document. Mercifully, he handed it over, saying in perfect English, "Make sure you don't die! If you die, I die!"

Three nights later, 'Writ Powl' was cleared to play in Moltrasio's next game in the tournament. All my documentation was given the thumbs up, I took my place on the field for the whole game and the match was drawn 1-1. We were now in second place in our group. After the game was over the talk amongst the squad and the management in the dressing room was not about yet another mediocre performance, but the result of studying a print-out of the other teams' results in the competition and their positions and goal averages in relation to ours. From it, we knew we had to win our following game on the Saturday evening and the three points we would get from that result would be essential to make sure we advanced into the next round. To take one point from another draw would leave us depending on other teams' performances to decide our destiny for us.

The next game we took part in was played in a temperature of twenty-eight degrees and it was keenly fought. Unfortunately, after being disallowed a blatant penalty, we were eliminated from the competition after only three games. If we had scored from the penalty spot, we would have won 3-2 but our only consolation was that the result, a 2-all draw was against the eventual winners of the competition. That evening Del Meglio invited the whole team to eat pizza and drink beer at a *trattoria* on the way back to Moltrasio.

The following year we did it all again, but not with all the same players. About six members of the squad could not make it but Del Meglio, being his usual resourceful self, dug out some replacements who were actually better players than the ones he had employed the year previously, especially one whom I had never seen before and suspected was an imported 'ringer' and not a Moltrasino at all, although I found out later that he was, and lived very close to me in Via Besana. I was soon put straight about him. He was twenty-eight years old and had, in his earlier years, played for Juventus in Seria A and later for Como in Seria B and when he started to play, his experience and skill showed. We also had a new goalkeeper, who turned out to be more than adequate. With these better players, Moltrasio had a good tournament and we went all the way to the final. The last game of the tournament against a team from Milan had some needle about it because we had beaten them 3-1 in an earlier round and they were out to get revenge. They had also won the trophy twice in the last three years, which seemed to give them an air of arrogance, as if the winning and ownership of the prize was their right. Del Meglio hoped this attitude would lead to their downfall.

The game started very brightly and the opposition looked very capable, fast and aggressive. Fortunately our star player was performing brilliantly for us and it was obvious early on in the game that our opponents were wary of his ability from the previous game and they tried everything they could to stop him playing. Our goalkeeper was also performing heroics keeping their shots out, but after consistent pressure they went a goal ahead after half an hour. We did well to recover and levelled the score by half time. The second half was not so good and our star player could not make it out of the dressing room because of a recurrence of a swollen knee problem and, sadly, after that we went down 3-1. Eight games in twenty-one days in June temperatures was gruelling but everybody had enjoyed themselves, especially me. To get the opportunity to play a different style of football and to experience playing abroad with some excellent players was a treat.

After the game we were all very tired, especially as we had lost. The winners were obviously jubilant, and by the energy they displayed whilst they where doing their lap of honour, it looked as if they could have played for another ninety minutes. Both teams were presented with medals and the victors were handed a truly enormous trophy. There was a sweet note for our goalkeeper, who was awarded a special plaque for the best 'keeper in the whole tournament and, much to his pleasure, 'Writ Powl' received a plaque for best defender. The opposition's number eleven won the plaque for the best forward, which wasn't surprising. He was one of the fastest players, either professional or amateur, I had ever seen and he scored all of their three goals in the final. We found out later that he was an Italian Olympic hundred-metre sprinter who also happened to play soccer.

Although I didn't realise it at the time, the tournament turned out to be the last time I would ever play football on grass in an eleven-a-side team, and although we didn't win the trophy I now look back on it as a fitting end to my career. I continued to play five-a-side on shale pitches for a few more years, which both earned me a lot more friends and further strengthened my place in Moltrasio society.

Chapter 10

Lavoro Regolare -
Regular Work for Nicola

WHEN WE LEFT the UK, the recession had really set in. In mainland Europe there did not seem to be any sign of a downturn, but there were warnings from the BBC World Service that the threat of the recession we had managed to run away from was looming and was likely to hit the rest of Europe by 1993.

And then, bang on cue, it happened.

In such circumstances, a self-employed artist like me is always one of the first casualties. His work is a luxury to almost everyone and it can dry up, quite literally overnight. After fifteen months as Italian residents, our bank balance had neither grown nor decreased, and from this, we surmised that we must be doing okay, but to help cushion against financial downturn that might come our way, and help us continue living in Italy, I suggested to Nicola it might be a shrewd move if she found some work. Better still, she should get a permanent job as quickly as possible.

Nicola is not a natural housewife. To her, a career is an important part of her life. She had had a good winding-down period since leaving her job in Godalming and had become a little bored reading Christine's library for the third time and not doing anything in particular, but the question was, what could she do? Although she had been an experienced legal secretary in England, she had no working knowledge of Italian law, so the chances of finding similar work were pretty slim, if not non-existent.

Ever since we'd arrived in Moltrasio some of the locals would vie to sit beside 'Powl and Nicol, i due inglesi' when we were out socialising, so they could practise their very limited English on us. Some others enquired if Nicola gave private language lessons. This gave her the idea that she might set up a private language school, working from home. Her initial idea was to place a postcard in the local newsagent's window, advertising English lessons. However, the newsagent placed doubts in her mind when he told her that unfortunately he could not display it in his window without having a taxation stamp attached to the bottom corner.

She did not understand exactly why this was necessary, nor how to go about getting one and so, sensibly, she went to the Municipio to make enquiries. No one there knew either, but the deputy mayor advised her to go to Como to ask higher authorities, because the laws regarding taxation had been changed recently and that they would know better. She had no intention of taking a round trip of eighteen kilometres to Como and back to track down the correct office and official in charge for such a small matter and was in a quandary about what to do when, in the village a few days later, she happened to bump into somebody she knew who had helped her sew some of the carnival costumes. She told Nicola that she had recently advertised her household goods for sale in the same newsagent's window, adding that the newsagent's hesitancy was because the correct stamps had not arrived in the post office and it was likely to be some time before they did. She also told Nicola that in the meantime it might be better to go to the local barber and ask him to stamp it, as he had permission to stamp things that need stamping with the Town Hall seal.

It would cost her three-hundred lire (fifteen pence). In the end, the barber stamped the postcard with his little embossing machine for nothing. Why he held this authority was a mystery to us but at least it was a bit more information gathered and stored, should we need it again.

For all that effort, she got one pupil, a boy of sixteen who wanted to be an airline pilot and who needed to study English urgently. His parents paid the going rate and he learned quickly. Others came to the house in twos and threes because they had worked out that they could get a cheaper rate for a group session than they could for a one-to-one lesson. Some others came asking for conversation only, without wanting to write anything or use textbooks, which really meant that they did not want to pay for Nicola's time. They wanted to treat conversation as a casual social gathering where people spoke English in preference to Italian. This way, they imagined, it would be regarded as being 'just a bit of fun' and that bringing along a bottle of wine was satisfactory payment. After a few weeks of this, some of the village children began to arrive with their English school homework in the hope that she would do it for them, for free. Word had got about there was someone who was a 'soft touch' living in their village who worked for nothing. In the end, Nicola became disenchanted with teaching English at home and gave it up.

The next plan was to see if she could find a regular, paid job. To do this she put an advert in the local newspaper, listing her professional skills and bi-lingual abilities, with English as her mother tongue. The first reply caught her completely on the hop. The week before Nicola had placed the advertisement, Christine's daughter Isabel had stayed at the house with her new boyfriend, whose name was Giovanni. When the phone rang that particular night, Nicola answered it.

"Ciao," the caller said, "I'm Giovanni."

Nicola did not know any other Giovanni she was familiar with, and although he didn't sound like Isobel's boyfriend, she presumed it was him 'phoning, because he used the familiar term, 'ciao'. Italians only use this with somebody they know well. It's instilled into them from childhood to respect somebody they don't know and always use the polite unfamiliar expression, otherwise they risk causing offence.

"Ciao!" she replied, "Come stai, Giovanni?" "How are you?"

In replying with the familiar term, Nicola invited the caller to continue the conversation, but he went quiet. To get him to say something, she asked him what he was doing, but immediately wished she hadn't, because when he told her, she hung up in disgust.

It appeared that, to the Italian red-blooded male, the thought of 'English lessons taught' by an English female is the equivalent of a British male seeing 'French lessons offered' by a French female. After the call was over, she said she did not know whether to be frightened or flattered because it was the first dirty 'phone call she had ever received. When a second caller tried it on, she was more wary. This one made the pretence of wanting to make an appointment to meet her with the purpose of interviewing her for a job, but he never actually said what sort of job, and when Nicola asked him for more information she quickly discovered his ulterior motives.

After two more quite unsavoury late-night 'phone calls, during which Nicola learnt some more examples of obscene Italian slang that she might have preferred not to have learned, she became very wary when the phone rang at an unsocial hour. I started answering them and, not surprisingly, the callers always hung up when they heard my voice.

There was a fifth, genuine, call from a language school twenty miles away offering her two hours work per day, four days per week. These seemed to suit the requirements of the individual students, not the teacher, meaning that she could be on call all day for two hours work. The money on offer was poor and the distance to travel was long, with no travel expenses included and absolutely no chance of a permanent position in the future. With this, Nicola abandoned her ideas of earning a living by teaching English.

But it's often the way of these things that an opportunity comes along when you least expect it, and Nicola found herself a permanent and long-lasting job in the most bizarre of circumstances. One spring day, we took a walk to the village of Urio, higher up the mountain and further along the lake to the north of Moltrasio. By the time we got there, it was lunchtime, and we saw a small hotel with a mountain bar with a spectacular view of the lake and wandered in for a drink. The hotel was run by a Scottish lady by the name of Sandra, an elegant redhead from Glasgow in her late fifties with an outgoing personality, who had been married to an Italian for over thirty years. We paid many more visits to the hotel and when we got to know Sandra better she would keep us amused with her eye-opening stories about her younger days in Glasgow, over thirty years ago, when she was a young policewoman.

One of her regular customers in the hotel bar was another Glaswegian who lived in an apartment in nearby Cernobbio. His name was Alex and he was an exploration engineer engaged on contract work for an oil company based in Milan. He had a large family in Paisley and he would fly home for long weekends whenever he could. These visits kept him in touch with the Scotland of the day, and he would gather up savoury tit-bits of information about home to relay to Sandra, and occasionally fetch back a bottle of his favourite Cragganmore twelve-year old single malt whisky, which he would keep behind the hotel bar for his own consumption. He had worked on and off in Italy for six years, in the south for the first four years and, later, in the north, but he could hardly speak a word of Italian, mainly because he was one of those people who expected the whole world to speak English for his own convenience. He had such a thick accent that if he had taken the trouble to learn Italian, he might have had trouble making himself understood, and even when he spoke English we couldn't understand him until our ears became tuned, hence his frequent visits to see Sandra, the only person in the entire area apart from us he could talk to.

Underneath a gruff exterior this stocky little fair-haired man possessed an obtuse sense of humour and, being strongly patriotic, always referred to himself as 'Braveheart'. As a native Glaswegian and a member of a protestant family he was naturally a fanatical Glasgow Rangers soccer supporter, and completely blinkered towards any other team's existence in the world. In conversation he wouldn't allow the name of Glasgow Celtic, the other Glaswegian Premier League team, to be mentioned. His irrationality didn't stop at Celtic. He wasn't that keen on anybody or anything that wasn't Glaswegian and he certainly wasn't keen on the Germans or the French. He boasted that on his flights home, no matter how desperate he was to relieve himself, he always waited until the plane was over France before he visited the toilet. Alex wasn't at all unfriendly to Italians (it was only their football teams that provoked any hostility in him) and he would socialise with the local customers in the hotel bar every weekday evening after work and all day at weekends. His accent would get thicker by the dram and although the locals only spoke Comascan to him, which bore little relation to Italian and certainly none to Scots, they somehow all managed to communicate and have a great time.

He also came up with some very odd ideas. Soon after we started going to the hotel, Sandra and her husband had the hotel interior painted white. Alex tried to persuade them to have more imagination and paint all the bedrooms royal blue, Glasgow Rangers' shirt colour, and buy bedspreads with Rangers motifs. His idea was to attract Scots to stay at the hotel by making it into a theme bar, thereby doubling their revenue. He added that more Scots would stay at the place if only they imported some decent whiskies! He once formed the 'Como Glasgow Rangers Football Supporters Club' and wrote to the Scottish club, declaring himself the founding member and chairman, which, amazingly, they recognised. They sent him regular newsletters from the club, plus lots of memorabilia and clothing to give to the members of his supporters club. More importantly for himself as chairman, it put him at an advantage when it came to acquiring tickets to the important fixtures when he returned home. Eventually, Glasgow Rangers' management started to get suspicious, and they asked him how many club members he had. When they found out that he could not prove that he had any at all, they terminated all connections.

It was when we were with Alex in Sandra's bar and the twelve-year-old malt was doing the talking for him that he came up with an apparently ridiculous idea, the circumstances of which would unintentionally land Nicola a job. The twenty-fifth of January, as any self-respecting Scot knows, is Burns Night and Alex had noticed that the restaurant, which could seat a hundred and twenty people, happened not to have anything special booked on that night. Why shouldn't Sandra, he suggested, celebrate the birthday of Scotland's national poet by holding their own Burns Night?

"You're in Italy now," Nicola tried to remind him, "the Italians have never heard of Robbie Burns. The only Robbie they know is Robbie Baggio, the footballer."

"Aye, you're right," he slurred, "We can invite him as well."

Sandra must have also had a few drams of the same malt that night and agreed to his idea. Then and there Sandra, a Stewart, and Alex, a Buchanan, joined forces to organise a celebratory dinner, with a little help from we two English people.

On the night, the restaurant was packed. There were some genuine Scots, friends and contacts of Sandra's, who had arrived from all over Italy. Besides these, there was a mixture of Italians, Swiss, Germans, Austrians, Italians, Irish, two Australians, one New Zealander and, including us, three English. The genuine Scots had arrived for the gathering of the clans in full Highland evening dress, and everyone else managed to find something Scottish to wear, either the full highland regalia or at least something with a tartan design. Alex had found a theatrical costumiers in Milan who had a lot of Scottish regalia and so Nicola hired the complete traditional Black Watch tartan outfit for me, including kilt, sporran, socks and buckled shoes, For herself, she hired a twentieth century ladies' equivalent of the same outfit, with a tight knee-length skirt, wide leather belt, bonnet, white shirt and a tartan sash with an emerald clip. Sandra herself looked extremely elegant in her Stewart sash and brooch.

On offer was a selection of some outstanding single malt whiskies: the Glen Ord, the Highland Park, the Longrow, the

Tamdhu and the much-appreciated eighteen-year-old Glen Morangie, all served to the accompaniment of live pipe music. Alex had decked the bar out the day before in Glasgow Rangers regalia left over from one of the parcels the club had sent him. Most people tried to ignore it as they entered the hotel. The traditional Burns poetry reading was carried out by, of all people, a Norwegian lawyer who lived in Moltrasio. He also volunteered to take on the role of Master of Ceremonies. He had done his homework to perfection and, according to Alex, he was the best Master of Ceremonies he had ever seen. The sole piper, self-taught, was a little Italian from Milan who piped in the haggis with true pomp and ceremony. He had rehearsed his performance a couple of nights before and had got it just right, but on the night it was somewhat foreshortened, apparently due to the intake of a little too much whisky. (Sandra had not told him she had the music already taped as backup in case he fluffed it.) There was authentic Scottish country dancing performed by a troop of Italians also from Milan, hired specially for the occasion. They later gave us all lessons, resulting in kilts being swirled in every direction.

Even before he succumbed to the effect of sampling the many single malts, Alex said that it was far better and more genuine than a lot of Burns Nights he had attended in Scotland. So much attention to detail had been paid. Of course neither Nicola nor I could comment; it was a first for us and we had to pinch ourselves to remind us that we were in the foothills of the Italian Alps and not the Scottish Highlands.

It was at the dinner table, over the haggis, neeps and tatties that Nicola's job opportunity arose. I found I had been seated next to the Vice Consul General from the British Consulate in Milan, and after the two of us had taken a few drams of the golden liquid we started to get to know each other a little better. He was a Geordie with an indubitable passion for Newcastle United FC and the only other English person present apart from Nicola and me. A good quality island malt often has a habit of disconnecting the brain from the mouth, and after a short while it must have got the better of me because, completely against the run of the conversation, which had been almost entirely about Newcastle FC, I heard myself asking him if he had a job at the Consulate for Nicola. It can alter a man's behaviour too, because without as much as a 'by your leave' I left him chatting away about some soccer inconsequentiality and staggered across to the other side of the room, to drag Nicola away from the table where she had been placed. She was desperately trying to remember enough about Scotland from her school history lessons to explain to a large contingency of tartan-clad Germans who Robbie Burns was and why they were there to celebrate him. I guided her back to my table and pushed her in front of the Vice Consul and left them alone for a few minutes to discuss him offering her a job! When I came back, he began fumbling about in his jacket pocket, which seemed to take an eternity, but he eventually produced a curled up visiting card. Then, instead of giving it to Nicola, he presented it to me and then he told her to ring him at his office about a vacant secretarial position.

Two days later, Nicola telephoned the Vice Consul, but had a hard job getting him to remember where he had been the previous Saturday night, and an even harder job reminding him who she was and why she was calling. Nevertheless, he invited her to Milan for a pre-interview chat later that same week. I went with her, partly for moral support and partly in the hope that when he saw my face alongside hers he might remember our three-hour lament over the trials and tribulations of his beloved Newcastle United.

When we did actually meet he didn't give the slightest hint of recognition of either of us. Before Nicola went into his office for the interview, he seemed keen to tell us about his previous evening's visit to La Scala Opera House when he, his wife and two friends went to see La Traviata. Apparently when they had arrived to take their seats they found there were four French people sitting in them. After much wrangling in an already packed auditorium, the manager had to be summoned five minutes before curtain up to sort out a double-booking error and calm European relations between France and Britain. On a 'first booked' basis, the French contingent had to give way, which seemed to make the Vice Consul General enormously pleased. As this tale seemed to have given the conversation an informal tone, I risked a gag about his beloved football team.

"One sure thing," I said, referring to Newcastle's woeful performance, which was causing their fans to stay away in droves, "you and your friends wouldn't have a seating problem watching Newcastle at St. James' Park."

This crack made the Vice Consul's chin hit the floor. Nicola looked daggers at me and I'm sure she thought that I'd not only offended the man but had blown her job opportunity even before the interview had begun. Thankfully, all was not lost. Three-quarters of an hour later she arrived back to where I was sitting in an adjacent waiting room and told me that she would be starting work at the beginning of next month.

"He'll confirm it in writing," she added.

This was fantastic news, because it guaranteed that we could stay in Italy for as long as we wanted, we could reckon on a regular amount of money coming in each month but most importantly it would satisfy the bureaucrats in a country obsessed with permits and documentation. Having *lavoro rego-*

lare, regular work, and all the relevant paperwork to show for it means everything in Italy.

That night we went up to Urio to Sandra's hotel to celebrate the good news with her and Alex. Later on, when Sandra's back was turned, Alex told us that after the Burns Night, there had been a bit of a 'stooshie', as the Scots call an argument, behind the scenes at the hotel. Apparently, two evenings before the actual Burns Night, all the frozen haggis arrived safe and sound from Scotland, sent by express courier in a special sealed container. Sandra thought she could now relax, only to discover that Nico, the head chef of the hotel, blew his top at the idea of having the haggis thawing out in his fridge. He would not, he declared allow such 'disgusting rubbish' near good food. At this, Sandra's Scottish blood boiled over and her red hair stood on end. Relations between these two had been strained for some time and this insult to her heritage finally blew them apart. On top of that Sandra's husband, Gherado, made a grave error and to his matrimonial detriment, sided with the chef, rather than with his wife.

Sandra had managed to pass off the Burns Night in her normal outgoing, professional way and nobody would have known there was anything deeply wrong, but after another two bust-ups with Nico within the same week, she stormed out of the bar for the last time. We began to visit the bar less frequently, because without Sandra, it just wasn't much fun any more and when Alex returned to Scotland permanently, we stopped going completely. Two years after Sandra left, the hotel was closed and earmarked for conversion into apartments, so the moral of the story might well be not to say anything nasty to a Scot about haggis. We kept in touch with Alex for the next three years, but then one day Alex's wife 'phoned from Glasgow to tell us that they had been waiting for a train when he keeled over and hit the ground, stone dead from a massive cardiac arrest. He was just fifty-six.

We were well into our second year of living in Italy and the period of our *permesso di soggiorni*, 'our permission to stay' permit, had expired. Paradoxically, our stay was illegal according to Italian law, but not so by the European Union law, although we were not about to argue the case with the Italian authorities. We had knowingly pushed it to the limit simply because we did not want to put ourselves through all the rigmarole, the anguish and the free-for-all in the Questura all over again to renew our permits. However, when Nicola received the confirmation letter from the British Consulate to start work it was imperative for her in particular to bring all her paperwork up to date or she would never be accepted for work by the Italian authorities. This time with the aid of experience and a hard-bitten attitude, she applied for and received a five-year permit with only limited aggravation.

For me, the bureaucracy was still worrying, exasperating and annoying because, as a self-employed foreigner the form filling seemed to be compounded to a nonsensical degree compared with what I'd been familiar with in the UK. I gathered that even Italians who run their own businesses despair of getting everything correct, so how did I stand a chance? I was now supposed to make quarterly IVA (VAT) returns, which meant taking a day off work and queuing up for hours in a Como office with hundreds of other people, all irritated by the procedures, only to be told what I had anticipated, that I had got it all wrong and I must try better next time.

By happy coincidence, one of the women who had helped Nicola with the costumes at the carnival held a position of some authority in the IVA office. We bumped into her when out shopping in the village and Nicola poured out to her all the problems we were having in trying to pay our dues and how we desperately needed help. The next day we were invited to sit down in the comfortable privacy of her office in Como, where we were served coffee and brioche by a member of her staff while she completed and processed the forms for us. I could have kissed her, but instead we presented her with two-hundred cigarettes, which I am sure she appreciated more.

What we experienced are examples of some of the downsides of living in Italy, and they can discolour the view of an idyllic lifestyle in a beautiful country. Renewing car tax in January or the half-year can be a similarly painful event, because it seems that Italians wait until the very last day possible to pay their dues. Just the thought of visiting the relevant office, which would be packed with folk frantically filling in forms they could not understand with their time to complete them running out, is daunting, but we had no choice but to join them. Added to which we realised that we had not received all the registration documents we needed for the car we had bought some months before. We risked a fine if caught driving around illegally, so we had to pay a visit to the Automobile Club Italiano office to procure the missing forms and pay a trapasso, an ownership transfer tax, which is applicable when buying a second-hand car in Italy. One has to come to terms with The System as quickly as possible, so that the pain of bureaucracy subsides, allowing the better aspects of Italian life to come to the fore. If for us the good side of Italy had not outweighed the bad side, then there would not have been any point in our continuing to live here.

Chapter 11

The End of an Era

DECEMBER CAN sneak up quietly: it only seemed six months rather than twelve since we had last been involved in the creation of the village nativity scene. Now, the month was upon us again. One Saturday morning, Nicola was shopping in the village when she bumped into Riccardo Del Meglio. He took her to one side and asked her if I would design this year's presepio and, what's more, take on the artistic control because Ovidio, who normally did the design, wanted to go to New York to visit his relatives for the Christmas period and he would be leaving very soon.

At the time I was painting a large ceiling for Count Borromeo in his palace in the centre of Milan. I was one month into the work, with two more still to go, so I wasn't around to hear Nicola's conversation with Del Meglio. She must have said something to the effect that I would be more than delighted to help in the village activity, and when should I start?

I must say I wasn't too pleased when I heard the news. As well as being busy with the project in Milan, I was looking forward to the Christmas break and a good rest. Secondly, I was wondering why on earth we kept allowing ourselves to be involved in something as uniquely Christian as the nativity. Back in the UK we had always remained distant from anything related to the local church because it made the both us feel a little uncomfortable, and yet here was Nicola trying her best to involve us in it. However, she put me firmly in my place about any negative thinking.

"The actual theological belief behind the Nativity scene is irrelevant," she said, "the point of the exercise is that it's a traditional village activity and its religious connotation is secondary. It is all part of the community bonding process and if you want to enjoy the benefits of living in this village, then we have to put aside our personal opinions and pull our weight."

I agreed she did have a point, and when I thought about it, it dawned on me that it wasn't possible to describe any of the people who produced the presepio as being spiritual or as regular worshippers. The only time any of them were seen in church was for family weddings, christenings or funerals, which, as almost all of them are related in some way, kept them busy in one way or another almost all year round.

The only instructions that Fillipo, our resident builder and project manager, gave me was that it had been decided by his committee to incorporate all the life-sized figures we had made the previous year into a different setting. On the surface, this sounded okay but to incorporate all ten life-size figures, plus plenty of equally life-size animals and keep the whole thing in proportion, the setting had to be big. At the construction meeting a week later I presented him and the regular crew members with a cardboard scale model. They nearly choked when they saw it. It was like a section of an MGM movie set, an extra little Italian hamlet to be added to Moltrasio, with a touch of Bethlehem thrown in. What I'd done in the model was to extend the village by designing a row of little workshops that incorporated the various local trades, with an artificial stream and a waterwheel that was supposed to power the machinery in the workshops. The whole set was to be erected in the Blacksmith's garden, as it had been every year, between the plants and the bushes.

I made my presentation just three weeks before the opening night, so with little time to spare, the whole crew began building as soon as the materials arrived on site. I insisted that this time I be given more time than last year to complete the scenic artwork: there was a lot of timber in the building work, which meant there was a lot more painting to do.

Three weeks later and well on time, the installation was in position and everybody involved with the creation seemed to be content with their work. It certainly was impressive and everyone was talking about it. It was so large that some of it stretched beyond the blacksmith's garden and down the high street, causing the older villagers to do a double take, believing for a moment that some new artisan workshops had been added to the district overnight.

In the first workshop was a knife sharpener working the foot pedal of his grinding wheel. The carpenter was next door. He was endlessly sawing the same piece of wood in half and next door to him was the blacksmith hammering out a horseshoe, with his young assistant squeezing a pair of bellows to keep the brazier in flame. Then there was the gardener hoeing his vegetable plot, with the herdsman in the background guarding his flock. (In this case goats, rather than sheep.) All of these figures were driven by the motor from Carlo's wife's industrial sewing-machine, connected to a series of pulleys with a continuous loop of nylon fishing line running from them so it controlled all the figures together. We borrowed it (without her knowledge) because it was the smallest and most powerful motor we could find. In fact the only figures not connected to the motor were the three principal ones in the stable, Joseph, Mary and the ceramic baby Jesus doll in its cradle.

More or less immediately after the village presepio had

been completed, and the opening ceremony had been concluded the week prior to Christmas Day, Riccardo Del Meglio let it be known he was looking for two volunteers to judge the annual village presepio competition and strong signals were coming towards us from his direction. Ovidio was normally part of the judging team, but of course he was away in the USA. When Del Meglio telephoned Nicola to ask her if we would mind standing in for Ovidio, as he needed somebody with an artistic eye, she enthusiastically volunteered us.

The village presepio competition was a completely separate event from the public presepio we had just set up in the blacksmith's garden. This was the first we had heard of this competition and we mistakenly assumed that we would be judging some small nativity scenes that local families, mostly children, would have made at home or school and brought along to the church hall. There we would award a prize for the best exhibit and they would all be left on display for a week or so for the rest of the village to view. We were glad to be of service. There'd be no real effort on our part; half an hour's work maybe and then we could go off and have a Sunday lunchtime drink with the old boys in the Bar Centrale.

We turned up at exactly ten thirty on the Sunday morning outside the church hall as scheduled and we were met by a group of four youngish people. The leader was an energetic chap who, we later found out, worked as a broker in Milan. After making sure everyone was present he announced,

"OK, now off we go!"

"Go where?" asked Nicola.

"With us," the leader of the pack replied, "Are you ready for a bit of exercise?"

Six hours later, after trudging around the extremities of the village, mostly upwards, across it and back up again,

Nicola and I were ready to kill Del Meglio. We had been well and truly duped. This was taking advantage of our help to the limit.

"Wait until I get hold of him!" Nicola kept saying as she struggled to put one foot in front of the other for about the ten thousandth time.

And it was a marathon. On a day when the wind chill factor brought the temperature down to freezing, we had to visit houses and apartments in outlying parts of the village that we did not know existed until that day. Even our leader, who did the organising annually as his contribution to village activities, had to use a map to find some of the participants' homes, and he had been born and raised in Moltrasio. It soon became obvious why the majority of the exhibits could not have been transported anywhere; many were either too big, or were almost permanent fixtures. Although some were smaller and took up only a side-table or an alcove in the hallway or front room, the majority ranged in size from a complete floor of an upstairs bedroom to half a garden. Another took up a disused stable with full-size figures set in straw, looking like the genuine Christmas card image we are all familiar with. One that we nearly awarded the prize to was built in a sand-pit, creating the effect of a desert scene with planted palm trees, half-scale figurines and pieces of mountain rock interspersed with little white houses made out of cardboard and thatch.

Every place we visited we were naturally introduced to every member of every family who had been involved in the creation of their work, all of them eagerly awaiting our decision. Some of the families pretended to be laid back about it all, but we could see that underneath their façade they were nervous. Others tried to convince us that their offering was the best and would explain the concept behind their idea and the amount of hours spent working on it. Out of the thirty or so we saw some were exceptional in skill and ideas. It was hard for us, and absolutely necessary not to divulge any expression of pleasure or surprise that might be seen as favouring an exhibit, when really it would have been nice to enthuse about their work. We could keenly sense the feeling that we were under close scrutiny from the second we entered a contestant's premises to the moment we left, to see if they could discover the slightest clue to how they had fared from any giveaway sign one of us might have let slip. We even took to mumbling between ourselves behind pulled up scarves, to disguise any discussion that the families might hear. We were informed ominously by our leader that if anything was leaked at this stage about who our favourites were, the consequences could be detrimental to personal safety. Any notes we needed to take, or thumb-nail sketches we needed to draw to be used later when we re-congregated back at the church-hall for decision making time, had to be done sneakily, behind gloved hands, or outside in the cold when we left the contestant's home.

The last house on our list was difficult to access, with the only approach up seemingly endless winding steps and a narrow passageway across a mountain crevasse. Where exactly it was, and whether we would ever find it again, remains a mystery to this day. The daylight was beginning to fade fast as we made our way along the path to the tall, dark, narrow, three-storey detached house. The heavy front door, once dark green but now faded, was half hidden by ivy. We immediately thought of those Hollywood horror films, where the vulnerable young hero and his fragile, attractive, wife-to-be have to leave their broken-down car in the middle of nowhere on a rainy night and trudge through dense woods towards the only light they can see, to ask for a night's shelter, only to find out, when it's too late, that they've made a fatal mistake. If I hadn't been with five other people, I don't think I would have gone near the place on my own.

When we eventually arrived outside the front door, one member of the group raised the heavy iron door knocker, which was so seized with rust he had to force it down with both hands to bring it into contact with its striking plate in order to make any sound. Then we stood back and waited hesitantly for a sign of life. After a minute or so the door creaked open, as we half-expected it would, and a tiny old lady, around eighty years old with her white hair tied back, peered round the door and asked us for our help to push it open. Once inside she greeted us courteously. We had half-expected the place to be covered in dust and cobwebs and smelling musty, but it was spotlessly clean, with an odour of wax polish. The terra cotta tiles in the hallway were highly polished and on them was a magnificent sideboard with some large bowls of fruit on it, and beside it two life-size black and white ceramic dogs.

The old lady showed us into the sitting room and turned up the wick of the oil lamp so we could see her nativity scene, which was placed on top of a heavy, dark-wood sideboard. Her artistic effort was very sweet, just like she was. She then asked us if we would like an aperitif. We had drunk plenty already, but as this was the last house we had to visit and after our half-kilometre trek over such difficult terrain we all accepted. She then turned and opened a side door, apparently leading to the kitchen, and shouted, "Mama, bring in the limoncello!"

A sprightly figure entered, carrying a tray of eight glasses and half a decanter of the familiar lemon liqueur that is found all over Italy. All of us either smiled or laughed out loud and so did the two ladies, who sensed our astonishment when we found out that 'Mama' was 101 years old! Nicola wanted to award them the prize there and then for just being so amazing, which was very understandable. I made towards the mother in case she needed somebody to take the weight of the tray, but was assured by the daughter that she was not infirm. We never saw either of them again after that day but we often enquired to some of the locals about their well-being. We found it amazing that these two old ladies managed to survive, without electricity, mains gas or even a road but they were living in the same way that others in these parts have lived for centuries, and who continue to do so. Of course, nobody who has lived here all their life seems to think of it as being out of the ordinary but Nicola and I were utterly amazed by it.

The eventual winner of the presepio competition was a pensioner we never actually met. His house was closed up because he had gone to his daughter's for the Christmas period, but because his exhibit was in his garden we were able to judge it by looking over the low garden wall. The first thing that struck us was its accurate scale and that everything he had planted was manicured to perfection. The whole exhibit was basically a rockery with bonsai bushes and trees lining a roadway, leading through the rocks to the stable at Bethlehem, but it gave the effect that it was part of an oasis of plenty. I've never seen the desert in the Holy Land but I imagine it would look just like this. None of it had been planted just for the duration of the Christmas period, but rather it had been cultivated over many years especially for this particular year's competition. Even the leaves of the bonsai and the miniature cypress trees were in scale with the figurines. It captured all our imaginations with its detail and precision, and we were struck by what must have taken hundreds of hours of dedicated labour to bring it to fruition.

The popularity of the committee's choice of winner was

hard to evaluate amongst the other exhibitors, but the local press, who turned up later to view and photograph it, seemed to be as entranced as we were. If there were any complaints over our final decision then there couldn't have been many because there was no denying it was of the highest quality.

After deciding the winner, we had one more issue to settle. If we were cold when we started our trek around the outlying parts of the village, we were warm when it was all over, thanks to all the walking and climbing we had to do, plus the ample amount of alcohol we had received (always making it clear we could not be bribed). Some of us had discarded hats, scarves and gloves. Throughout it all, Nicola and I had a picture of Del Meglio sitting at home enjoying a nice, fat Sunday lunch and a warm siesta by his log fire, but we held our tongues and refrained from complaining to the rest of the group. It wasn't their fault we had got the wrong idea of what judging the presepio was all about and so we both agreed to soldier on uncomplainingly in true Christian Christmas spirit, as God-fearing residents of Moltrasio. That was, until we had caught up with Del Meglio and got our hands around his neck. We now knew he had led us on rather sneakily down the wrong path by letting Nicola believe that we would be doing the community a big favour without having to do very much. If there was ever a next time he asked us to do something regarding 'village activities', we knew we would have to be more aware about what our dynamic little friend was asking us to do.

As it happened, we didn't see Del Meglio for some weeks after Christmas because he moved house to a hamlet higher up the mountain that was well away from the centre of village activity. By the time we did see him again we happened to be in a wine bar having a great time. Although between drinks I did manage to mention to him the rough terrain and the extreme cold he'd subjected us to, it seemed irrelevant to pursue the matter further because it was well out of season and so I decided not to say anything. He with his usual cordiality responded by slapping me on the back and saying "Grande Powl, tu sei bravo!" and invited us to have a large drink on him for our efforts.

As January drifted away and the carnevale approached, we were ready for our call to the usual meeting place around the smithy's anvil, but it seemed to be very late arriving this year. Carnevale week got closer and closer but still we heard nothing. We already knew that Italians habitually leave everything to the last minute but this was becoming impractical. The amount of work generally involved in the preparation of carnival meant that for this particular year it would be impossible to build and paint anything in time. Perhaps the Bella Ghita did not need our services this year, or maybe the Niasce faction had kicked up a fuss and complained to Del Meglio that there was a treacherous household within their boundary and that we mustn't be utilised by the Bella Ghita. At this point, we did not know what to think.

The truth, as we soon discovered when we met Riccardo Del Meglio in the village, was that there had been a row amongst the Bella Ghita committee and they would not be entering in this year's carnival. The majority of the usual volunteers had apparently become tired of being taken advantage of, there was no new, younger blood showing an interest in replacing them and a lot of the older members had agreed that enough was enough and pulled out. The previous year Nicola had seen the start of the rot when the castle drawbridge had stuck on our Robin Hood float and Enzo had fallen out with Umberto. Then we heard that our friend Ovidio the carpenter had dropped out because he had also had enough and gradually the unrest filtered through the whole faction until they all lost interest. There was no individual to blame. Village activities took up a large amount of time and energy and these people, over the years, had done more than their fair share of providing entertainment for the villagers to enjoy. It was a sign that the times were, as the song goes, a-changing.

So, for ten minutes we felt redundant, until Del Meglio had the bright idea that we could judge the four remaining factions that would be taking part. Before we accepted, Nicola asked if there was any hidden agenda we should know about, remembering the experience of two months previously when he had asked us to judge the village presepio competition. He calmly assured her that all we had to do was give marks for the best float, best costumes and best-choreographed routine. As foreigners, he saw us as the ideal neutrals, and it was a bonus that we had artistic talents and previous experience as participants in the event. He presented Nicola with a clipboard and some forms to complete, along with instructions to be at the starting point so as to assess what the floats and the costumes were like and to award marks out of ten for the best theme each faction had chosen and its artistic merit.

On the whole the standard was good, but not great. There was nothing outstanding between any of the factions involved as far as theme ideas went and we had to do a lot of conferring with each other to try to find a winner. In the end we selected the Borgo faction. They had chosen 'The Chinese Year of the Dog' theme for their float, which was technically good, and the actors did a well-choreographed dance routine in character with their chosen idea, which we decided earned them first place.

At the end of the procession, we went with Del Meglio to the balcony above the Bar Centrale, where he introduced us as the judges. He thanked us publicly for our time and effort and announced who the winners were in reverse order, to great applause and obvious enjoyment from the winners. When it was all over we descended the stairs from the balcony to take our leave and to walk home, when we were suddenly accosted by a crowd from one of the losing factions who had been waiting to demonstrate their displeasure at our decision. The whole scene quickly became quite menacing and we were almost knocked off our feet in the jostling. The only thing that kept us upright was the fact that we where sandwiched between hundreds of people who had turned up to see the presentation and it was almost harder to fall down than to stand up. We were incredulous of how seriously these people had taken the whole event. We had always considered it to be a bit of weekend fun and that whoever turned out to be the winners or losers wasn't of much consequence, but this wasn't how it was for this group of native Moltrasini. Their language and aggression were particularly alarming. Nobody caused us any actual harm, but the leader of the pack, an unkempt greasy-haired male of around thirty-five, who stank of strong alcohol and garlic, grabbed Nicola by the collar with both hands and pulled her towards him until she told him to become rational and to let her go. Fortunately he did relax his grip but continued to demand why we had not chosen his faction as the winners. Nicola demonstrated her courage and her contempt for his loutish behaviour and told him straight to his smelly face that the decision had been taken because the winners were the best. When he'd absorbed what she had told him, I thought he was going to become psychotic, because he started foaming at the mouth as well as shouting and gesticulating like a madman. Somehow, we managed to pull ourselves away from him and his mates and take shelter inside the bar, and with the aid of the bar owner we managed to slam the door shut and lock it until they had cleared off.

Again, we felt like blaming Del Meglio for finding ourselves in another predicament. We had not understood the expectations the competitors had of an adjudicator and perhaps he had not been straight with us about this. What we originally thought would be a nice stroll following carnival along the street on a warm February afternoon turned out to be a rough and tumble, with Nicola visibly shaken for an hour or so after the event. From then, along with our chums from the Bella Ghita faction, we too decided 'enough was enough'.

In June, the palio came and went, and like the carnevale, the committee members of the Bella Ghita excluded themselves from the preparatory work and did not take part in the event. After that, lethargy seemed to spread rapidly throughout all the factions and it affected all the village activities in general. More seriously, it hit the chief organiser and president of everything – Del Meglio himself. He withdrew his involvement and resigned as president of everything and consequently everything folded. The nativity competition, the palio, the carnival and the village presepio in the blacksmith's garden ceased to exist. He even resigned as manager of the GS Moltrasio after twenty-one years in charge. He, the soccer club's principal sponsorship raiser and the organiser of all the village events, had thrown in the towel and so without him, none of them were able to survive.

The festa is still held every July at the campo sportivo, and the local council still runs a schoolboys' seven-a-side soccer team. But long gone are the days of the other village activities, along with most of the people we associated with.

We see Del Meglio about twice a year. He has a section of the harbour down by the canoe club where he rents out boats by the hour and we occasionally hire a motorboat off him.

After the death of a relative, Enzo and Ada moved into their family home further up the mountain, well away from the village centre, so we see less of them than we used to. Fillipo, the local builder, is now so successful we hardly see him at all. His business is now a public company and he is just too busy to be involved in anything outside his work. Ovidio, our carpenter friend, has also become very busy and Umberto the blacksmith still continues to pound away at his anvil, but he seems much subdued these days and we only see him when he's blowing his trumpet in the village brass band or dancing at the festa. The rest of the central village characters seem to have gone to ground or have, as Ada would say, "Passed away to a better place". Still, we feel privileged to have taken part in these events, which served to bring us close to the community, to get a deeper understanding of the northern Italian character and, most of all, to have made some truly wonderful friends.

Chapter 12

Moving House and Some New Flatmates

WE HAD BEEN living in the Masins' house for three years, when, almost to the day we moved in, Christine called to tell us that her daughter was about to start studying for a degree at the University of Rome, and her son would soon follow. This meant they would have to sell their house in order to raise the necessary money to pay for both courses and find themselves a new home, and for us it meant having to find somewhere else to live too. This caused us a little anxiety at first, but then we had stayed in Italy for two years longer than our arbitrary deadline and if after that deadline we had decided to stay, we always knew that sooner or later we would have to move house. Suddenly it was decision time and we had an urgent discussion as to whether or not we truly intended to stay in Italy or move elsewhere. We talked about going to Spain, briefly, and about moving back to England, but these considerations were soon knocked on the head because it would mean starting all over again. As we were really enjoying living in Italy and, more importantly, we both had work, we decided to stay. We discussed the idea of buying a place in Italy, preferably in Moltrasio, but this would have first meant selling our house in Godalming, then looking for a house to buy. All of this would take time, which was what the Masins didn't have, so we decided to look locally for somewhere to rent for a few more years and review our situation at our leisure.

Nicola decided to ask the shopkeepers in the village centre if they knew of anywhere to rent. She had talked to me about occasions like this in the past, when we would need assistance from the locals, and that it was as well we took care of our reputation to be regarded as bravi, decent people, instead of stronzi. For sure if we were regarded as the latter the locals would not give us any information whatsoever about where we could find a property to rent. They were certainly not going to put the word about if it meant that a couple of 'shits' were about to move in next door.

In our three years in Moltrasio we'd got to know pretty well everyone and we now thought of it as home. We really wanted to stay here but it wasn't going to be easy to achieve, because in the first few days of looking on our own we only found places in other villages we could afford, or a few holiday residences in Moltrasio at tourist prices, when of course we wanted to pay the prices the locals pay. Like a lot of countries with a big tourist industry, Italy has an unofficial two-tier price system, one for the locals and one for foreign buyers, such as Germans, French, Americans or, indeed, us. Being English was not that common for the region, but even so we would be classified as tourists and therefore just as likely to be expected to pay the upper price bracket. We quickly found it was vital to tell local residents we hadn't met before that we were, after having lived there for three years, permanent residents and not foreign tourists. That is why it was imperative for us to become as local as possible as soon as possible.

We didn't like the idea of having to move further afield, where we didn't know anybody, so we decided to ask our friends and any local contacts we could find if they knew of anywhere in the village we could rent. One of the first people Nicola asked was Eleanor, the wife of Pino, the butcher. She told Nicola that she'd heard there was a place in the centro-storico, the historical centre of the village in Via Recchi, and as she accepted us as being *bravi* she volunteered to find out for us if it was still available. She said it was owned by a middle-aged widow whom she knew quite well, but did not see very often.

Things remained quiet for some weeks, then, out of the blue, Eleanor telephoned to say that she had recommended us to the widow as being bravi and she was interested in showing us around the apartment. We grabbed the chance and went to see it straight away. It was part of a three hundred year old building and above a disused butcher's shop, with a front door that opened directly onto a set of narrow stone steps that led up to the village. It was small and unfurnished with only one bedroom, no central heating and no gas and the stone kitchen sink had one cold water tap hanging loosely on the wall. Worse, there was no garden and no terrace or balcony where we could relax in the sun. On the plus side, the apartment had bags of character and we had really taken a liking to it. It was situated in a much prettier part of Moltrasio, with a favourable piazza outside and to the side of it was a strong waterfall running down the mountain that used to power the waterwheel of the old granary. Also the view from the kitchen window, looking over the centro-storico was truly wonderful. The houses seemed to jostle for position, their roofs and painted stucco walls creating a pleasant, composite patchwork of terra cotta, burnt orange and yellow ochre. After living in a four-storey, three-bedroomed, detached-house with all mod cons and two gardens it would certainly mean that we would have to do some adjusting, and it left us thinking for a while. Could we turn it into a place we could both enjoy living in?

Because we liked the place so much, we decided to see if

we could come to an arrangement with the owner over the terms of the lease, and we soon agreed she would pay a plumber to put in a modern boiler, have the gas connected and replace the stone stink with a new one and we would pay for the installation of the central heating. Then, before we moved in I spent four weeks painting the apartment, having the central heating put in and furnishing it. I had to, because it was uninhabitable by modern standards, we wanted to stay in Moltrasio, and it was the only place we could find at such short notice at a rent we could afford.

In the time we had lived at the Masins' house, I had accumulated a pile of art materials and associated artists' equipment, but we set aside the problem of finding somewhere to store it all for the time being while we agreed terms. After we moved in, I quickly found out there was no room in the apartment for me to produce my oil paintings and watercolours, so I needed to find a studio and storeroom. It seemed like a stroke of luck that soon after we had moved in, the old butcher's shop below that had been closed for thirty-seven years became available to rent. We'd not had the opportunity to look inside the shop, but judging from the outside, I thought that it might suit my purpose ideally.

It was during the negotiations for the shop that we discovered the full story. The owner's late husband had been the butcher who owned the shop and when he died, Pino and Eleanor decided to rent the property from him, thereby holding the butcher's licence to stop any likelihood of competition. They had been content to rent the shop off of the widow for all that time, even though they never did a day's business from the premises, continuing to trade from their original shop further up the stone steps that ran outside our front door. When I approached the widow and asked her about the possibility of renting the empty shop, she informed me that Eleanor and Pino had not paid the rent for the last half year and it was due in advance. When I told her I was interested in taking over the old shop and converting it into an art studio, she said she would make further enquiries for me and see if Eleanor and Pino still wanted to continue renting the place.

Two large supermarkets had opened near to Moltrasio in the early nineties and had taken a lot of business away from the smaller shops in the surrounding area. Eleanor and Pino had realised that there wasn't much likelihood of another butcher ever opening up again in the village because the two that were already there were finding it difficult to compete with supermarket prices. A few days after I'd approached our landlady about taking on the old shop, Eleanor and Pino arrived at our front door to speak to me about taking over the lease and when I told them I wanted it for an art studio and was not planning on a career change and taking up butchering, they willingly ended their tenancy and handed me the keys.

Having a studio and workshop literally downstairs was very convenient because I could both show my work to the public and have much more space to store our belongings. We also found living in the central part of the village very attractive and very sociable, because the piazza outside was a pedestrian zone and we met so many people as they walked by. The foreign tourists that happened by my studio said they had not witnessed anything like the ancient village before. Most of them had just arrived from the hustle and bustle of the real world, from their manic existences in the twentieth century they called civilisation and suddenly they had found themselves in a time warp. Apart from Nicola, I was just about the only person in a wide area that spoke English and because my studio door was always open, I would be bombarded with questions from English and American tourists who had been dying to speak to somebody who could understand them. They all said that the village had a calmness, a peace and a harmony on the eye that gave them real contentment, and what most of them wanted to know was where they could rent a holiday home, because they felt they wanted an instant lifestyle change and to swap places with me. Some visitors to the village were so knocked out with the place that they spent most of their holiday arranging a place to stay for the following year, and confiding amongst themselves that they must keep quiet about the village. "We want to keep it for ourselves," they'd whisper.

Because there was, and still is, nothing in the way of museums, grand houses, smart shops or public gardens in Moltrasio for the tourist to spend money visiting, the village hardly gets a mention in the guidebooks. For the discerning visitor who isn't interested in ticking off the 'must-see' items in the guidebook or isn't a shopaholic, the fact that there are none of these commercial interests makes the place all the more desirable. Of course, if it did have something that attracted the average tourist, I doubt we would have chosen to live there and we would have continued our search for one of the ever-decreasing number of unspoilt beauty spots.

But there was more life in the village than the human residents and the tourists. No sooner had we settled in to our new surroundings than we discovered that the piazza was a haven for a large population of feral cats. We had recorded ten residing in the immediate proximity, but an accurate head count was difficult, if not impossible. The early spring, which was when we had moved house, was the beginning of the rutting season for the little darlings. Our bedroom window overlooked our landlady's garden and the nightly cats' chorus coming from it was becoming extremely noisy and was seriously disturbing our sleep, and with the mating season in full swing and the scent of the females attracting quite a few more, there were some mighty bust-ups and a great increase in the noise level.

After a few more weeks we noticed that one of the females, a tabby, was becoming rounder by the day, which made us very alarmed, because we knew that this would yield lots of irresistible, fluffy babies, the kind we are suckers for. Sure enough, a few weeks later the tabby walked past my studio door looking very much slimmer, which only meant one thing – in three to four weeks' time we could expect to see her out for a stroll to show off her latest litter.

One morning in early June, I heard the same mother cat meowing more than usual outside in the piazza, so I went to see if she was all right. I followed her gaze down the road, towards a tiny black and white kitten that was struggling up the slope, as if it were pulling a ton weight. I slowly approached it and even though it tried its best to scamper away, I easily picked it up. It was a male, and he was one of the most gorgeous babies imaginable, with a black hood over a white face and a coat as soft and as shiny as silk. Kittens of this age are generally pretty lively creatures and when I picked him up I discovered why he could not get away like he should. It was because a large hole had been torn in his abdomen and some of his intestine was hanging out. By now his mother was giving me real grief, meowing and fretting, but when I offered the kitten back to her she ran off in the opposite direction, leaving me, literally, holding the baby.

Our only regret about moving to Italy was that we had to leave Lucy, our dear cat, behind. We had considered at great length whether or not we should bring her with us, but if the one-year trial period we had given ourselves hadn't worked out, she would have had to go into quarantine when we returned to the UK. Nicola's sister had been willing to take her for whatever time we spent out of the UK and it turned out they were both having a happy time together. We asked for, and received, regular reports on how Lucy was and it appeared she wasn't missing us at all.

That evening, when Nicola returned from Milan and she saw the tiny kitten, she knew I had fallen in love while she had been out at work. Three quarters of an hour later we were inside the vet's surgery in the next village where he told us that he did not think there was much chance that the kitten would survive, as the hole was massive in proportion to the size of his body. He did not know if he could stretch the skin across the gaping wound, but he said he would try. While we were there, he found a dog's tooth inside the hole, which explained what had happened. We telephoned the vet's secretary every few days to see how his progress was, and he seemed to be surviving. Two weeks later, when we went back to collect the tiny creature, the vet told us that he had clung onto life beyond expectation. His future was sealed – we had found a replacement for Lucy and once again we had taken on the responsibility that goes with having an animal. That was something both of us had said would never happen again, but knew in our hearts probably would.

The following spring a sleek, white feral that regularly roamed the piazza was seen to be putting on weight around her midriff. Sure enough, a few weeks later she too passed by the studio looking her svelte self again. And, four weeks later, right on cue, she began parading four babies around her territory in the piazza. Our neighbours began throwing their hands up in horror at the sight of more kittens, all with a potential to soil their gardens unless, they told us, they were poisoned pretty quickly. When we heard this we were horrified and adopted three more kittens immediately, as well as taking on the feeding of the rest of the feral animals.

We came to discover that only a small percentage of Italians are any good at looking after pets. Cats have a particularly rough time and are treated like vermin. Dogs fare slightly better, but there are still too many residents who have the wrong motive for owning a dog and a lot of them regard them as guard dogs first and as pets a very poor second. Also, dogs are often used as status symbols behind big gates of smart villas. The intention of this is supposed to indicate to the passerby that the owner must be rich and has something worth guarding. It would seem that the higher the gates, the larger and more visible the dog or dogs are likely to be. The dogs apparently act as a living invitation to any burglar who might be 'casing the joint', telling him that there are some prize possessions to be had if he's prepared to take the chance of getting ripped to bits.

Cats cannot guard anything, therefore they are low in the Italians' reckoning. "What is the use of a cat, or any other pet," they say, "if it cannot earn its keep?" Then the same people add, "Of course, some of them do catch rats, and cats are also good to eat." At first we thought we had misheard the last part of this statement but when we heard a neighbour expounding on the gastronomic delights of eating cat with polenta as a winter dish and how she and many of the locals appreciate the way a plump cat roasted over an open fire and the local maize dish compliment each other perfectly, it began to dawn on us that they, or at least some of them really do eat cats. I think she must have thought that when we said we were cat lovers, she thought we too enjoyed eating them and it had never entered her mind that somebody should want to keep a cat, or in our case cats, as a pet, feeding it solely so that it can have a nice life rather than fattening it up to be eaten at a later date. To her way of thinking, and many like her, anybody who spends good money feeding an animal for no practical purpose must be insane.

The practice of eating cats is alien to British sensibilities, but it's not hard to understand why the Italians choose to do so. They must have suffered a great deal after countless invasions and occupations of their country since the end of the Roman Empire, often being left to starve. World War II left such a legacy, and when we had first arrived in Moltrasio, there were still a number of people around who suffered under the Nazis and the memory of that brutal time is as vivid to them as if it had happened only yesterday. But in times of plenty it seems peculiar that a few of this older generation still liked to eat cats and, worse, are not too fussed whether they are feral or somebody's pet. One night a group of us went to a *trattoria* in a village on the opposite side of the lake, next to Enzo's home village of Lemna. When the waitress presented us with the menu we saw on it '*gatto con polenta*' – cat with polenta. According to one member of our group, the proprietor will accommodate a customer bringing in a cat the day before they are due to eat there and the chef will prepare and cook it for them.

When another female gave birth in our landlady's garden, the headcount of ferals in the close vicinity of our apartment rose to twenty. It was plain for anybody to see that the man from the council would be round to lay his poison if people started to complain about the amount of cat poo they were having to contend with. At this point, Nicola decided to take control of a worsening situation and she set out to have them

ll sterilised. With the patience of a saint and the aid of several
ins of Whiskas cat food, she gradually gained the confidence
of our feline neighbours, sitting for hours at the foot of the
tairs to the apartment with the front door wide open and a
owl of freshly-opened cat meat at the ready, coaxing these
nervous, always wary, often completely wild creatures to come
a little closer each day. At first she had no success at all while
he was sitting near them. Of course, as soon as she moved
away there was a free-for-all for the food. Gradually, though,
he gained their confidence one by one, ingeniously using the
evening breeze coming down the road from the mountains to
assist in blowing the irresistible smell of the food in their di-
ection. The poor, skinny creatures, desperate for nourish-
ment, could not resist the temptation any further and began to
et her touch them whilst eating. Then, as calmly as they would
allow her, she would pick one up, then snap it into the cat basket before the creature realised what had happened, call to me
o stop watching TV and fire up the car engine so we could
ush him or her to the vet for sterilisation.

Nicola finally captured all twenty ferals, one at a time,
which was amazing, although the result was achieved at some
onsiderable financial cost. The next part of her programme,
which turned out to be as equally difficult as the cat baiting,
was to educate our human neighbours. She wanted to make
ure they understood the effort she had exerted and the ex-
ense she had incurred in taking control of the situation, to
ry to ensure that they understood why she had taken on such
esponsibilities and get them to take on a responsible attitude
hemselves. She told them that she had done something posi-
ive to resolve a problem that should have been sorted out years
earlier, but this was all new to them and most of them weren't
nterested at all. Some gave her verbal support but there was

never any financial assistance offered and she knew they did
not really understand why she was doing what she was doing.
They surely must have been wondering why this English
woman kept banging on about animal welfare, and persist-
ently telling them that it was everybody's responsibility to take
care of them properly and not to go putting poison down as a
cheap, short term solution to a long term problem.

For a few months everything seemed to calm down and
encouragingly, the flow of pregnancies abated, but we had noticed that the population of feral cats had gone down from
twenty to thirteen. Some of the cats we had taken to the vet to
be 'done' had disappeared. We wanted to know where they
had gone, and why! We hoped they had not been eaten but anticipated that they probably had. Eventually we would get
some clues.

After about one year of living in our new apartment, one
of the four domesticated cats, a small female tabby we had living with us, did not come home one night. This was unusual
because cats are habitual and she always came home at the
same time. I was distraught and for days and nights afterwards
I looked everywhere for her. Nicola put the word out that one
of our cats had gone missing and she hoped it had not been
eaten. She was told that this was most unlikely, as it was the
height of summer and cats only get eaten with polenta as a
winter dish. Nothing was heard for two weeks, then, Marco,
one of the local council workers, discovered her down a ravine
in the waterfall, drowned and bloated. How did she get there,
we wondered, and why?

On further enquiries a young girl told us that she thought
she saw an old man who lived in the house beside the stone
footbridge push the cat off the wall into the ravine. She
claimed he did it because he had done it before to another cat

I was ready to pull him out of his house and push him down the same ravine, even if he was eighty years old, but Nicola stopped me, telling me that there was no proof that he'd done it and we couldn't take the word of a young girl who only thought she saw what she saw.

Still to this day I think there was proof that this person had murdered one of our babies and I am sure that Nicola kept the whole truth away from me for my own good. This was one of those times I wished my Italian were better, so that I could have made some enquiries of my own.

Then, the following winter, another beauty, an all-white, fluffy longhair we had adopted disappeared mysteriously. This was really odd, because we had taken her in when she was a tiny kitten roaming the piazza. She had only recently started to go out of the house, but had never gone further than a few yards, preferring to sit for hours beside the front doorstep, never moving. I think it was a pre-meditated act by some greedy passer-by who fancied a cat for dinner and had whipped her away. From then on, we put collars on all of our cats and Nicola did the rounds yet again, informing all the neighbours about the latest victim and asking them not to mess with our cats. However, the problem of teaching the ignorant was not yet resolved and every time we thought we were getting through to them something else would happen that made us think that we were going backwards instead of forwards.

One night around midnight we heard a muffled noise outside the front door, then the sound of someone running off into the distance. The sound of footsteps outside our door was not an unusual occurrence, as the door opened onto steps that were a regular thoroughfare to the village centre. A few minutes later we heard a faint mewing sound and it was not one we were familiar with. When we opened the front door, we saw that somebody had dumped a box containing a tiny kitten on our doorstep. Next morning, after the gorgeous little creature had had several good feeds, Nicola set off in a determined mood, verging on anger, with the box including the baby under her arm to root out the perpetrators and to give them a stiff lesson in how to take care of their animals. Amazingly, she was successful in locating them and when she returned and before I could ask her how she'd got on, she said, "I gave the whole family a severe scolding they'll never forget and they assured me they will never do anything of the like again!"

A few nights after that, somebody else dumped a runt in the piazza. This time we were not able to trace the owners and according to a neighbour who was in the habit of peering through her lace curtains at everything that passed by, they'd driven up the road in a car at midnight and then dropped something out of the door. Word was getting around about feline welfare, but either it was the wrong kind of word, or it was being conveniently misinterpreted. "If you ever have a cat problem," the wisdom seemed to be, "then take it along to Piazza Recchi where the two English who are soft in the head live and they will take care of your problem for you, free of charge." Slowly but surely, after many lectures on animal safe keeping and how shameful it must be for the people of Moltrasio having two foreigners in their midst doing their mopping up for them, we started to win through.

We looked after our four official cats better than we looked after ourselves. They were fat and happy and they received the best medical attention money could buy. Sandro, the mobile vet, visited them regularly on his cross-country motorbike to administer check-ups and the neighbours were happy in the knowledge that the remaining feral cats in the area had all been neutered and defended their territory, keeping other cats at bay and preventing a return to how things were before. In the summertime, all of our babies would lie in the studio window basking in the sun and more than one person has told us, "They are a picture fit to paint."

Chapter 13

Italians in General, and our Neighbours in Particular

ROMAN CATHOLICISM is still strong in Italy, but it means different things in different parts of the country. In the south, especially amongst the women and in the rural areas, religion does have a strong influence and traditional values still hold firm. In the north, the original religious or spiritual significance plays less of a part, but it is now more of an influence on lifestyle. Attendances at Sunday mass at Moltrasio's church of San Martino were, and probably still are no better or worse than in any other church in the western world: it is more of a custom based on an upbringing founded on a fear of God, with the people feeling that it is good for their souls, whether they are truly devout or not. Attendance was, and still is very much a social event and the community, especially the older ladies, use it to catch up on any gossip they may have missed out on since the last church service. The men are far less keen on attendance than the women, with something like one in eight of the congregation being male. If the church of San Martino was not filled on a Sunday morning, the Bar Centrale would be, with bianco sporco drinking club members playing cards and waiting reverently to escort *le moglie*, their 'sinful' wives, home.

Virtually all Italians will have been born to a Roman Catholic family and baptised into the church, although they may choose to change their religion or abstain from it later in life. As an almost universal doctrine, the Roman Catholic faith has, down the centuries pervaded all walks of Italian life. This has its good and not so good points. The not so good aspects are that it perpetuates dogma, particularly regarding original sin and contraception and it might be said to have had a repressive effect on the Italian people. The good parts, the ones we appreciate about living in Italy are that the church has instilled through the catechism a code of good behaviour and respect for others. We find the people honest, kind, generous, well behaved, well mannered and generally civilised. Crime against the person is rare. Petty theft is also rare and if there is any, it's usually perpetrated by ethnic minorities. We find that Italians appreciate the best things in life, be they the very traditional or the very new, and we believe that their heritage and their culture is one of the best there is. They don't insist on throwing away the good things in life just because they cannot be measured in financial terms, diving in a headlong rush to follow the spiral of financial growth. I have found that the attitude of the Spanish and the French, both of which are Catholic societies is similar.

Britain today is, to a greater or lesser extent the opposite. Unfortunately its heritage and culture have become eroded almost to the point of extinction, which is a huge tragedy because once gone, it will never return. In its quest to create a rich society (rich in what, is the question), Britain has washed away its own foundations, leaving it vulnerable to unsustainable sub-cultures that will incubate and eventually replace the one that has evolved over centuries, along with a generation that once remembered it.

For the visitor to Italy, or for anyone who wants to stay long term, it's helpful to know something about the very real north-south divide that bisects Italy. For a start, from a social point of view, it helps if the new resident, especially one in a small village, knows who is related to whom and who has or hasn't got southern connections. Then, particularly in conversation, there is less of a chance of putting your foot in it.

This north-south divide is very distinct and there is an unvarying war of words between the two separate regions. The subject can, if brought up in conversation rile even the most passive northerner to the point of exasperation, and a sense of injustice is deeply embedded in some of them. Northerners in general think of anyone living south of Rome (some say south of Bologna) as ignorant, lazy *terroni*, (peasants) and the root cause of the northerners' discontent is they believe there is an unfair distribution of wealth. The reality is that there is very little work in the south, and the southerner receives a lot of state handouts as a result. Thus the northerner often regards the southerner as living off the fruits of his labour, soaking up his tax revenue like a sponge.

They also know from past experience that any financial handouts from the government or the EC that are paid to the southern half of Italy will end up in the pockets of the Mafia, because they have had a hand in everything that happens in the south. The northerner knows that time and again after some do-gooder politician is elected, be it to the Italian or European parliament, and thinks it is about time something was done about the plight of the downtrodden Italian southerners, they will start to pour money into the territory. Then the mafia will say, 'Thank you very much' to their naïve benefactor and nothing will be seen, nor heard, of the money ever again.

Surprisingly, southerners do not disagree with the northerners' derogatory opinions of them because they know how much truth there is in it, and instead turn the blame onto a succession of inept governments for their unfortunate circumstances, lack of investment, lack of opportunity, lack of infrastructure, lack of control over the Mafia and general lack of everything as not being of their own making. To show he doesn't give a damn about what the northerners say, the southerner will flick the underneath of his chin with the back of his hand, at the same time referring to northerners as cold, humourless stronzi, who are not true Italians, but really Swiss.

At some point in his life the southerner will have to make a decision whether to continue living in the south, or to migrate north to find work and face being classified as a second-class citizen for the rest of his life, or try his luck abroad. If he chooses to move north, he will first attempt to contact other southerners already settled there, asking them to take him in and to help and protect him from the northern prejudices he will almost certainly encounter. Generally speaking, the southerner will stand out in the north because of the darker colour of his skin, which is in marked contrast to the paler skin of the northerner. In fact, northerners are sometimes called 'white Italians'. The southerner will also sport a crop of thick, healthy hair as black as jet. Because of this colouring, the northerner will often claim that southerners are in reality 'useless Arabs'.

If any English person were asked to describe what a typical Italian looks like, they would probably describe a southerner; someone with olive skin, swarthy good looks and a vigorous crop of black hair and they would probably think of him working as a waiter in an Italian restaurant. Northern Italians and most Brits would not recognise a northern Italian on sight; there are far fewer of them in Britain, because so few need to leave Italy to seek work, because they have it all already.

While I was painting a mural for a Swiss client near

Zurich, I met two brothers who had left their village in the southern region of Calabria over thirty years before. They told me they were so poor they had had to cycle the 1,200 kilometres to the north of Italy because they couldn't afford the train fare. They said they had gone north to take up the offer of a government incentive to relocate some of the impoverished southerners and became bricklayers. A few years after they had moved north, they learned that Switzerland was in desperate need to expand its manual labour force and had set up a similar scheme to attract downtrodden foreigners into their country to do their dirty work for them. With much better rewards on offer than they had in Italy the brothers were just two of many opportunist Italians who moved those few kilometres over the border. The brothers are now very successful, owning a large construction firm and living in impressive style in Winterthur, a town in the German-speaking canton of Zurich. It has to be said however, that they made their pot of gold by working every hour there was, seven days per week, for many years and through the callous exploitation of other migrant builders from the Baltic States they employed as labourers, demanding that they too worked non-stop, and for little financial remuneration.

Another southerner I met, a resident of Moltrasio was Dino, a Sicilian who worked for the council maintenance department. He told me that in the late nineteen-seventies when he and his family lived in Sicily his eldest son, then nineteen was approached by the Mafia who wanted him to sell drugs. They made him, as the saying goes an offer he could not refuse. When Dino found out about this he immediately told his family to pack as many of their belongings as they could cram into their car and they fled the island under the cover of darkness that same night, driving as far north as they could to escape the arm of the Mafia. They ended up in Moltrasio, which was just about the last hamlet in Italy they came to before reaching the Swiss border.

Even now, when the north-south divide crops up in conversation, Nicola has a bit of fun at my expense, by jokingly telling northern Italians that I am a terrone, a peasant. She will then explain that a north-south divide also exists in Britain; only it's the opposite way round from the Italian one, with the north being the poorer half. "Paul was born in the north," she would say, "Near Liverpool." For a brief moment the Italian northerners give me a startled look, because Nicola has made them think that they might have an undesirable in their midst.

If she tells southerners the same thing, their reaction is often completely different. They look at me with sympathy and may even start to regard me as one of their own. They think that as a relative newcomer to the north of Italy, I had to endure the same hostilities and bigotry as they did when they first arrived. At times like these I am often offered bucketsful of compassion and even offers of help. Of course I don't need any, but mud often sticks! But what confuses the southerners most is why a 'British terrone' should choose to live in the north of Italy. They believe I must be either lost, stupid or mad, or perhaps all three, because from their point of view if, like me they could live wherever they wanted to live, then the very last place they would choose would be the north of Italy!

In general the Italians have a positive, keen and refreshingly enthusiastic attitude towards life. They are also gregarious and they radiate a vigour that has to be admired but I often wonder if life always merits their outward endeavour. Maybe they believe that the more you put into life, the more you get out of it, but one thing is sure that as a whole, they expound a lot of nervous energy all day long. To the foreign observer, it appears that they live on the edge for the sake of living on the edge and are consciously prepared to put themselves through this mangle of anxiety, never stopping to think for a few moments why, when most have absolutely no reason to do it.

Seeing this sort of behaviour, it's easy to get the impression that Italians have a state of innate insecurity, but they are not insecure at all. It seems to be something that has evolved through the generations and it has now become the expected behavioural pattern, particularly amongst women. There is one advantage to come out of this self imposed high stress factor, and that is, there are very few cases of obesity amongst Italians, as if this state of high tension assists them in appearing to be vital, interesting and vivacious. In fact the complete reverse happens; instead of attracting people towards them even though they may look good, their stressful state of mind can turn them away, especially turning men against women.

Two extreme examples of this state of high tension were Signora Eleonora and her younger sister Livia, who lived on the north side of the Piazza Recchi. Their state of nervousness and tension was not an act or a piece of theatre, but their true selves. Even Italian women found it hard to come to terms with the sisters' hyper-metabolic condition and it will come as no surprise that both were as thin as rakes. Eleonora, the elder by about ten years was in her mid-fifties and was actually the eldest of four daughters. The two other daughters married and flew the coop years before, leaving the family home, a converted medieval mulina, a flour mill, for their two unmarried sisters to live in. Eleonora and Livia were not typical inhabitants of this area of Italy. Whereas most people in our surrounding neighbourhood were generous and friendly to a fault, these two were the complete opposite, and it was this oddness in their nature that made them interesting, if often frustrating and even infuriating, characters.

Ela and Liv, as the two sisters called each other, were fastidious in everything they did. Liv was a fabric designer by profession and was always dressed very fashionionably. Ela, a retired florist also dressed well, with an eye for style. They were impeccably dressed at all times, even when gardening or doing housework. Both worked tirelessly in their garden, buzzing like insects around their flowers and for them housework was a twenty-four hour a day chore that never seemed to be completed. I wonder to this day where they got their energy. With stick-like frames they were well past their prime yet both toiled like young slaves to keep everything in order. Their ancestry was Swiss, and perhaps this was the answer to their fastidiousness and they typified the reputation the Swiss have gained for being precise, clean, well-behaved, upright citizens.

You might think that they would have made perfect neighbours, but this was far from the case. In fact, no one in Moltrasio liked them. The locals would stare at them and huddle together to whisper about them as they passed by, and pull faces behind their backs. One day, our curiosity got too much for us and we asked Tomasso, an old gardener who regularly passed our apartment on his way to his allotment, why they were so unpopular. He seemed to act as a spokesman for the rest of our current neighbours and he loved to talk.

"Why do you think they live in such a huge house?" he told us, "Haven't you noticed that the outbuildings where they park their cars are bigger than most of the houses we live in? Look at the size of their terraced gardens and those huge wrought iron gates. They have electric motors to open them. Doesn't that say something about them?"

He must have seen the perplexed look on our faces. We

hadn't really thought about it. After all, there were plenty of huge houses around the lake area, many of them with automatically controlled gates.

"They got all their money in times of hardship," he continued, "When ordinary folk like me were going hungry. During the war, the family sold flour on the black market to people who had money. The likes of us they lied to and told us they had nothing for us. When we were starving, they were making a profit. And they are Swiss, not Italian. Everyone knows that. They had connections over the border, trafficking contraband into Italy."

I knew that it took fifteen minutes to reach the Swiss border from Moltrasio by car and during World War II the border crossings were manned by the German army. Traversing any of the mountain paths above Moltrasio, which were the main smuggling routes is about a five-hour slog on foot each way, so to take this route, carrying illegal goods, the smuggler would have had to transport enough to make it worth his while, probably using a squad of carriers or pack mules. The Germans knew about these mountain paths, and cut side and underground holes where they concealed themselves. The remains of these excavations can still be seen today. The smugglers would have trafficked in currency, gold, silver, refugees and escaped POWs, cigarettes and desperately required foodstuffs like grain and meat, as well as goods that were easier to conceal, like the sweetener, saccharin, which fetched a good price on the black market in deprived Italy. Using either route, the smugglers would have been quite conspicuous, so if our friends were leading us to believe that the two sisters' family were smuggling grain from Switzerland into Italy on a large scale, right under the noses of the German army, to and from a country dubiously regarded as neutral and a supposed safe haven throughout the war, it is pretty plain that they would have been in collusion with the Germans to get away with it and survive.

But these uncorroborated tales were all I ever heard about the sisters and their family. When I pressed my neighbours to find out more, they could add nothing to the story and I got the impression it was all a mixture of myth and gossip that had been passed down over the generations and there was nobody left around who remembered the truth about why the family was unpopular. It is possible to assume that because the locals had been raised from childhood to believe that the sisters' family was disliked by tradition it had become folklore to slander them: after all the partisans rooted out and shot collaborators after the war was over, so the sisters's parents would never have survived to have a family if there was any real truth in the stories.

Tommaso, a veteran communist partisan, was considered to be one of the learned elders amongst his friends and associates. After he had told us what was generally believed about the sisters' family, I discovered he was a *Milanese*, a native of Milan who moved to the village in the 1950s, so it raises the question of how he knew these stories that stemmed from the war if he hadn't lived through them. We can only put it down to the darker side of community life, where a community closes ranks against an outsider who is perceived as unpopular.

Any foreigner residing in Italy has to understand and accept why some Italians behave like they do if he or she is to get along with them. For instance, many Italians have a sense of self-importance, and as a matter of course they will push their way to the front of a queue and not give way. Our two female neighbours epitomise this behaviour. In centuries past the country suffered repression and invasion many times over and the occupiers victimised its people, none more so than the German army during the war, when there wasn't enough of anything to go round and so the only way to get what was available was to grab it! Also until recent times, Italians had very large families where the individual had to push and shove to survive against heavy odds, but in times of comparative plenty it is hard to accept self-centredness when nobody needs to strive to survive any more and in general the modern Italian knows how to behave, otherwise the environment would be a very hostile place to live in.

It is possible that a non-Moltrasino might have felt sorry for the two sisters and be sucked into believing that what they had to endure was unjust, that they were two lonely spinsters crying out for husbands and they didn't deserve to be treated as outcasts because of some foul rumour spread from questionable origins. It might be possible for the outsider to think that they would have made perfect wives for the type of men that seek a woman who wants perfection in all that she does; the sort of men who require their houses to be spick and span, with everything in their lives precise, sterilised and in order. Unfortunately, they did not make any effort to endear themselves to the village folk or to try to change the villagers' opinion about them. In fact, not only did they not try to be liked, it seemed as if they tried not to be liked.

Living right opposite them, I had the opportunity to observe them at close quarters, without, I hope them knowing I was doing it and I to have to admit, like the rest of the Moltrasini I could not take to them either. They were completely self-involved, even blinkered to everything and anybody outside the perimeter of their estate. Except for close relatives, it was as if nobody existed outside their sheltered domain. I tried to overlook this self-isolation and I tried to like them and imagine that perhaps it was the rest of the village who got them wrong, that they were subject to a witch-hunt and that they had become like they were through some sort of self-defence mechanism. If I felt in a devilish mood I took enjoyment from testing them, by relating news bulletins about what was happening in other parts of the village and who was doing what, and then waiting for their reaction. I quickly found out that they were completely uninterested in anybody else's existence except their own. When I praised one of the locals for doing something good for the community it made them visibly shake and invariably they would cover their ears in an effort to denounce what I'd just told them. They would then scurry away as fast as they could, as if I were a cruel ogre who had been sent to destroy their immunity.

These 'Sisters Grim' always used the unfamiliar *lei* pronoun with everybody they were forced to converse with, even with the neighbours they had been to school with and had known for over half a century. Their only exceptions to this were their relatives. They didn't take part in anything that happened in the village and they contributed absolutely nothing to the local surroundings, except to moan about everything, and that of course got up everybody's noses.

And they would rush everywhere, all the time. Everything, but everything had to be done on the double without a second to spare, as if life were too short to finish all the chores that needed doing, and everything, including time itself had to be in its place. They did everything to an ordered programme, to a set, weekly schedule that neither man, beast nor act of nature should ever be allowed to change. If anybody tried to alter their living pattern, or interfere with it by arriving in the middle of something they regarded as imperative, they would get short shift and were ordered to make an appointment to see them at a properly convened time. Seasonal weather patterns would cause the sisters all sorts of grievances. If the weather and the temperature were not precisely as they deemed it should be for the time of year, and therefore did not suit their requirements, then God help these creations of nature and they would give them a strong piece of their minds. They would comment daily on the weather forecast as if the fates were constantly against them, and only them! If it was cold, it was too cold. If was hot, it was too hot. If was wet, it was too wet. If it was dry, it was too dry. There were times when I actually began to feel sorry for the weather, because it could never please The Sisters.

As one would expect, they would inflict their impatience on the local tradesmen. To them, a male was a useful tool, put on this earth to serve their needs; a workhorse, there to be utilised when they could not manage a household chore for themselves. He would have the physical strength that they required and they were only interested in those who possesed a practical ability that they could put to good use. Otherwise, a man would serve no useful purpose. Unless he was a relative or an emergency repairman, a male was very rarely allowed to enter their property. If something in their home needed repairing or replacing, they would demand that the appropriate tradesman come out and fix it immediately. They would not listen to excuses and wherever he was, or whatever he was doing, he had to stop immediately and come and attend to them, because their needs were greater than anyone else's. After he had attended to what he was called out to do, their attitude was that, for all they cared, he could crawl away and die. That is, until the next time he was called upon, when he better raise himself up from his grave pretty sharpish or there would be hell to pay if he arrived late.

Throughout the month before we were due to move into our new flat, I worked solidly there, carrying out all the repairs and maintenance needed so we could move in. One spring afternoon, the front door was open and I was stood at the top of a stepladder, wiring up some light fittings. The sisters entered and stood silently, watching me working. I don't know how long they had been there, because they stood behind me and only when I sensed their presence did I turn around to see who it was. They reminded me of two middle-aged versions of the mystical children from the John Wyndham novel *The Midwich Cuckoos*, with their beady golden eyes riveted on the pair of new, starched white bib-and-brace overalls I was wearing. At the moment I turned around, Nicola arrived and to break the eerie silence, she told them that I was very practical and could turn my hand to most things. At hearing this, the sisters' hardened lips showed a glimmer of a smile and their eyes glowed with a piercing, laser-like sharpness and their heads moved in a rhythmic, tick-tock motion like a precision Swiss watch, winding the seconds away. Little did I know it at the time, but I had arrived like manna from heaven. Here was I, a practical male, a future workhorse, living more or less on their doorstep, available to be called out at any hour of the day or night.

From that day on, I was summoned to their sanctuary on more 'dire emergencies' than I care to recall. I was required to remove a broken key from a front door lock, and then ordered to buy and replace the lock the next day. I was presented with two IKEA wall cupboards, a vanity table and a TV cabinet to assemble, told to plane the bottoms of three jamming doors, which, by the look of the marks etched deep into the marble tiles must have been sticking for decades, all of which were done as an emergency call-out. I succeeded in making an enormous, fully decorated Christmas tree stand upright after it had toppled over. (As it was Christmas Eve, I suppose it was a legitimate emergency.) I drilled various sized holes in numerous walls and bits of wood, fixed a very large, valuable eighteenth-century gilded mirror onto a wall, painted their picture frames and framed their pictures. I was summoned to remove offending spiders from their bathroom sink, clear dozens of dead rats and mice from their terrace and then told to carry the offending creatures well away from their property and dispose of them by dropping them over the garden wall into the waterfall (surreptitiously, or risk a fine from the Comune) then told to make sure they wouldn't miraculously revive themselves and target them personally ever again. Even when a creature had been dead for hours, or even days, if the sisters had discovered it on their property, wherever it may be I was duty-bound to attend to the problem that same minute. Once, I had to remove a stag beetle that was minding its own business, half way up an olive tree, near their vegetable garden, some fifty metres away from their house, simply because it was inside their boundary. The sight of it just being there caused them hot flushes, bordering on the panic, so it had to be eradicated. On another occasion they expected me to batter an adder to death with a spade and then do the same to a large scorpion, for no better reason than that these poor creatures had made the mistake of wandering onto their side of the fence. When all of these deeds had been done, they showed no sign of gratitude. Instead, it was as if I'd suddenly become a hindrance and they could not get me off their property fast enough. They would usher me through the big iron gate and slam it shut behind me, enabling them, at double-quick time, to carry on living their kind of normality.

Every second of every time I was called out to slave for them I asked myself why I was doing it. After all, I am supposed to be an artist, not their personal handyman. What was this hold they had over me? I asked myself. It was as if I had been cast under a witch's spell. Why couldn't I bring myself to say 'go to hell' each time? But when the next time arose I would remember why I did it. It was because, geographically we were such close neighbours and I appreciated my peace and quiet. Their lips would quiver, and they would appear to be on the verge of crying hysterically until I agreed to do the deed! They had learned how to twist me around their little fingers, just as they had with every other 'useful' male that they had come into contact with throughout their lives. Then and only then, when I had satisfied them both would they dismiss me, allowing me to go back to living my own life.

There was a paradox in their make-up, which was revealed when I was summoned to do the most unsavoury of jobs for them. Outwardly they appeared timid and fragile, and on occasions they would fall to pieces and act like frightened little girls, which they threatened to do if their ever-pressing needs were not immediately met. But underneath they were as tough as a pair of old leather boots. When I had to undertake one of the aforementioned unsavoury tasks, (for example, a half dead, pregnant rat that had been opened up on their steps - admittedly by one of our cats) they could stand and watch me clear up the whole mess. They might appear to have had the need to cling to each other for support to lessen their shaking but at the same time they would peer through open fingers, covering half closed eyes and stifling retching noises as though they were about to vomit simultaneously. In the meantime they would have gathered in readiness all the correct instruments I needed to finish the creature off, and they would pass them to me one at a time. They would then expect me to scrub the area with a selection of disinfectants and hose it down. Why, I continually asked myself, if they had the stomach to watch these acts, didn't they do them themselves? Why I wondered, did they suddenly have an incapacity that threatened to turn them into jelly, when they were more than competent to handle everything else they were associated with in their lives by themselves? It left me wondering why they continued to live in this world if they couldn't stand to live amongst the insects, reptiles, rodents and fellow humans that inhabit the place.

It might be that the sisters' way of life was an adverse reaction to the close proximity of houses in this part of the village, with the tall stone buildings huddled closely together on such a small amount of level land. We, and every other resident found that it was necessary to open all the windows and shutters when the weather was hot to encourage the movement of air through the houses. Sometimes, it was possible for us to hear every word that was being said in a neighbouring household, to observe all the things our neighbours did outside their homes and, from an oblique angle it was possible to see everything that was going on inside. It was taking neighbourliness to the extreme.

Usually, the residents of our village carried on with their daily lives, conforming to standards that were acceptable to the rest of the community but on odd occasions something happened that caused them great embarrassment. Such an incident occurred with Gina, who lived on the opposite side of the piazza in the top-floor apartment of a converted villa. She was a classic southern stereotype, who had arrived in Moltrasio with her parents from the south coast of Italy years before and she had married into another southern family who had also settled in the village. The villa where they lived was old and run down, with a dilapidated roof and a gravity-defying conglomeration of twisted brick chimneystacks. Gina's husband, Carlo and their son were builders. Gina herself was a *casalinga*, a housewife of the traditional southern Italian variety; short, stocky, uncompromisingly tough and of an indeterminable age. As regular as clockwork at six-thirty every single morning, fifty-two weeks of the year, after her washing machine had finished its cycle (and if it wasn't raining) she would lean as far as she could out of her kitchen window and hang her washing onto a drying frame that extended over the piazza. And because it was permanently on display, her washing was as much a feature of the centro-storico as the antiquated roof and chimneys above.

One day, when the spirit moved me, I leaned out of our bedroom window and did a small watercolour featuring their roof and the interesting chimneystacks. I also happened to include Gina's washing in the picture. When it was finished, I hung it on my studio wall for sale.

Every Sunday, some of the more senior ladies of the village followed the same ritual; mass, Sunday lunch, an afternoon snooze and then a *camminata* a stroll around in small groups to visit other senior ladies, chatting endlessly and collecting more ladies on the way. A good proportion of these groups stopped by my studio, mainly as a halfway rest point and for a drink of my bottled water rather than to buy any paintings. A couple of Sundays after I'd finished the watercolour of Gina's apartment, Gina and her group popped in. After the usual salutations and a drink of water, Gina fixed her attention onto the picture of the exterior of her abode.

After pausing to absorb what she was looking at, she clasped the sides of her face with both hands and yelled out, "Jesu Cristo!"

Now this was very strong language indeed for a devout

churchgoer like Gina to use and it received instant attention from her lady friends, who scuttled over to see for themselves what she was swearing about. Still with alarm in her voice, she bade me come over to where she was standing. She then turned a finger to the picture and began tapping forcefully on the glass, making it rattle in its frame.

"Che cosa è?" she demanded, "What is this?"

At first I thought she had called me over to point out some architectural error to do with the roof or the chimneystacks, but I followed the line of her forefinger, which was pointing out her washing.

"That's your washing," I said.

"Yes I know that!" she replied abruptly. "It's not that I'm pointing at. It's those!"

On closer inspection I saw what had made her take umbrage. It was a pair of her *mutande*, her knickers hanging at the front of her washing display that I'd painted. She said that it was already insulting enough that I'd selected her crumbling roof and chimneys to paint, because for years people around the village had made rude remarks about them.

"It's bad enough being married to a builder," she went on, "When he's at home, he only wants to sit on his backside and watch football on TV, when all the time, the house needs re-roofing. He might be a good builder when he's working for somebody else, but when I need something doing he tells me where to get off."

But she hadn't finished. "What is so interesting in particular about you wanting to paint my knickers?" She demanded, "And what's more, my knickers are not grey! My knickers are WHITE!"

At this, the rest of her group burst out laughing, which roused Gina's already delicate mood and to add more insult to injury, one of her friends, Silvana said to her, "Go on then, show them to us and prove they are white!"

Then to wind Gina up even more, she added, "Gina's knickers are grey because she doesn't use Dixan soap powder, she uses a cheaper brand!"

At this, Gina continued to throw even more verbal daggers in my direction. Despite all her commotion, I tried to calm her down and explain in non-technical terms that her undergarments only appeared to be grey because they where hanging under the shadow of her roof, but this did not wash and with a scowl on her face she turned and stomped out of the studio, leaving her chums behind in her wake.

Half an hour later, she returned, still irate, but this time with husband Carlo in tow. We went through the whole performance again. After Gina had berated him, telling him that he should be ashamed of himself for letting their roof fall to bits, Carlo did not know which way to look, but for the sake of a peaceful life, he was forced to side with his wife's disgust at having her underwear on display on my studio wall for all and sundry to see. He then asked me as politely as he could if I wouldn't mind taking the picture down. Gina became less peeved when I agreed to do so, but she wasn't content until she'd watched me put the picture in a cupboard in the back room. What's more, she insisted that it had to be stored face down. I was sorely tempted to remind her that, even as she spoke, the real ones where hanging in their usual place outside her kitchen window for every passer-by to see, but I thought better of it. However, anybody with a keen eye would have seen that from the next day on, when Gina hung her knickers out to dry, they were always placed in a less prominent position on her washing line.

But that wasn't the end of it. The following Sunday, Gina,

on her regular *camminata* and dressed in her Sunday best, brought four different women friends along to my studio to have a private viewing of the picture. Straight away, it was obvious that she had invited her friends to add support to her outrage. She marched into my storeroom, found the picture in its hiding place inside the cupboard and held it up for her group to see.

"Just look at it!" She declared. "It's beyond me why he wants to paint my knickers, and this monstrosity of a roof when there are so many beautiful things in the village to paint pictures of."

By their confrontational air, I sensed that two of her gang of four had arrived to do battle with me and probably intended finding out if they had a pervert with a clandestine fetish for women's underwear living amongst them. However, when they actually saw the tiny watercolour and realised that Gina's knickers were but an incidental part of the picture and not the principal feature, and it seemed that only Gina had taken offence, their expressions took on a deflated look, and they looked at her as if to ask what all the fuss was about. One of them even said she liked it, and told Gina that she considered what I'd produced was an architectural record of the village.

The following week, Gina brought another group along to give their critical opinions. The good news for me was, after many discussions over the picture's content, the consensus started to turn in my favour and Gina began referring to it as 'my picture in the cupboard'. After another week and another visit, she allowed me to put it back on the wall again, and then she took me to one side and tentatively asked how much it would cost to buy.

Two weeks later, I sold it to an American gent and when Gina found out, mixed expressions of horror and disappointment passed over her face and she blamed her absent, incompetent husband for not buying it for her earlier. Her friend Silvana continued to tease her, saying, "Your grey *mutande* are now as famous in the USA as they are in Moltrasio!"

Chapter 14

Eating and Drinking, Italian Style

JUST ABOUT every family in the village has a private vegetable garden or an allotment, called an *orto*. In these plots, laid out on terraces cut into the mountainside, they grow vegetables of prize-winning quality. This success is helped by a southerly wind that guarantees a bumper harvest every year, so there are almost none of the disappointments the British amateur gardener may feel, no feeling of wasted energy, no negative thoughts of paving over the vegetable patch and installing a barbeque, or creating extra living space by erecting one of those out-of-keeping conservatories.

When we lived in Christine and Giorgio's house we had not been able to grow any food because the garden was fully mature, with plants, bushes and trees and it would have been wrong of us to dig anything up. There was no land at all attached to our new apartment, nor were there any allotments available to rent at the time we moved in. My father's family were market gardeners and rose growers and as a youth my Saturday job was working for my uncle in this line of business, so when I saw just how well everything grows in Italy I felt a bit frustrated at not being able to grow anything myself.

Everybody in the village knew that we, living in our small, first floor apartment, didn't have an *orto*, and so throughout the growing season our neighbours would inundate us with fresh produce. Every morning from springtime onwards, when we would open the front door to let our cats either in or out, we would find a large bag of goodies on the doorstep, usually washed and dressed, ready for us to use. In the spring, we would see lettuce in at least half a dozen varieties, followed by parsley, sage and basil, and later in the summer we would receive cucumbers, carrots, courgettes, runner beans, cabbage, aubergines, apricots, plums, pears, walnuts, hazelnuts, and tomatoes by the kilo. It was hard not to become complacent in the growing season and expect that we would not have to shop for greengrocery for weeks or even months, and even to become reliant in the knowledge that we would have enough produce delivered to our front door to keep us going for some time, all of it out of the goodness of our neighbours' hearts.

If any plant is inextricably linked with Italy, it has to be the tomato. During the growing season, the sun will have been penetrating the fruits for weeks, ripening them and sweetening them, and when they are ready, we take delight in gorging ourselves upon them for the whole of September, when they are at their most plentiful. I challenge anyone to find me a better lunch than freshly-picked tomatoes, warmed by the sun, with buffalo mozzarella, black olives, some fresh oregano, a dressing of ground black pepper, a pinch of salt and some extra-virgin olive oil, accompanied by a fresh *panino*.

All over Italy, the season of fresh tomatoes is followed by the season of *polpa di pomodoro*, when everyone who grows tomatoes pulps down what they cannot eat, for use over the coming months. Every serious Italian gardener has a special machine that pulverises whole tomatoes, including the skins and seeds, into a pulp. He then par-boils the pulp, pours it into bottles, adding only a sprig of basil to each, and then caps the bottles. Often as much as a hundred kilos of tomatoes are ground in one go. As we sat by the lake during cool September evenings, watching the sun set over Monte Bisbino, we were sure to hear the sound of someone grinding tomatoes.

Polpa di pomodoro is used as a base for a lot of Italian dishes, so families grow as many tomatoes as their patch of ground will allow, so as to have enough to pulp and store. A 650mm bottle provides enough for the sugo, or sauce for a pasta lunch for a family of four. Fortunately for us, almost everyone produced more than they needed and we were often given the surplus, so I made sure I had a ready supply of empty bottles of the right size. Beer bottles are best for this job, and the hardest work I had to do around this time of year was to drink the golden liquid from as many bottles as I could, and then hand over the empties to a friendly neighbour and wait for them to be returned, full of the delicious red pulp.

September was also Enzo's time of year, the month he lived for; the other eleven were spent in expectation of a bumper crop of his beloved *Boletus edulis*, the famous wild *porcini* mushroom. The season would only last for four weeks and they had to be picked in the early morning after a lengthy spell of rain, when the temperature was low and when the *funghi* had absorbed enough moisture to bring them to their fattest and tastiest condition.

At this time of year he would change character, becoming tense and feisty, and his normal life pattern would alter perceptively. When he was satisfied that the time was right, he would sneak into his car at three-thirty in the morning and without starting the engine, roll it down the hill from outside his house. Then at the last minute, he would start the engine and make his way over the Swiss border to a place he kept to himself, a seemingly limitless wood he was told about decades before by an old man on his deathbed, where there was an oasis of wild *porcini*. There were two reasons why Enzo kept this place a deep secret. Firstly, he was breaking the law by sneaking into another country without going through a customs checkpoint, and worse, he was filching a vegetable product and taking it back over the border. He would have faced some severe fines if he were caught. Secondly, he knew people (though he certainly wished he didn't know them) with commercial interests who wanted to take the crop for themselves. Wild mushrooms are highly prized in this part of Italy and can fetch a good price when sold to shops or restaurants, so the short picking season can be very competitive. Sometimes these people would try to follow him in their cars to find out where it was, but, fortunately for Enzo, they never did.

Enzo was not interested in selling his crop, only in stacking his freezer with enough *funghi porcini* for the rest of the year, which would complement Ada's risotto, or her *cassuola* of stewed steak and vegetables, which she served with polenta. When the season was over and he had brought his harvest home and washed, chopped and stored it all in his freezer and made sure there was no evidence left carelessly lying around to brand him as a poacher, he would relax and return to being his normal self. Having evaded the customs authorities, outwitted the Swiss gamekeepers and no longer under threat from highway brigands he would be free to brag about his prohibited treasure to people like us, who did not covet his prize and posed no threat to him. Quite amazingly, some of the mushrooms he harvested were enormous, weighing up to one kilo each. Even more amazingly he told us that they grow to that size in a day and a night. The flavour of porcini mushrooms when cooked is exquisite and they possess three times the flavour of commercially grown mushrooms. Nicola and I both remarked that, as with the tomato, we had never tasted a mushroom properly until we came to live in Italy.

The Moltrasini eat a lot of game. Moltrasio village centre is situated two hundred and fifty metres up a mountain track, and the game is caught in the mountains and woods behind the village. They make use of every part of the animals they catch and also of the farm animals they keep. Hare sauce with tagliatelle makes a good starter, as do pasta parcels filled with a *besciamella* sauce and *funghi porcini*, followed by a *primo piatto*, a first course of risotto, with either mushrooms, chicken or goose livers. They also eat a lot of sausage, tripe, pigs-trotters and *osso buco* (literally 'bone with a hole'), veal shanks cooked in white wine and tomatoes. A typical *secondo piatto*, a main course, in Moltrasio might be either wild boar in red wine, or roast donkey, venison, wild-goat, pheasant, veal or goose, usually with polenta, although of course the traditional accompaniment for *osso buco* is Risotto Milanese, flavoured with saffron. And if a household is splashing out they'll have a rack of rare roast beef with potatoes roasted in lard.

Lombardy is not a good grape growing region and only thirteen commercial wines have been distinguished as DOC wine – *Denominazione di Origine Controllata* (Controlled Denomination of Origin), and only two are of the higher DOCG rating – *Denominazione di Origine Controllata e Garantita* (Controlled and Guaranteed Denomination of Origin). Franciacorta, a sparkling white wine made in the classic method, where it is fermented in the bottle similarly to Champagne, is one of the more popular Lombardian wines. Valtellina Superiore from Nebbiolo and Oltrepò Pavese are both full-bodied reds. By comparison, the neighbouring northern region of Piedmont has forty-six DOC wines, the highest number for any Italian region, and four DOCGs. Another of Lombardy's neighbours, Valle d'Aosta ,which is the smallest region in Italy, has an impressive array of twenty-five different DOC wines.

The wine drinker with an eye to saving money will club together with his brother or cousin and buy their table wine twice yearly directly from a *cantina*, a wine producer, at cost price, in either the Veneto or the Piedmont region. They will load up a four-by-four truck with up to six fifty-four-litre demijohns. The lower half of these massive vessels is covered in plaited cane, which is twisted to form two strong handles, and when full, they need two even stronger men to move them. These people usually spend a whole day travelling there and back to obtain their favourite tipple. They spend even longer siphoning it off into bottles, but when and only when, the moon is on the wane! One autumn, I put my fifteen-litre demijohn onto the back of a truck heading for the Veneto. When it returned my intention was to transfer the wine into 750mm bottles that same evening, but I was told by the truck driver to wait for a waning moon! Around these parts they believe that the flavour of the wine alters noticeably because of the forceful power of the moon, and if it is not on the wane then any sediment in the wine will not settle properly at the base of the bottle.

Much of the wine growing in Lombardy is done on a small scale, by a householder, usually trailing vines around his allotment to make a bordering fence between his patch and his neighbour's or, better still, serving a more useful purpose by encouraging the vine to grow across the family pergola, where the large flat leaves form a canopy that shades the terrace from the sun when the family dines outside. If there happen to be some decent grapes to make a few dozen bottles of wine , then that's a bonus.

The Moltrasini make their wine from the deep red 'Americani' grapes, which are local to the lake area. From early October, the same gardening enthusiasts who gave us their fruit and vegetables in the spring and summer would start harvesting these small grapes. They are far too fiddly to eat individually and have a consistency of soft jelly, but although they are sweet, they leave a gritty, unpalatable texture in the mouth and each grape has at least a dozen pips. They do, however, make a full-bodied, medium sweet wine, which tastes perfectly fine to a layman like me. But this wine, I discovered, was not to everyone else's taste. Some of the locals told us that the residue made a far better grappa, which is not a good recommendation for the grapes, because it is often said that anybody with any know-how can make grappa from the leftovers of almost any vegetable matter.

After he has made wine, the Moltrasino will make grappa from the mush of skins and pips left in the bottom of the pan after the fermented wine has been strained off. He will put this mush, called *pomace*, into his still, boil it up then sit back and watch the vapours rise up and transform into a clear liquid without a trace of the colour that the red grape skins had imparted to the wine.

Grappa is a kind of moonshine, with an alcoholic content that can range from forty to eighty percent. Most Italians have drunk grappa at least once in their lifetime. Some people drink it once a day; others drink it many times a day. For the first timer, the unexpected harsh flavour takes a certain amount of getting used to and at first it can be something of a shock. There's a story about a grappa aficionado who needed to visit the dentist and he did not want to have an injection in his gums, which would leave him with the effect of the anaesthetic for several hours. He opted instead to give his mouth a good rinse around with a large shot of grappa to knock out all his nerve endings before the work commenced.

Grappa is mostly drunk as a digestive at the end of a heavy meal, either in a separate glass alongside the coffee or poured into the coffee. Some people prefer their grappa warmed and they will drink the coffee first, then pour the grappa into the still warm, empty cup. Most households have a selection of grappa kept in the cupboard which they will only bring out when friends come around for a meal. There will normally be a couple of commercial brands which will have been made from the residue of commercially-grown grapes like Chardonnay, Prosecco or Pinot, with maybe sweet herbs or sticks of oak added by the distillery to make it palatable. These will be acceptable to most, but in addition there will be a couple of grappa made by the host, or by a friend of his.

The homemade stuff can be different altogether from the commercial product. Over the years there have been a number of home distillers in Italy who have produced a course raw spirit with a dangerously high methanol content that has given grappa a bad reputation. That's not to say that grappa is always unsafe to drink. It comes from humble origins and it was frugal Italian farmers who discovered it by using what was left over from pressing their wine. A good deal of expertise has been passed down over the years to make it safe, so that it doesn't rob the drinker of his eyesight or render him impotent.

Grappa can be a source of fascination and a topic of earnest conversation and some hardened drinkers will put themselves through all sorts of rigours in sampling un *grappino*, 'a small measure of grappa'. It is always drunk neat and taken in small measures. The idea of taking a larger glass, equivalent in volume to a treble gin or vodka, is inconceivable to the aficionado. The experienced grappa drinker will normally ask some questions about the bottle placed in front of him before actually taking the harmless-looking liquid. Certainly he will want to know its alcoholic volume. Next, he will judge the smell, then the clarity. He'll also want to know who made it and when it was made. These are important questions to be asked if the potential drinker wants to get home without the aid of a stretcher. There are some people in the village who have a good reputation for making grappa and some who haven't and if you are invited to try some, it's advisable to make sure that it is made by a person with a good reputation. Hygiene conditions are also important when home brewing and it's comforting to know that the bottle set on the table was washed properly before it was filled. Some dodgy distillers won't bother washing the bottles, because they believe that the high alcoholic content of grappa will sterilise the bottles for them. This, in case you are in any doubt, is certainly not the case! It's best to drink homemade grappa in the company of the person who made it, if only to make a close inspection of the said distiller to see if he is at all *compos mentis*. For sure, there is not going to be a label on the bottle giving information about the distillation process, so other than careful observation and a tentative sip before downing it, there is no other way of knowing if one is about to drink another man's poison, unless you're not bothered about meeting your own maker sooner rather than later.

Some homemade grappa can be very smooth and palatable when expertly distilled and it can do the job it is meant to do without destroying millions of brain cells in one session, or make the liver ache rebelliously for days after. Both Nicola and I drink grappa, and it serves to deepen our bond with the locals, but we only take it occasionally and in token quantities. At dinner parties, the conversation between members of the male fraternity present will turn to comparisons of different grappa. It is unlikely at this stage there will be any women present; sensibly, they will have moved well away from the dining table. At these sessions, there will be a substantial selection of grappa on offer, all in individual queer-shaped bottles, and it is customary for the men to try at least six types and to pass comment on each one. If I was present at one of these occasions I found it advisable to listen and learn, mainly for the good of my future health. I also learnt that grappa can have a subversive effect on the drinker, bringing on the bravado, and he might tell stories of how so-and-so drank two whole bottles in one night, and then made love to four women, all in the same bed.

A law was passed not so long ago to protect the distiller from himself by restricting the home production of grappa to three litres per year, but this limit is flagrantly ignored. If Alberto, a near neighbour of ours, had obeyed this law, he would only have made enough to satisfy his needs for one week! When Alberto, a retired plumber with a six-foot girth, made grappa he became very *allegro* (lively) and at some point during the distillation process he would always call me into his workshop to sample his latest supply. Alberto's still displayed his plumbing skills and artistry to the full. The most prominent part was a large copper tank, with a conglomeration of pressure gauges and tubes connected to it. The most important part was a narrow tube spiralling out of the top of the tank, and at the end of the tube was a spigot that controlled the flow of the clear, condensed, lukewarm spirit. For the visitor going into his workshop from the fresh air, the strange, sweet, earthy aroma of the steamy vapour mixed with fumes from the gas jet burning furiously underneath the still could make a person feel heady even before trying a shot or two of his tipple.

Alberto would have his *pomace* boiling from early morning until late into the night for several days, and he would sit by the still, controlling the gas pressure throughout the whole distillation process, vigilantly watching every single drop as it emerged. He would coo melodiously over his liquid, like a father drooling over a newborn baby. When word had got around that he was running the still, his pals would arrive to sample it, and pass comment. Every time a visitor popped his head around the workshop door, he would down a glassful, symbolically to wet the baby's head. No wonder he got through a whole year's legal quota during the distilling process alone!

Another favourite *digestivo* that is commonly made at home and is safe to drink is limoncello. This pleasantly flavoured, bright yellow liquor is made by infusing the zest of lemons in grain alcohol and adding sugar and water to taste and is served in thick glasses that are first chilled in the freezer compartment of the refrigerator. Some restaurants will serve it free of charge at the end of a meal, and with an alcohol content of around twenty-five percent, it is acceptable to everyone.

Characters the likes of Alberto will not be around for much longer, and when he invited me into his workshop to sample *un grappino* I always felt honoured by his gesture. The likes of people like Alberto and Enzo have helped mould the environment for others to enjoy. They represent times gone by, but they are not re-enactments of an historical TV series nor in a feature film. They are for real. I have often had to pinch myself to realise I'm not living in a different time sphere and I appreciated every second when in their company. Fortunately in Italy there are still pockets of resistance to the world of progress, but for how long their traditional way of living can be allowed to continue is the question.

One of the principal reasons for our living in Italy was to sample its different food varieties and the best way to do that was to follow the crowd or listen to recommendations from *conoscitore*, the experts, about where to eat enormous amounts of delectable grub at a discount price. In Italy there is a two-tier price system in restaurants, one for foreigners and one for locals, and so we found it best to attend these gastronomic extravaganzas in the company of faces familiar to the local restaurateur until ours also became familiar.

As well as enjoying food and wine for its own sake, the Italians treat eating as a social occasion. Since arriving in Italy we had attended several very satisfying lunch dates in the local area. Without fail, every second Sunday in May there would be the annual Moltrasio *gita di primavera* (springtime outing), a coach trip for the elderly. Each year the destination would be a different one, but normally it would be a town or city within a two- to three-hundred kilometre radius, with something interesting to see that could be reached by lunchtime. Most importantly it would have an accommodating restaurant where the day-trippers could enjoy the highlight of the day, the mangialonga. This, literally translated, means a 'long eat'; in other words a blow-out lunch. Although we were technically too young to qualify, Enzo invited us to a trip that had been scheduled to go to La Valtellina, an area north of the lake around seventy kilometres from Moltrasio, famous for its vineyards, first to visit a cantina to taste the wine and then to visit a traditional trattoria for some outstanding food. The organisers were past masters at getting it right when it came to choosing a restaurant with prices so low for the quality on offer it made one appreciate the moment like no other. They were not allowed to make mistakes – it wouldn't be worth the wrath they'd have to endure if they did. Enzo's offer sounded too good to refuse and so we greedily accepted. The trip turned out to be far better than anticipated.

At the cantina we were given a short tour around the arched underground cellars where thousands of bottles of wine were all neatly stacked in rows, but the main reason we had stopped there was so everybody could sample the sparkling white Franciacorta and the rich, red Valtellina Superiore. A small canapé buffet had been prepared for us on the outside terrace of the cantina with some of the wine we had just seen, but Enzo advised us not to drink too much because there would be litres of wine served at lunchtime and it was important to have a clear head and to leave a space in the stomach for the delights to come in the trattoria further up the road.

Half an hour after we left the cantina, the coach pulled up outside our trattoria, the two-hundred year old Crotto Rustico. In the garden was a three lane *campo di bocce*, a gravel courtyard area for playing Italian bowls, and so I joined Enzo and some of the other men on the trip for a few rounds accompanied by a few more aperitifs until the *a tavolo* ('to table') call came, when we abandoned the game and went inside for the next four hours to pack away some truly wonderful food.

The speciality of La Valtellina is *pizzoccheri della Valtellina*. *Pizzoccheri* are pasta ribbons made from coarse ground buckwheat flour and semolina with mixed herbs. It is served with potatoes, *coste*, or cabbage and two types of Valtellina cheese. The pizzoccheri is added to the potatoes and cabbage part way through the cooking process, then the mix is drained and mixed with a butter, garlic and chopped sage sauce. Everybody on the trip wanted to try the Crotto Rustico's pizzoccheri, but not until we'd packed down several courses of other guaranteed delights on offer first. The four-course menu also included an unlimited amount of Valtellina wines per person and on closer examination it contained further unanticipated courses between the set ones.

To start the drinking we had Prosecco, followed by the white Fran1corta. To accompany it we picked at *grissini al rosmarino*, rosemary flavoured bread sticks, and *bruschette*, small pieces of warm toast dripping in garlic, fresh anchovies and slices of *prosciutto crudo*, cured, raw ham laid on top. There were four choices of *antipasti*, starters. I had homemade ravioli filled with *funghi porcini* and Nicola had a platter of cold meats, olives and sweet, wild onions that was a meal in itself. Some people had two different starters and there were seconds served with all the courses we had throughout the meal. After the starter was cleared away we were then served *frittata liscio*, thin, plain omelettes. Then we had a wine break.

A *primo piatto*, a 'first plate', is served before the *secondo piatto*, or main course, and it can be big or small, as some people have it as a main course rather than as a *secondo piatto*. Not on this trip, however, as everybody ate everything put in front of them, because it was too delicious to turn down. On offer were *tortelli con fegato di anatra e mele in grappa*, pasta, with ducks' livers and sliced apple in grappa, or *pizzoccheri di Valtellina*.

Between the first and second courses we had a choice of either *risotto all'isolana*, risotto with small pieces of cubed chicken, smoked ham, young peas and sweetcorn, or *uovo in soufflé con pancetta affumicata*, a smoked bacon soufflé. Some people ate both. Then we had a green salad to digest what we'd eaten and a brief rest for another wine break. The *secondo piatto* was a choice of fish or meat. I had grilled perch with smoked king prawns and tuna *carpaccio* in a *besciamella* sauce with potato fritters, and Nicola, who doesn't like fish, had lamb chops marinated in a basil and parmesan pesto, with new potatoes and young spinach leaves. We then had a selection of Valtellina cheeses, accompanied by an appropriate wine.

Dolce, desert, was a choice of *canoli Siciliani* with *gelato*, pastry tubes filled with mascarpone and candied fruit, served with plain ice cream or ricotta mousse with nuts in warm chocolate, accompanied by a selection of desert wines. One of our group was celebrating a birthday, so the kitchen had prepared an enormous layered sponge cake, packed with rasp-berries and myrtle berries, with the lady's name piped onto it in jam. We all had a slice of that, plus more Prosecco to toast her along with the café and either grappa or *amari* (liqueurs). At the end of the lunch Enzo reminded the men folk that the game of *bocce* in the garden hadn't been completed. It never was, because our stomachs were so full that none of us could move from the table.

We enjoyed this trip so much that we accepted invitations to go on four more. The second went to Cremona to climb the highest bell tower in Italy, the third to Verona to see the bal-cony reputed to be the inspiration for Shakespeare's *Romeo e Giulietta* and the fourth to the coastal city of Genova to visit the port and the underground aquarium. In Genova our *man-gialonga* consisted of a huge seafood extravaganza. For rea-sons I cannot recall, we did not go on the trip the year after that. The destination was Padua and it turned into something of a disaster. The cause of the trouble was our friend Ada.

The trips always set off at seven o'clock in the morning, prompt, but couples would begin queuing for the coach at least half an hour before its arrival, for the simple reason that there would be fierce competition to grab the front seats, or seats as near to the front as possible, before anybody else. Although the majority of day trippers would arrive with their spouses, as soon as the coach driver opened the doors the women would abandon their husbands and make an unashamed charge for the coveted front seats, staking a claim on them for the remainder of the day. Hubby would then sit as close to his missus as he could, but this would generally be around the centre of the coach, depending on how quickly he was out of the starting blocks. In other words it was a mass free-for-all, ending up with the women at the front and the men to the back. The reason for this rigorous competition and the resultant segregation was, we discovered, not for the best view, but a less obvious one; because they hoped that sitting in the front of the coach would prevent travel sickness.

According to a detailed report we received from Gina, the wife of the organiser (and the owner of the [allegedly] grey *mutande*) the day after the trip to Padua, Ada and Enzo turned up five minutes after the coach doors had opened and, very disappointingly for them, they had to sit at the very back. Despite Ada having taken all the accustomed remedies before leaving home, and sucking boiled sweets continuously, the inevitable happened. Whether or not it was psychosomatic or not, Ada's travel sickness was bad and the coach had to stop several times en-route to accommodate her. In the end, after everybody having their say about what and what not to do about Ada's sickness, the driver decided to do a big detour to find the out-patients department of the nearest hospital. They eventually found a small regional hospital. As it was a Sunday, there was only a skeleton staff on duty, so Ada had to wait for over an hour to be attended to. By the time the doctor allowed her to get back on the coach it was 12:25pm and the organiser of the outing announced that the restaurant he had booked way back in January was still over eighty kilometres away, and they had just five minutes to get there for the booked time. He then had to make the painful decision to abort the trip for that year and return to Moltrasio.

Gina added that the annoyance and the disappointment were considerable, and there was a great deal of stern finger-pointing and unsympathetic, even foul and abusive, language aimed at Ada, with some people even saying they should have abandoned her hours ago in the first autostrada lay-by they came across. Others decided, between themselves, that they should have left her in the hospital to recuperate, then picked her up on the way back later that evening. Apparently some even wanted to see her dead!

From our experience of these trips, we could well imagine the displeasure, because Italians are not the most retiring or patient of people when something displeases them. For the regulars on these trips, the annual outing is a big event, but the majority are not particularly interested in the coach excursion itself or in the sightseeing. No, they are there solely for the *mangialonga*. Some trippers would even refrain from eating for up to twenty-four hours prior to the meal, solely with the intention of packing down as many courses of delectable food and wine as their stomachs could accommodate.

In Italy food is of great, if not absolute, importance, and thousands of hours of discussion, preparation and consumption are spent in any individual's lifetime concerning this subject. Therefore one can imagine why everyone on the trip was so upset by having their day out spoiled by Ada's travel sickness. In fact, the following year at least half of the regular crowd, a party made up of people who did not suffer from travel sickness, formed their own separate *mangialonga* coach outing. There are no prizes for guessing who was not invited to join the party.

The irony is, that on the more successful trips we have

been on, lunch can take up to an average of four hours of non-stop eating, hence the name *mangialonga*, and yet, strangely, it's been our recollection that with stomachs full and waist-lines bulging noticeably nobody has ever complained about travel sickness or nausea on the journey home. In fact, the majority are eager to continue their munching and guzzling and will plead with the bus driver to stop at just about every road-side food outlet en-route, to sample even more regional gastronomic specialities. They will gorge themselves on Parma ham in Parma, on Gorgonzola cheese in Gorgonzola, on *pesto alla Genovese con gnocchi* in Genova, take more than one glass of *liquore di Saronno* in Saronno, or Lambrusco in Modena, and take in as many biscuit and chocolate factories along the highway that the driver can be persuaded to stop at, so they can buy even more extravagant specialities to take back home.

Chapter 15

Gianni, George, and Benito

ONE OF our neighbours when we lived in the Masins' house was the fashion designer Gianni Versace. In the mid 1980s he bought and restored the massive Villa Fontanelle situated close to the lakeside and he used it as his regular home when in Italy. Apart from having a superb location, it was conveniently located for his fashion headquarters in the Via Montenapoleone in Milan. There had been a rumour for some years that Gianni was interested in buying and restoring the Villa Passalacqua in Moltrasio, Boris's old home and the largest building in the village, even larger than his own Villa Fontanelle, to house a permanent Versace museum that would have been open to the public. It would also have made good use of the then run-down Passalacqua, but this never materialised and subsequently the Villa Passalacqua was fully refurbished as a five-star property for rent.

Although Gianni and I lived next door to each other, the closest I ever came to meeting him was in the year before his death. The driveway to his villa is located at an awkward angle to the road and, because there was a blind spot, there was a large mirror fixed to the wall on the opposite side of the road to help drivers make a safe exit. On this day, I was returning from Como (admittedly I was driving at more than the speed limit) when Gianni drove out of his driveway in a black Range Rover with darkened windows. Either he did not look, or he misjudged the speed I was doing, because as I came around the corner, we both had to swerve to avoid each other. Neither of us had to brake hard, but had we not reacted quickly, I would have rammed him side-on as he cut across the road to the northbound lane. It was unmistakably him, because I recognised his designer stubble and his famous silver hair, which shone out from the dark interior of his car.

The Versace family was hardly a topic of general conversation amongst the locals in Moltrasio, but were just a few of the many rich and famous people who live around the lake, the stars of TV and film and the world of high fashion who regularly inhabit the gossip columns of the glossy magazines. They were not regarded as being real people who led real lives, not having to deal with the humdrum chores of day-to-day existence like the rest of us. That is the common perception, and for the most part it is true, but Nicola still tells a joke about the time we lived next door to Gianni Versace. We shared the same rubbish container, which was parked in the road between our two residences. She says that at night, she would peep through the curtains of the upstairs bedroom window, waiting for the moment when Gianni put his black plastic bag in the bin. Then, when he had returned to his villa, she would take a torch and rummage through his refuse, in the hope of finding a little designer number he had discarded that she could fit into!

In a country without a monarchy, the Versaces, along with other famous names in the fashion, entertainment and industrial worlds, are akin to royalty. As often happens in a republic, there seems to be a need for famous figureheads to fill the void left by the absence of a royal family. Gianni Versace's funeral became the biggest event in Moltrasio's recorded history and, for a few weeks, put the tiny village firmly on the international map.

On July 15 1997 at 4pm central European time, news came that Gianni Versace had been shot in the head outside his Miami villa. As the shock incident had taken place over six thousand miles away in the USA, the people of Moltrasio assumed the incident would be kept over there and that was where he would be laid to rest. However, forty-eight hours later his brother and sister brought Gianni's ashes back to Italy in a gold casket, and to the tiny cemetery in Moltrasio, and all media attention immediately switched from Miami to our village. The Versace family expected to be able to place Gianni's ashes in the village cemetery, but unfortunately the mayor had to break the bad news to the family that all places were already allocated to local families and even though the Versaces were rich and famous, he had to tell them that it would be unfair to the residents if precedence were given over their heads. Gianni was fifty years old when he was killed. As neither he nor anyone else in the Versace family appeared to have made any plans for his final resting place, they took up one resident's kind offer of a space in her family tomb in the interim, as she herself, although old, was in good health and didn't anticipate that she would need her spot for a few more years.

The international press and paparazzi arrived en masse at the cemetery to witness Gianni's sister carry the solid gold casket containing his ashes to this temporary resting place and to try to get photographs of celebrities, supermodels and work associates, all connected in some way with the Versace family, as they visited the gravesite. Nearly all of these people passed my studio door on their way up the steps to the cemetery and for a further three days visitors arrived non-stop to pay their respects, until the cemetery was ankle-deep in flowers, wreaths and tributes and the mayor had to organise gangways between them to enable people to enter and exit. At seven each evening, the cemetery gate was locked and a team of security guards was posted there throughout the night to keep out those riff-raff who seemed to have a perverse need to visit the man's resting place out of hours, especially as there had been a couple of attempts to steal the gold casket.

Then, just as world interest was calming down and the flow of visitors seemed to abate, press attention switched back to Miami, as the US police department declared they were closing in on Andrew Cunanan, described as a 'spree-killer' and the prime suspect for Versace's murder and they began showing live action on TV of the manhunt.

A few days later the media spotlight switched back to Moltrasio as the casket containing Gianni's ashes was taken to a packed Duomo di Milano, the cathedral of Milan, for the official funeral service. Once again, Moltrasio was highlighted as a large contingency of people escorted the funeral carriage from the village to Milan, from where the whole world could watch the service live on daytime television. The most poignant part for me was watching Elton John, one of Gianni's bosom friends, who was sitting in the front pew next to Diana, Princess of Wales, weeping openly on her shoulder while she cradled his head. This was only six weeks before Diana's premature death in Paris.

When the funeral service in Milan was over, the cortège returned to Moltrasio's tiny cemetery and his ashes were once again returned to their temporary resting place. A couple of days later, and seven days after Gianni's murder, the Miami police announced that Cunanan's body had been found in a house-boat only half a mile from Gianni's villa. It was alleged that he had committed suicide.

For months after the funeral, weekend visitors continued to come to Moltrasio especially to look for the Versace's final resting place, but most went away confused, because he was housed in somebody else's tomb and there was nothing to indicate that his ashes were there. Gianni's sister Donatella and his brother Santo took over the residency of the Villa Fontanelle and the Versace family built a marble tomb in the garden. When the building work was complete, they transferred his ashes there, well out of the public gaze.

The following summer, an elaborate exhibition of Versace's designs and costume creations that he had produced for some of the most glamorous women in contemporary society, including many of the late Princess Diana's clothes, were put on show at the Villa Olmo in Cernobbio, only two kilometres from the Villa Fontanelle. The exhibition began in time to catch the start of the tourist season and ran throughout the summer months, before being dismantled and put on the road to travel the world's exhibition centres. The exhibition opened with all the pomp and ceremony normally accorded to a visit by a head of state, such was Versace's standing in Italy at the time, and according to Nicola who attended the inauguration for VIP's, the exhibits were stunningly presented on the opening night.

The British Consul General in Milan, along with many ambassadors and international and Italian dignitaries, had received an invitation for the official dinner and opening ceremony. It happened, he told Nicola, that he had a previous engagement that night (although Nicola did not believe him) and he asked her if she would represent him at the inauguration. At that time, Nicola's position at the Consulate was as a commercial officer's assistant. Her job was to liaise between Britain and Italy on the import of fashion goods and accessories into the Italian fashion trade and to assist British companies interested in exhibiting and exporting to Italy. She also sought distribution agents in Italy, organised and set up business deals, proofread contracts, translated documents and made representation on behalf of British business interests. She clearly knew more about fashion and the fashion business than the Consul General, added to which she lived only two kilometres from the Villa Olmo, which saved him a ninety kilometre round trip. When he offered her an extra day's leave as a bribe if she would go, she willingly agreed. In other words, she said, he did not want to go. The extra day's leave meant she had time at home to prepare herself to look her best for an evening in the spotlight. She left that evening dolled up in a new, all black outfit, with silver high-heeled shoes. She looked fit for any fashion catwalk.

My only involvement in all this was that I was to drive Nicola to a side road alongside the villa a few minutes before the opening ceremony was due to begin and then disappear into thin air, as all good chauffeurs are required to do. The only snag with this arrangement was my car, which was a very modest, twelve-year old, Vauxhall Cavalier. Thanks to the long, extremely narrow lane, sandwiched between two massive sixteenth century stone walls that led up a steepish gradient to the piazza outside our apartment, almost every inhabitant's car has scratches on it from the walls. My ageing Cavalier was no exception. Taxi drivers refused to pick us up from the house, knowing there would be a real chance they would scrape the vehicle that earns them their living. Not surprisingly, Nicola was not keen to wobble the three hundred metres down the mule track in high heels to the lake road where a taxi might, or might not, arrive on time, so I was obliged to volunteer my services.

When we arrived at the Villa Olmo, there was a large, highly organised and very obvious police presence already in place. There were road signs everywhere to direct the arriving limousines and the other extremely expensive luxury cars, and every one I saw seemed to carry a single dignitary. For a few moments I was closed in between a gleaming black stretch limo on one side and a spotless white Mercedes on the other, each delivering their VIPs to the front steps of the villa. This caused some policemen to approach my car, probably thinking I had slipped through their security cordon, but I stepped on the gas and left them in my wake as I aimed for the side road where Nicola wanted me to drop her. Here she alighted, collected herself and walked to the entrance, clutching her Versace evening bag containing her official invitation card, thus avoiding her personal embarrassment and the reputation of the British Government, by arriving at such a prestigious event in an old English banger. Before she got out of the car, Nicola told me to go home and wait for a phone call to pick her up around eleven-thirty, and to make sure I parked on the opposite side of the villa, well out of the glare of any street lighting and under the cover of darkness and to remain there until she arrived.

Before I left, I was curious to watch Nicola's arrival at the front steps of the villa, so I did a reverse U-turn, making sure I was far enough away from the police cordon to be out of their immediate vision. Outside the villa, two parallel lines of about thirty *Carabinieri* (the national police force) formed a guard of honour up the steps. All were in immaculate black dress uniforms, patent leather riding boots with spurs, dress-swords at the waist and their famous hats with the large, crimson plume in the centre that makes every one of them look at least seven feet tall. As Nicola walked elegantly up the steps, they stuck out their chests, clicked their heels together, lifted their right elbows level with their right eyes and, to a man, saluted her.

"Good old Nicola," I said to myself out loud, "it's about time you were appreciated." It was a scene for the scrapbook, the opportunity for her to be a real VIP for an hour or so. Shame I'd forgotten the camera.

Back at home I diligently waited for the call, so I could do my bit for Britain abroad and pick up one of her VIPs, but it never arrived. Instead, I heard the key turning in the lock ten minutes before I was due to leave for the villa. It was Nicola, letting herself back into our apartment, shoes in hand.

"What's the problem?" I asked.

"No problem," she replied, "I'd seen enough. I enjoyed the exhibition, it was beautifully presented and Versace's designs were fabulous. I let my presence as a British representative be known, which was why I was there, and when the dinner and the tribute speeches were over I telephoned for a cab, made my excuses and left. Anyway, my new shoes were killing me."

When I pressed her to see if she could get accustomed to being a VIP, she replied, "It was ghastly, because I didn't know anybody to talk to and nobody else seemed to know anybody to talk to either." She then added, "The Swiss Ambassador kept following me around all night, and when he tried to get me into a corner away from the main body of VIPs to chat me up, I gave up and came home."

American film star George Clooney is another lakeside resident. He bought the Villa Oleandra from US Senator John Kerry's super-rich wife, Teresa Heinz Kerry, the former wife of the late Senator John Heinz and heir to the famous H. J. Heinz foods fortune, just before husband John announced his candidacy for the US presidency. 'George', as he is called by the locals, is still at the height of his fame and adoring female fans of all ages continue to congregate around the gates to his villa. In 2004, part of the movie *Ocean's Twelve* was filmed in the street right outside his home and the film crew blocked it off for three days. He then made a TV advert for Fiat in the same street and all the traffic had to be diverted well away from the Via Regina Vecchia. After that, George thought it prudent to write an apology to all the residents for the inconvenience of having a super-star living in a medieval village and the confusion that surrounds it. In the meantime he built a footbridge spanning the road and purchased a disused workshop on the opposite side and had it converted into a gymnasium. He then bought and restored the nineteenth century Villa Margherita next door, to house his guests. A section of the community were opposed to any more interruptions, and there were rumblings that such a tiny village could not sustain George's business affairs any longer. But they don't know their luck – the continual parade of visitors and paparazzi who still arrive, hoping to get a fleeting glimpse of the star brings in revenue to the shopkeepers and bar owners. And the residents themselves benefit from the knock-on value of their properties, thanks to the growing number of celebrities who seem willing to pay a premium price to live besides Lake Como. Now, most of the locals have changed from brooding to rubbing their hands with glee.

Whilst Gianni Versace and his work were loved and admired worldwide, and the eminently likeable George Clooney, with his huge fan base, continues to enhance the prosperity of the area, Lake Como has also been associated with some pretty dark characters. Perhaps the most notorious was Benito Mussolini. Mussolini was one of the most influential figures in shaping modern Italy. After the Great War, the country was on the verge of chaos and Mussolini presented himself to King Vittorio Emmanuelle III as the only person capable of setting Italy on the right path to prosperity. The king appointed him as head of government, and by 1925 Mussolini had proclaimed himself as *Il Duce*, 'The Leader'. In 1929, after suppressing all opposition, Mussolini turned Italy into a one-party state.

His aim was to change the country from an inward looking, parochial and inefficient agricultural society into a modern manufacturing one, with the emphasis on exports. When he introduced his public works scheme he encouraged as many people as he could to give up farming and move to the cities to work in factories. Initially, the prosperity that this generated made Mussolini a popular figure. The legend goes that he was the first man to get the trains to run on time, but, like so much of what the world believes of Mussolini's achievements, this was pure propaganda; most of the work to renovate Italy's previously run-down railway system had been done before he came to power.

But his ambitions got the better of him and during the 1930s he tried to match the former glory of the other great European nations by building an empire. Italy already occupied Libya. To add to this and to worldwide outrage Mussolini invaded Ethiopia. His support for the Spanish Civil War added to his international infamy and in 1940 he dragged Italy into the World War II, allied with Hitler's Germany. In 1942, along with the Germans, the Italian army was driven out of North Africa by the Allies who, in 1943, invaded and liberated Italy. The end came in sight for Mussolini when he was deposed by the Council of Fascism as their leader, followed by deposition as supreme political leader by the king. The Italian public too were tired of the futility of war and they turned from loving him to hating him. By the end of 1943, Italy had changed sides and helped the Allies drive out the Fascists. In April 1945, Mussolini and his mistress, Clara Petacci, along with a small group of his supporters made a bid to escape into neutral Switzerland, but they were intercepted by Italian partisans moments before they reached the border crossing. A couple of days later, in the pretty village of Mezzegra, just up the road from Moltrasio, the partisans placed him and Petacci against a wall and, without any attempt at a trial, shot them both.

After the war, having removed the monarchy by referendum, Italy got itself together and became the fourth largest economy in Europe and the seventh largest on the planet, its name synonymous with the great style, high fashion and exclusivity the modern world desired. It exported almost everything and anything it could produce, in vast quantities. But like just about every other European country, Italy would suffer a downturn in prosperity in the twenty-first century that would have an effect on all of its citizens and residents, including us.

Chapter 16

Settling Permanently

OUR APARTMENT in the Via Recchi had really been too small, and for the two of us plus our four cats it had been like living in a caravan, but we had adapted to it. Like all the homes in the village, the floor area was small, but the ceilings were three metres high. We bought high wardrobes for the bedroom and to provide adequate storage space in the kitchen I'd fitted two tiers of wall cupboards and adapted a stepladder so we could reach the upper ones. Yes, we had become very settled and contented living there, and were becoming better off as the country pulled out of recession.

Then, suddenly we were shaken out of this comfortable position by a series of three highly significant events. The first one happened early on the morning of September 11 2001 when an Al Qaeda faction destroyed the twin towers of the World Trade Center in New York City. A few days later Al Qaeda's leader, Osama bin Laden, issued the prophetic words, "The world will never be the same place again." The secondary effects of that atrocity did not do my business, or anybody else's, any good, as tourists fled Italy on the first available plane home.

Five months after that, on January 1 2002, the second blow hit. It was the day the euro was launched, and it affected everybody in mainland Europe. It finished off any hope that the slump of the tourist trade caused by the September 11 atrocity was only temporary as practically overnight the price of a holiday rose by twenty-five per cent, in line with the rise in the cost of living in the euro zone. That spring, when the holiday season was supposed to be starting, the few foreign visitors that did visit my studio all remarked on how expensive they found Italy to be, compared with their previous visits when the lira was the currency. Today, if the same tourists came back to any European country, not just Italy, they would probably faint when they discover that prices have virtually doubled since 2002.

The third reason that caused us alarm for our well-being, and one literally close to home, happened on the evening of the eighth anniversary of our living in the apartment above the old butcher's shop in Moltrasio. It was three months after the advent of the euro when a hand-delivered letter dropped onto the doormat, informing us that the rent on our flat would rise by twenty-five per cent with immediate effect. As if this wasn't bad enough, a month later another letter arrived, demanding a separate rent rise of around thirty per cent for the studio. My immediate reaction was to confront our landlady over these considerable increases, but after further consideration, we decided to direct our energies into moving house.

On asking around, it appeared that rents were being hiked up all over the local area. Likewise, thanks to the euro and what you might call the 'celebrity effect', property prices were escalating beyond reason around the lake, so rather than squabble over the rent of our flat, or waste time hunting for something we could afford, buying a place of our own became our most immediate goal before we were priced out of that market too. Unfortunately we were in for another shock. After viewing only three properties for sale in a few days we discovered we already had been priced out of Moltrasio, which had suddenly become the twelfth wealthiest community in the whole of Italy. For such a tiny village to hold its own with the big cities was some accolade, but we could not hang around to appreciate it before it reached number eleven!

Up until the moment that our rents had been increased we had not seriously considered buying a property, but now that we had made the decision to buy, we knew we would have to look further afield, unless a miracle happened and we won *il Lotto*, the national lottery. Seven years previously we had sold our Elizabethan cottage in Godalming, but had been hesitant about re-entering the housing market again. At that time off-shore investment rates had been satisfactory, but now, following the slump in the bullish stock market boom of the early 2000s, the drop in interest rates and the uncertainty of the worldwide economy, people had returned to buying bricks and mortar as a secure investment and we were being left behind. Suddenly we found ourselves trying to compete against a large influx of highly paid Italian and international soccer stars, both present and past, as neighbours, plus wealthy industrialists, business tycoons, oligarchs, property developers and well-known celebrities, the likes of film star George Clooney, for highly desirable lakeside properties.

So what were we to do? For nearly a year we went through an indeterminate period of feeling cornered and worried about the way life was panning out, with little hope on the horizon that we would ever be able to claw our way out of our melancholy. Besides, any commissions for my artwork were practically non-existent due to the slump in the economy and, thanks to the strong euro, the short supply of tourists. Then, from out of the blue, a minor miracle happened, when one evening an excellent four-bedroom property appeared on an estate agent's website. It was a modern villa, built into the hillside just thirty metres off the main road along the lake, with three floors, terraced gardens, wide balconies on each floor, a garage and a spectacular, uninterrupted, 27 kilometre panoramic view over the lake. This was a property we could really get excited about, especially as it was one we could actually afford. All this and it was only ten kilometres further up the lake from Moltrasio, in the appealing, lively and unspoilt village of Argegno.

Five months of bureaucratic paper-shuffling later, we were the proud owners of this large white villa. We had already realised that saying goodbye to Moltrasio and its residents was not going to be easy, because in the fourteen years we had lived there we had become extremely fond of the place and our neighbours regarded us as part of their family. We were looking forward to living in our own home in Argegno with our four adopted cats, but on our last day there were hugs and tears aplenty as we said our farewells to our friends and neighbours. They said they would miss us a lot, but a lot of people felt hurt, almost offended, as if we were letting them down. We kept trying to reassure them all that we would be back to see them, and I tried to make light of the situation by repeating we were only moving down the road and that it was purely for economic reasons we were going. I think Nicola did persuade some of the younger ones that we had been forced out by circumstances, but we knew the older generation were not convinced. To them, we were changing allegiance and nobody should even consider wanting to leave their village. The mountainous nature of Italy divides the country into different cells or units and until the advent of modern day communications, each one was practically isolated. It made close communities of the villages, giving each its own identity, and once anybody becomes accepted into one, it is not a simple thing to turn one's back on it and leave.

In leaving Moltrasio we experienced a similar feeling to the one we had when had turned our backs on England and crossed the departure lounge at Gatwick airport fourteen years previously. It had not been easy to say *arrivederci* to it all and acknowledge the waves of the farewell committee as we drove down Via Recchi for the last time. As we drove away, there was a real hullabaloo from the back seat of our car. Our most difficult problem in moving out had been to find four cat boxes that would fit into the car so that we could transport all the cats to Argegno with as little physical and mental trauma as possible and we prayed that once they had arrived in their new surroundings they would not plead to, or attempt to, return to their birthplace.

Another concern throughout the house buying process was how our new neighbours would regard two strangers moving in who had just bought the largest villa in the whole village, the type of building the rich, faceless and the self-opinionated normally reside in. Would the locals of Argegno refer to us as being either *bravi* or *stronzi* behind our backs?

Although Argegno is only ten kilometres along the lake road from Moltrasio, Italian law meant that because we were changing community we had to apply for residence permits again. Fortunately, the computer age has made some things in life a lot easier. Obtaining permits is one of them and we received them relatively quickly compared with fourteen years earlier. Basically, all the policeman at Argegno Comune had to do was check with his counterpart in Moltrasio that we were who we said we were when we visited him. We had our old residence permits with us to disprove any doubt and so it was only a matter of renewing documentation from information that already existed.

But for all of that, it was an exciting time being a house owner once again, and once more I had a project to tackle. The villa in Argegno was huge, and our problem was what to do with the large expanse of floor area in all of the rooms. The villa was only thirty-five years old, but it had been empty for three years. It was built on three floors, covering an area of two-hundred and thirty square metres per floor, with rectangular proportions, four double-bedrooms, open staircases, lots of large windows and marble tiled floors and we looked forward to spreading out once more. It had not been painted, inside or out, for at least twenty years, so it required a lot of paint and a lot of time to apply it. It had some art-deco features, so I decided to furnish it with the latest minimalist look in interior design, utilising the classical Bauhaus school of furniture and echoing the 1930s theme of ceiling fans, mirrors, chrome, steel and float glass for the rest of the decoration. The garden covered four thousand square metres with a good proportion of it having a fifty-degree gradient up the mountainside. It was semi overgrown and so urgent chores would keep me busy for well over a year, including pruning the twenty palm trees, all six metres high.

Then there was the village of Argegno to explore. It is close to the lake shore, with easy road and public transport access following the lakeside road. Behind the road, the small houses and shops cling to the mountainside, with narrow cobbled passages running between them and a stream that runs down, under a bridge on a curve in the road and into the lake, where there is a small marina beside the market square. Further along the road there is a cable car that runs up to Pigra at the top of the wonderful, rural Intelvi district. This village has dizzying views of the lake and has a culture and dialect completely different from those of Argegno. The cable car journey takes just six minutes, so the trip up to Pigra is one the visitors try not to miss.

With twenty-four different varieties of freshwater fish in the lake to choose from, the people naturally eat much more fish in comparison to the mountain-dwelling Moltrasini. At weekends and on public holidays a lot of Milanese arrive to sample lake food and the local culture. Down by the lakeside, in the *trattorie* and restaurants of Argegno, perch risotto is one of the favoured dishes with the chewy, creamy, short-grain Arborio rice that comes from the Po Valley district only forty kilometres away in Arborio, in what is reputedly one of the largest rice growing areas outside of China. Carnaroli rice is also a local favourite for making risotto. Lavarello, a type of freshwater salmon, grilled or oven baked with butter and sage is a highly recommended speciality. So is Missoltino, which is very special and unique to Lake Como. It has a strong flavour and certainly an acquired taste. It is a small oily fish about the size of a mackerel and is only caught in March. It is first cleaned, then sun-dried, then salted and pressed flat in plaited wooden cases with bay leaves and then left until the winter months. It is served warm with polenta, accompanied by a full-bodied Barbera from Piedmonte. As it is a preserved fish, it can be eaten all year round, but there is such a demand for it that after the winter is over it is difficult to find a trattoria that has any left. Agone, freshwater shad, is another favourite. After it has been gutted, it is rolled in flour and deep fried for thirty seconds, then marinated in white wine vinegar with wild thyme and then bottled for some weeks, before being warmed through and served with a mixed grill of lake fish or with salad. Whitebait is also enjoyed, first tossed in flour and fried in olive oil for a few seconds, then drained and served hot in a basket.

All of the fish, including trout, pike, eel and bream, landed in our part of the vast lake are caught daily by a single fisherman. The terms of his licence are strict, only allowing him to trawl for fish that are in season. He provides all the hotels and restaurants in the central area with his catch and he is also the only person allowed to sell fresh water fish to the public. Conveniently for us, his shop happens to be in Argegno.

Getting to know our new neighbours was comparatively quick compared with our first weeks in Moltrasio, because although at first we thought we might not know anybody, we remembered that Sandra, who had organised the Burns Night twelve years earlier, now lived in Argegno with her husband Gherado, and so we went to find them to tell them that we would soon be neighbours. After the fracas they'd had over the haggis, when Gherado took sides with the chef about 'putting disgusting rubbish next to good food', they had kissed and made-up and they had tried to forget that the acrimony they'd had ever happened. Gherado in particular was most helpful when introducing us into the local society, because it is his home village and so he was more than willing to enlighten inquisitive residents as to who and what we were and from where we had moved. He was most valuable for me because whilst Nicola was working in Milan and I was left on my own, he would invite me to the spot where the all-day card playing, wine drinking, dialect speaking, early retired men of the village meet up daily. They are the eyes and ears of every Italian community and it is important to meet them early on because of the influence they have over all the other residents. It was a real case of déjà vu, inasmuch as the scene was the same as Moltrasio, the difference being that we met in the Bar Onda instead of the Bar Centrale.

The one thing that gave me some security when I first met

the locals was that I could now speak Italian and I could actually communicate with the people he was introducing me to, whereas when we lived in Moltrasio I used to just smile and nod agreeably at I knew not what. But under some circumstances speaking Italian in Italy is not always an advantage. The locals in the Bar Onda preferred to converse in their own dialect, which was different from the one in Moltrasio, and it became tedious for them to have to translate what they were saying into Italian for me so I could understand.

Trying to learn a dialect is extremely difficult if a person is not brought up listening to it, because although Italian dialects are in general written languages, they are not taught in schools and, in practice, apart from the occasional abbreviated Italian word, they seem to comprise a lot of grunts. After Nicola and Christine had pushed me hard to learn Italian and forget about English, I found everybody in Argegno was telling me to forget about Italian and learn to speak the local dialect!

I particularly enjoyed the weekly *il Club di Lunedi*, the Monday Club, held in the Bar Onda. It was organised by Luigi Ortelli, Argegno's equivalent of Riccardo Del Meglio, and he had a similar strong personality and an infectious, inbuilt cheer about him. The Monday Club was attended by a dozen retired or current restaurateurs from the area because Monday was their day off and so they all met up at ten-thirty in the morning to discuss all subjects imaginable. At the same time they would consume several bottles of vino, several plates of sliced salami and hams and maybe some wild onions and duck pâté on *panino* for *aperativi* before lunch. The weekly reunion was always referred to as the Church-going Club, and it was for men only because they attended to escape their wives and they were supposed to be going to the eleven o'clock mass in the local church. Maybe they convinced themselves that their wives believed they were going to mass, but they all must have returned home smelling of alcohol, so one must assume their wives were glad to get their retired and otherwise bored menfolk from under their feet for at least one morning a week!

As much through the Monday Club as anything, the village members came to accept us, the English couple who lived in the big house up the road, as part of the community. Another method we used to make our faces familiar was to shop in the food market and frequent the *trattorie* in the main piazza. We also remained in residence throughout the year and not solely for the summer season and so we attended anything going on in the community, but I stopped going to the Monday Club when the organiser suddenly died. The club continued to flourish without Luigi but I thought it best to leave them in peace to talk in their dialect without my having to keep interrupting their fun by asking a kind person to translate for me everything that was said.

In some ways I missed going to the club, even if it was only to have a drink at an economical price, but Monday wasn't my official day off, like it was for the members in the restaurant business. I had work to do in the form of art commissions and I still didn't have a studio ready to work in. The villa we had moved into might have been big but until an open terrace on the first floor, which had been the previous tenant's games room, had been converted into my studio then I had to work in a spare bedroom. To complete the studio I had to do an extensive amount of plastering on the walls as well as calling in an electrician and a double glazing specialist to make an ideal space for painting in, because I knew that when it was finished, I'd have a staggering view over the lake as inspiration for my watercolours and a place to display them for sale. It was also necessary to get my studio completed *presto*, because our six cats (we had gained another two!) were applying pressure on me, demanding to sit in the expanse of new windows so they could soak up the heat from the sun.

For us two the attraction of Italy is a permanent one. Once tried, it remains in the blood forever. We couldn't do without the fix and we made sure that we got a regular dose of it by coming here to live. Even though the discomforts we had to battle through when we first arrived had not been easy, we could always see a light at the end of the tunnel and we felt that if we could survive to reach it, then the battle would have been worthwhile. Everything has its price and satisfaction at this level doesn't come cheap.

Italy holds the essence of beauty, formed out of a history that is ingrained, a history that has not been distorted by forward-looking elements that try to erode it. Italy has a resolute strength that radiates permanence, an atmosphere only time creates and it commands respect. Objects like a twelfth-century, carved stone footbridge spanning an ancient river, the hand-painted interior of a celestial cathedral, or everyday objects like an ancient drinking fountain, a set of stone steps, an old park bench take on a significance that is at once beautiful and this is recognised by visitors from overseas. Even the simple village we live in has details that merit attention because they are beautiful. On bright, sunny days you are somehow coaxed into looking at what is around you, to acknowledge it and realise that this day is special, that it cannot be brushed aside as just another day to pass through. Each day here insists on being appreciated, and even if the weather is off form, it still looks fabulous, and that is true for every season.

Chapter 17

Epilogue

When Nicola and I bought the plane tickets to Milano all those years ago, we told the travel agent we weren't coming back. We have kept our pledge, and to strengthen the bonds both with Italy and ourselves, we married in 2006. It had only taken us twenty-two years to get around to it, but true to all our experiences with Italian custom it was a bit of a pantomime. The ceremony was a civil one, it was conducted by the mayor in his office and it took him all of seven minutes. Nicola and I had booked the appointment two weeks previously at the *Comune* and completed and paid for the necessary paperwork in advance, but when we arrived for the actual occasion the mayor was in a planning meeting with an architect and it appeared he had forgotten he had to marry us. After fifteen minutes of waiting for him to conclude his meeting, Nicola told him that she hoped the ceremony wasn't going to take too long to complete, because she had just put polish on her marble tiles in the lounge and she needed to get back to buff it off before it dried and turned white!'

He might have done the whole ceremony in just two minutes, but it took almost five minutes to rummage through the store cupboard and find his official green, white and red *Tricolore* sash. We actually thought he was looking for some more forms to fill in, but instead, he triumphantly produced this sash, crumpled and dusty, which he proudly pulled over his shoulder. Then he realised he needed two witnesses, so to hurry things along, Nicola and I dashed into the Bar Onda next door and found two willing people, who just happened to be the mayor's brother and sister-in-law.

Ceremony over, we took the mayor and our two witnesses to the Bar Onda for a celebratory drink. Two hours later, Nicola realised she'd forgotten all about her polished floors, and anyway, she didn't care, because she'd downed a few too many glasses of bianco sporco to do anything about it. However she did finish the job the next day, but why worry about such details? We had achieved our dream; our ambition of living in a country where every day brings a joy to the soul, and that was what truly mattered.

Earlswood Press